AMERICAN PEDIATRICS

AMERICAN PEDIATRICS

*The Social Dynamics of
Professionalism, 1880–1980*

SYDNEY A. HALPERN

UNIVERSITY OF CALIFORNIA PRESS
BERKELEY   LOS ANGELES   LONDON

University of California Press
Berkeley and Los Angeles, California

University of California Press, Ltd.
London, England

Copyright © 1988 by The Regents of the University of California

Library of Congress Cataloging-in-Publication Data

Halpern, Sydney A. (Sydney Ann)
  American pediatrics.

  Bibliography: p.
  Includes index.
    1. Pediatrics—United States—History
I. Title. [DNLM: 1. Pediatrics—history—
United States. 2. Professional Practice—history—
United States. WS 11 AA1 H12a]
RJ42.U5H36 1988   362.1'9892'00973   87-30222
ISBN 0-520-05195-5 (alk. paper)

Printed in the United States of America

1 2 3 4 5 6 7 8 9

To the memory of my father
Jules Halpern, physicist

Contents

Acknowledgments

I am extremely grateful for the assistance of those who served as informants for this book: twenty-six pediatricians; two pediatric psychologists; and staff members of five pediatric societies, two child-health organizations, three private foundations, and five federal agencies. These individuals interrupted busy schedules and answered my questions with care and graciousness. Without their help, I could not have reconstructed developments in pediatrics following World War II. Special thanks to Morris Green, chair of pediatrics at Indiana University, who provided me with the mimeographed newsletters of the postwar Ambulatory Pediatric Association and to Melvin Grumbach, then pediatric chair at the University of California in San Francisco, who loaned me professional correspondences and memos concerning the evolution of pediatric endocrinology and was a sounding board for my ideas on pediatric subspecialties.

Many others helped me gain access to data on nineteenth and early twentieth-century pediatrics. I drew much of the book's historical material from the library collections at the Berkeley and San Francisco campuses of the University of California. Reference librarians there were of tremendous aid. Special thanks to Nancy Zinn, Head of Special Collections and Archivist at the University of California, San Francisco, who gave me exceptionally competent assistance on numerous occasions. In the course of tracking down difficult-to-obtain sources and in making extensive revisions to the manuscript after leaving the Bay Area, I used the services of archivists and librarians at eight additional institutions. I am grateful for their help and for that of the late physician-historian Samuel Radbill who generously shared the contents of his private collection on the history of American pediatrics.

In the formative stages of the research, I benefited from the intellectual support and criticism of sociologists Joyce Bird, Kathleen Gerson, Jane Grant, Barbara Heyns, David Hummon, Robert Jackson, Robert Mayer, Neil Smelser, Ann Stueve, Paul van Seters; American historian Samuel Haber; medical historian Gert Brieger; and health-policy analyst Philip Lee. Smelser, chairman of my dissertation committee at Berkeley, kindled and guided my interest in the study of changing social structures. Haber, also a committee member, was the source of innumerable insights into the history of American professions. Brieger made valuable comments on early drafts of the manuscript. Jackson importantly influenced my thinking about social processes.

I rewrote and added to the dissertation manuscript extensively before arriving at the final version of the book. A number of scholars made intellectual contributions during this phase of my work: sociologists Robert Bell, Richard T. Campbell, Arthur Stinchcombe, and Stephen Warner; psychologist James G. Kelly; and health-policy analyst Janet Perloff. Bell responded to several drafts of key chapters. Perloff's critique of a version of chapter 7 was the stimulus for its substantial revision. Kelly provided abundant comments on the entire manuscript.

The National Center for Health Services Research (NCHSR), Office of the Assistant Secretary for Health, supported the study that produced this book through grant number RO3 HS 03687. The Office of Social Science Research (OSSR) and the Department of Sociology at the University of Illinois at Chicago (UIC) provided resources to enter several chapters of the manuscript into the university's mainframe computer so that revisions could be handled more easily. My thanks to Barbara Heyns for facilitating my application to NCHSR and Robert L. Hall for his assistance in obtaining funds from OSSR. William Bridges and Christopher Ross, colleagues in the UIC sociology department, helped me solve problems downloading computer files containing book chapters from the university mainframe to my personal computer. Bridges provided generous practical assistance when malfunctioning software threatened to erase a chapter of the book. I am indebted to Brieger and to health-policy analyst Victor Rodwin for their help in shepherding the manuscript into publication. Finally, my thanks to the editors and staff at the University of California Press who have made the final stages of the book's preparation an enjoyably cooperative enterprise.

Chapter One

Introduction

American pediatricians offer a highly distinctive professional service. They are physicians of childhood, treating children's illnesses, providing care for healthy youngsters and counsel for parents. Supervision of well children is at the center of the pediatrician's domain. These physicians administer vaccines. They weigh, measure, and assess children, monitoring the course of growth and development. They offer normative advice to parents on the problems of child management and training. The advice-giving role of pediatricians is embodied in the figure of Benjamin Spock, author of the best-selling manual, *Baby and Child Care*. Through face-to-face consultations with such specialists, Americans seek to assuage the uncertainties and anxieties of parenthood. Pediatricians and the services they provide are widely recognized by the American public. In 1980, parents took preadolescent children for more than fifty-three million visits with pediatricians. This constituted 60 percent of all physician visits made by children under the age of eleven. Among children under two, the annual rate of office visits to pediatricians averaged 3.5 per child.[1] That year, there were twenty-eight thousand practicing pediatricians.[2]

But if pediatric care is highly sought after today, in historical terms it is a recent innovation. One hundred years ago, medical services dedicated to children did not exist. In 1880 there were fewer than fifty child specialists in the country, none practicing pediatrics on a full-time basis. A special term for the field was just being coined—the first child specialists called themselves pediatrists rather than pediatricians. Medical supervision of healthy chil-

1

dren would not be routine for many decades. Americans seldom arranged for private physicians to see their children and parents that did consulted general practitioners not pediatricians.

The advent of specialized medical services for children was not an isolated phenomenon. Since the mid-nineteenth century, some two dozen specialties have emerged and about three times that number of subspecialties. Each of these medical segments offers a discrete variety of medical care. Over the years, specialty divisions became a standard feature of medical practice. Surgery, ophthalmology, psychiatry, orthopedics, and cardiology became household terms. Internists, obstetricians, and pediatricians supplanted general practitioners as frontline physicians. In 1923, just over 10 percent of American physicians were full-scale specialists, a proportion that grew to 20 percent in 1940.[3] Entrance into specialties redoubled following World War II. By 1985, the earlier ratio was reversed with only 12 percent of physicians in the fields of general or family practice.[4] Today the overwhelming majority of physicians are trained and practice in a restricted area of medicine.

Many accounts of the factors underlying these trends identify scientific progress as the principal cause of specialization and physician choice as the primary vehicle. Conventional wisdom holds that medical knowledge is so vast that practitioners cannot assimilate its entirety. Specialization divides knowledge into circumscribed areas which practitioners can realistically hope to master. But explanations of physician choice do not explain the complex organizational changes which accompanied progressive specialization. The long-term trend toward specialization is widely recognized yet few outside the profession are familiar with its organizational features. Medical specialties are not simply divisions of science and practice. They are highly structured occupational units and their emergence involves the creation of new professional institutions. These structures include specialty associations, certifying boards, and standardized training programs. Specialties are institutionalized as separate departments and units within hospitals and medical colleges. They articulate distinct professional ideologies and sustain unique professional roles.

The history of medical specialization in America is characterized by waves in the founding of occupational structures. Specialty societies proliferated in the final third of the nineteenth century. Regular medical school departments appeared in the first two decades of the twentieth century. Certifying boards multiplied during the 1930s and specialty training was standardized in the late 1930s and 1940s. With the stabilization of residency programs, specialties assumed their mature form. Following World War II, subspecialties emerged and the number of specialists rose substantially. But the basic occupational institutions were established by the late 1940s. These structures—associations, departments, certifying boards, formal training programs—provided a foundation for manpower trends of the postwar period. Where did these structures come from? Why and how did they evolve? The present study addresses such questions as it examines the long-term development of one medical segment.

This book tells the story of how pediatrics emerged as an organized professional unit within American medicine. It follows the development of pediatrics from its inception in the final quarter of the nineteenth century to its secure establishment in the 1930s and 1940s and through the rise of pediatric subspecialties following World War II. Its principal focus is emerging occupational structures and the processes through which they evolve. Examining such processes implies attention to the vicissitudes of professional labor: the narrative explores the work patterns, perceptions, and activities of successive generations of child specialists and the changing contexts in which they practice medicine. It is a social history, one which considers the impact of collective action and a broad range of societal factors on the unfolding organization of a profession. My concern with occupational structures and social processes makes the study fundamentally different from previous accounts of the rise of pediatrics. There are already a good number of histories of pediatrics, most written by members of the specialty. The bulk of these accounts fall into one of three categories: scientific histories which trace advances in knowledge and treatment of chidren's diseases, biographies of eminent contributors to the field, and depictions of the accomplishments of pediatric associations. Several general histories of the specialty combine these strategies and add to them consideration of some social factors operative in the specialty's development.[5] Approaches of the first type predominate and, in these, pediatrics is conceived of as a division of medical science. The present study is a history of medical institutions, not an account of innovations in diagnosis and treatment.

The book concerns both the unique features of pediatrics and the general patterns through which medical specialties evolve. While remaining faithful to the particulars of the case, I strive to identify patterns and processes that may be common to other occupational segments. My starting point is the assertion that the rise of medical specialties in America is a variant of the phenomenon social scientists call professionalization. While not identical to the development of freestanding professions, the emergence of medical specialties is understood best when viewed in the light of scholarly literature on the rise of professions.[6] Medical segments are occupational collectivities. Like professions more generally, they seek to improve their standing and exert control over the social and economic organization of their labor. Some additional comments on the sociological study of professions will clarify these assertions and the book's perspective on medical specialization.

Specialization as a Variant of Professionalization

Social scientists use the term *professionalization* for a number of distinct empirical phenomena. One referent is changes in the occupational structure of industrializing societies whereby professionals make up an increasingly large portion of the overall work force. In America, this trend has proceeded during the whole of the twentieth century. Between 1900 and 1970, the professional and technical sector grew from 4.3 percent to 14.0 percent of the total labor force.[7] The shift took place less through expansion in the ranks of preexisting professions than through the inception and growth of new professions. These proliferated in America during the late nineteenth and early twentieth centuries and included social work, nursing, and ancillary health professions.

Another referent of *professionalization* is efforts made by such newly emerging occupations to assume the form and acquire the standing of older professions like medicine and law. Sociologists disagree as to what constitutes the essential basis of professional status. Some emphasize a systematic body of knowledge; others point to autonomy in the performance of work, authority, or market control. But it is clear that developing professions mobilize to secure professional privileges and struggle to maximize collective control over the conditions of their labor. Toward these ends, nascent professions adopt the occupational institutions of established professions and claim attributes viewed as typical of this class of occupations.

Professionalization has also referred to a transformation which older professions undergo with the advent of modern industrial capitalism. Beginning in the second half of the nineteenth century, professions like medicine responded to changing social and economic conditions by rebuilding professional institutions and struggling for enhanced legal protection of occupational boundaries. Among their goals were greater control over the conditions of labor and the protection of expanding markets for professional services.

Finally, *professionalization* may refer to the emergence of specialized occupational units internal to a profession. Specialization is not always sufficiently well developed to be considered a form of professionalization. In many instances, specialties are rudimentary or informal organized groupings. Even where internal differentiation is well developed, occupational structures may be absent. In law, for example, specialization is pervasive but the profession as a whole has resisted the creation of formal specialty divisions. There are no specialized educational tracks and very little certification.[8]

Medicine is one of the professions in which internal differentiation is most thoroughgoing. Yet here the extent to which specialties emulate professions varies cross-nationally.[9] Medical segments are less highly developed outside the United States than they are within it. But within American medicine, specialties have assumed much the same form as freestanding professions. Indeed medical specialties in the United States function and are organized like professions within a profession.

American medical specialties are like professions in a number of different ways. First, there are substantial similarities in social organization. Freestanding professions establish occupational institutions which function to control and regularize recruitment, entrance, and professional practice. These structures include occupational associations, standardized training programs and, among well-established professions, university-based teaching and research branches. Through these institutions and organizational divisions, professions transmit professional culture and prescribed occupational roles and advance their intellectual foundations. Medical specialties in the United States have analogous occupational structures. Today there are twenty-three fully institutionalized medical specialties and about three times that number of formally constituted medical subspecialties. Virtually all specialties and subspecialties have their own professional societies. Pediatrics alone has six not including regional and subspecialty associations.[10] Training for specialty practice is standardized with separate residency or fellowship tracks established for each specialty. Residency programs constitute a formally organized tier of professional education which follows the four years of undergraduate medical school. Fellowship programs are yet another tier of professional education. These follow medical residencies and provide training in medical subspecialties. Specialty divisions are integral to the organization of academic medicine with nearly all specialties institutionalized as separate departments or departmental divisions within American medical schools. Furthermore, each specialty articulates an ideology which delineates the tasks and purposes of the field and defines the unique features of the specialist's occupational role. The resulting professional cultures are distinct from those of other specialties and from the culture of medicine as a whole.

Second, like professions more generally, medical specialties structure markets for the delivery of services. Several sociologists have underscored the importance of market consolidation to the course of professionalization. Building on the work of Max Weber, Jeffrey Berlant and Magali Larson argue that evolving professions systematize new services, present them to the public as recognizable and desirable commodities, and move to consolidate and control the market for service delivery.[11] Professional licensure is one tool in market control, providing legal monopolies for the provision of services. Like freestanding professions, medical specialties offer distinct professional commodities and organize markets for service delivery. In the United States, specialties are regularized divisions of the overall market for medical care. A system of specialty certifying boards operates like licensing bodies. There are twenty-one regular boards (and two conjoint boards) which control formal entrance into the twenty-three primary specialties and more numerous subspecialties. The boards examine individual candidates and specify a course of graduate education requisite to certification. Historically, certifying boards preceded and provided impetus for the standardization of residency training. Each board is an autonomously constituted private corporation. While their governing councils include representatives from the AMA and other major professional associations, the boards are controlled by their respective specialty societies.[12]

The board system is unlike professional licensure in that certification has no legal status and is entirely voluntary. There are neither judicial nor formal professional sanctions against any licensed M.D. practicing in a medical specialty for which he or she is not certified. Indeed many physicians conducting specialty practice have never passed board exams.[13] However, board eligibility—completion of specialized residency programs requisite to certification—is often required for hospital staff privileges in a specialized field and, in many professional communities, is essential to the construction of colleague referral networks necessary for viable specialty practice. The occupational boundaries established by specialty certification are ones which members of the medical profession can cross. Nonetheless, the boards, along with standardized training programs, function to regularize specialties as arenas of professional practice and as divisions of the general market for medical services.[14]

Third, medical specialties share with freestanding professions a propensity to compete among themselves for status and resources. William Goode, among others, notes that professions vie for social rewards including power, prestige, and income. In his view, competition with other occupations is inherent in professions' attempts to secure preferred legal privileges. Competition takes place among established professions when developments internal to one lead to encroachment onto the terrain of a neighboring profession.[15] Among medical specialties, there is perennial conflict over market boundaries, a phenomenon most visible when new fields emerge or existing fields redefine their missions. Conflict is endemic within hospitals and medical schools where specialties compete for prerogatives and institutional resources.[16]

Finally, like professionalization, the emergence of medical specialties serves as a means for collective upward mobility. A number of sociologists point out that professionalization is a vehicle for group mobility. Everett Hughes, for example, depicts the emergence of professions as a form of collective social advancement.[17] Social historians link professionalization to the rise of the middle class. The professions expanded and multiplied during a period when the traditional bases of middle-class status were undercut by societal reorganization and the appearance of a new corporate upper class. The reconstituted professions gave the middle class a new foundation for prestige and social integration.[18]

Medical specialization serves the analogous function of intraprofessional mobility. Through the formation of specialties, collectivities of physicians raise their standing and improve their competitive position relative to that of other practitioners. As early as the mid-nineteenth century, specialists commanded greater prestige and accrued higher fees than general practitioners, this despite widespread hostility toward specialization among rank and file generalists.[19] In this period, it was largely physicians from the upper strata of American medicine who established specialized (or semispecialized) practices. Historian Charles Rosenberg attests to the existence of a well-defined medical elite within nineteenth-century American cities.[20] During most of the century, entrance into this upper strata rested largely on ascribed characteristics and social connections. With the reorganization of medicine and growing legitimacy of medical science during the late nineteenth century, older bases of prestige were thrown into question. At the outset, specialization was a way for an existing professional elite to reassert its social standing. The founders of the first medical specialty societies in America were, as a rule, from the medical elites of eastern seaboard cities. Early associations restricted admission and kept their membership homogeneous.[21] Entrance into the specialties was democratized before World War II with the creation of certifying boards and the standardization of residency training; specialization became an avenue of mobility open to rank and file physicians.

While the similarities between medical specialties and freestanding professions are extensive, at a certain point the analogy breaks down. Developing medical segments can rely on the occupational privileges of medicine as a whole in a way that has no parallel in the evolution of freestanding professions. The social standing of medicine rose substantially during the period in which specialties evolved. The emergence of specialties no doubt contributed to this improved status. But I will not pursue this observation for the moment. The point here is that individual segments drew upon the rising status of medicine in establishing favorable work arrangements and consolidating markets for their services. For the most part, specialties do not launch campaigns to win popular favor. Few have publicized separate codes of ethics in an effort to win public confidence or appealed to the state for aid in establishing occupational boundaries. With privileges and status conferred by the profession as a whole, legitimacy within medicine is the more central issue for an evolving segment.

The development of medical specialties is unlike that of freestanding professions in that some tasks of professionalization are handled by a superordinate occupational unit. Partly for this reason, the researcher's attention is drawn to features of occupational evolution not ordinarily emphasized in scholarship on professions. The present study highlights two dimensions of occupational development. The first is the importance of changing work patterns to the inception and consolidation of professional collectivities. Pediatrics was in the first instance a new division of professional labor. It came into being and evolved through shifting work patterns and through the response of practitioners to changing contingencies of labor. The second is the impact of surrounding occupational structures on the form of an emerging segment and the pace of its growth. Pediatricians repeatedly emulated professional institutions established by earlier medical segments and repeatedly responded to pressures that surrounding structures created. The emphasis on work patterns and occupational environments is new to the analysis of professions and at the heart of the account presented here.

Unique Features of Pediatrics

While searching for underlying and perhaps generic dynamics in the rise of pediatrics, the narrative attends to unusual features of the specialty and its historical development. Pediatrics is a field whose evolution is strongly influenced by ideological currents and social reform movements outside the medical profession. Changing notions about childhood and social movements promoting child welfare are important in virtually every phase of its history. These movements and ideological currents stimulate the inception and continued development of pediatrics as a professional entity.

In this regard, pediatrics differs from the bulk of medical segments. The majority of fully institutionalized medical specialties have their initial impetus in scientific and technical innovation. George Rosen, in a seminal study published in the 1940s, provides what is still an unsurpassed account of the original intellectual foundations of medical specialization. Rosen argues that discoveries made in Paris during the early nineteenth century created a conceptual basis for specialization. Until well into the nineteenth century, medical thinking was dominated by a unitary notion of physical illness which allowed for the existence of disease but not of diseases. French clinicians systematically correlated symptoms observed at the bedside of hospital patients with abnormalities in these individuals' organs discovered through autopsies. This coordination of clinical and pathological findings resulted in the isolation of distinct disease processes and the recognition that symptomatology indicates pathology in particular organs and regions of the body. The notion of localized pathology granted new significance to circumscribed problem areas; disorders of discrete organs and organ systems were now legitimate foci for clinical practice and investigation. The new conception of disease also stimulated technological innovation. Persuaded that the anatomical changes accompanying disease might have diagnostic implications, physicians sought ways to observe evidence of pathology in the living patient. They created instruments which both facilitated diagnosis and opened new avenues of medical treatment.[22] Most specialties in existence today are rooted in the treatment of a disease type or organ system (for example, neurology, dermatology, ophthalmology, and otolaryngology) or in the application of a set of technologies (as in surgery, radiology, and anesthesiology).

Pediatrics has its conceptual roots less in scientific and technical change than in the identification of health-related social problems. Its development is grounded in social meliorism and in a tradition of stewardship on the part of the American medical elite. Pediatrics is not alone in this regard. There are a number of social-problem based medical specialties including psychiatry, public health, and obstetrics. Social movements larger than the profession of medicine were critical in their formation and development as well. Like pediatrics, these fields arose during the late nineteenth and early twentieth centuries from meliorative impulses and from certain aspects of physicians' social role.[23] In addition to professional segments originating in the late nineteenth century, a number of social-problem based specialties and subspecialties have consolidated since World War II. These include family practice, geriatrics, and the still emerging field of adolescent medicine. While not linked to large-scale social movements, later entrants have gathered support from private foundations and from federal policy-making and funding agencies.

The social-problem based fields share a number of characteristics apart from their association with reform movements and state sponsorship. Practitioners in pediatrics, psychiatry, and public health earn lower average incomes than is typical among medical specialists.[24] In recent decades the fields have attracted disproportionately high percentages of women physicians into their ranks although female practitioners were excluded from the organized branches of these—and other—specialties during the late nineteenth and early twentieth centuries.[25] With the exception of obstetrics which is constituted as a surgical specialty, the social-problem segments have less status within medicine than most organ and technology-based specialties.[26] The precise reason for their lower status is difficult to pin down. Prestige differences may rest in part upon income, ascribed characteristics of a segment's members, the social standing of clientele, characteristics of professional labor, the segment's centrality to core occupational values, or its perceived intellectual foundation.[27] Physicians in organ and technically based specialties often depict psychiatry, public health, general pediatrics, and family practice as soft or unrigorous, much as academics in the physical sciences portray social science disciplines.

I am not the first to categorize specialties on the basis of forces that dominate their inception. Rosen points to a group of specialties which is rooted in demographic and social factors.[28] Furthermore, the identification of scientific and social-problem specialties parallels a distinction made regarding professions more generally. A. M. Carr-Saunders and P. A. Wilson—authors of the first major sociological study of professions published in the 1930s—distinguish scientific and institutional professions, the former stimulated by advances in knowledge, the latter by demands of social organization.[29] Subsequent scholars suggest similar dichotomies. Wilbert Moore, for example, differentiates professions arising from the "demand side" and those growing from the availability of new knowledge.[30] As is the case among medical specialties, professions seen as outgrowths of scientific progress are frequently accorded higher status than those generated by changes in social structure.

But while consistent with categorizations of the professions, the distinction between scientific and social-problem specialties is not free from ambiguity. Some specialties defy classification. Obstetrics is linked to social movements promoting maternal health; at the same time, it is an organ-based specialty. Internal medicine does not fit comfortably into either category. More important, it is not clear whether scientific and social-problem specialties undergo fundamentally different processes of professional evolution. The construction of a systematic body of knowledge is integral to the evolution of all specialties including the social-problem fields. Furthermore, a great many of the scientifically grounded specialties were influenced by social meliorism. Most of the organ-based specialties which appeared during the 1800s coalesced around specialized hospitals and dispensaries established in the third quarter of the nineteenth century. In that period, hospitals and clinics were charity institutions providing free medical care for the poor.

Secondary literature on scientifically based medical segments suggests that changing work patterns and surrounding occupational structures are central in the evolution of these segments as well. Indeed, attention to shifting patterns of labor might open the way to new insights in the study of a wide range of professions and professional specialties. But these comments are premature. The broader applicability and limitations of the study's findings are discussed in the final chapter after my analysis has been fully elaborated. In the meantime, the narrative attends to special features of pediatrics and its development while deferring judgment on how these features affect the underlying dynamic of professional evolution.

Pediatrics and the Professional Regulation
of Childhood

One thematic current in the book's analysis clearly has most relevance for pediatrics and other social-problem based specialties.

Pediatrics is one of a number of professions and professional specialties whose core tasks bear directly on the societal regulation of childhood and family life. Routine medical supervision of well babies and children became an established professional service during the third and fourth decade of the twentieth century. Its creation placed physicians in a fundamentally new relation to the American family. Specialists now counseled parents on the parameters of normal child development and dispensed advice on proper methods of child hygiene and training. They examined healthy youngsters on a periodic basis, frequently during infancy and at regular intervals through the remainder of childhood. Medical prescriptions on child management were not in themselves a new phenomenon. Child-care manuals written by physicians were popular in America during much of the nineteenth century. But never before had there existed a discrete professional service monitoring the growth and development of individual children. Nor had professional advice to parents been so systematically organized.

Contemporary pediatricians were fully aware that medical supervision of healthy youngsters involved a radically new relation to children and their families. They joked in professional meetings about taking over the traditional functions of neighbors and grandmothers.[31] They substantially revised earlier professional ideology, formulating a new professional role. The pediatrician was now "the child's family advisor," guiding parents—most particularly, mothers—in the emerging science of child management. This advisor was a technical expert on developmental benchmarks in children and the norms of age-appropriate behavior.

Ongoing changes bearing upon childhood went far beyond the specialty of pediatrics. Nineteenth and early twentieth-century reformers had conceived of childhood in terms of increasingly differentiated stages each with its own behavioral expectations. By the 1920s, these ideological currents had stimulated new academic disciplines focusing on child development. Researchers set out to catalog behavioral norms for each phase of maturation. Between the mid-nineteenth and the early twentieth century, Americans had established numerous institutions impinging on children and parents including schools, social welfare agencies, and juvenile and family courts. State intervention into family life had expanded through the enactment of child labor and compulsory education laws. For the most part, it was professionals who performed the work of child-serving institutions and agencies: teachers, child-welfare workers, juvenile court officers, child psychologists, and psychiatrists. These professions emerged concomitant with the rise of pediatrics and like it, they defined child serving as a primary task and knowledge of child development as a core expertise. Pediatric care for healthy youngsters was thus part of more general trend toward new forms of societal regulation of childhood, regulation implemented by newly consolidated professions and specialties.

In recent years there has been a growing interest among social scientists in the "professionalization" of family and private life and a number of disparate literatures bear on the subject. One literature considers the medicalization of social control and is a concern within the sociology of deviance. Another starts from a feminist perspective and focuses upon professionals' advice to women and its implications for family and gender roles. Several studies explore moves by contemporary family-serving professions to establish or renegotiate their position toward children and parents.[32] Goode places the phenomenon in the context of long-term historical trends, pointing out that professional intrusion into the family is consistent with rationalization, professionalization, and the expansion of state powers. It is consistent also with the American propensity to create technical solutions to normative problems.[33] Christopher Lasch sees child and family services as an expression of professional dominance and state power. While many argue that changes in family organization stimulate the growth of these services, Lasch reverses the causal sequence and claims that helping professions undercut the family.[34]

This book offers a perspective on child-serving professions not available in other treatments. By following pediatrics through a full hundred years of development, it identifies shifts over time in the profession's stance toward families. Two periods in the specialty's history have particular relevance for professional regulation of family matters: the 1920s when pediatricians first established themselves as family advisors, and the 1960s when a segment of pediatricians moved to expand the specialty's purview in the treatment of psychosocial problems. The book assesses the contributions of professionalization as a process as well as broader social forces in changing pediatrics' regulatory functions. The resulting analysis is more complex than many other treatments of child-serving professions.

My account suggests that the forces extending pediatrics' terrain differ for various stages in the specialty's development. It identifies forces encouraging heightened supervision of families and also those impeding further regulation. It challenges the notion that professional dominance alone sufficiently explains pediatricians' advice-giving activities.

Early in this century, large-scale social and ideological movements supported the professional regulation of childhood. Pediatrics capitalized on these movements but did not create them either alone or in concert with other professions. The book's substantive chapters discuss in considerable detail relationships between specialists' counsel-imparting functions and these broader social currents.

Constructing the Analysis

My strategy in conducting research for the book was to proceed inductively from the data. I first generated empirically grounded historical explanations and then worked to identify underlying social processes. My starting point was pediatricians' statements concerning the nature and purpose of the specialty. These appear regularly in pediatric journals and in the transactions of professional societies. An early finding in the research was that, over time, discontinuities occur in specialists' conception of pediatrics. Closer examination revealed that each of these ideological shifts coincides with a wave of institution building. Periodically, specialists mobilize to redefine their roles and build new occupational structures. (Chapters 3 through 7 of the book are organized around these temporal patterns. Each concerns a major transition in the specialty's historical development.)

Having uncovered sequences of normative and structural change within pediatrics, I then sought to account for these transitions. This meant examining the work patterns of contemporary specialists, their occupational environments, and the broader social context of their labor. Toward this end, I explored a very diverse collection of primary and secondary historical materials. Primary sources on events before World War II included pediatric journals and transactions, proceedings of child-health associations, reports of White House conferences on child health, and publications of the U.S. Children's Bureau.[35] I consulted a wide range of secondary sources on the prewar period: histories of hospitals, clinics, and medical schools; accounts of contemporary social and ideological movements; chronicles of the rise of American medicine; existing histories of pediatrics. Among the secondary materials, biographies of pediatricians were especially useful because they offer clues to the work patterns and career contingencies of early generations of child specialists.

Data on postwar events came from a different combination of sources. Published histories of pediatric subspecialties are scarce and provide limited information on organizational arrangements. I supplemented published materials with data gathered from interviews and from unpublished documents provided by several informants. These documents included mimeographed newsletters and memoranda of early subspecialty associations and professional correspondences of subspecialty leaders. I interviewed twenty-six pediatricians, two pediatric psychologists, and professional staff or administrative officers of five pediatrics societies, two child-health organizations, three private foundations, and five federal agencies. Among the twenty-six pediatricians interviewed, all but four held academic appointments; seven had served as pediatric department chairs; seventeen concentrated either on general or psychosocial pediatrics. I treated the data from interviews like documentary material. Informants provided background—otherwise unobtainable—on subspecialty associations, subspecialists' career patterns, and arrangements within contemporary medical schools and teaching hospitals.[36]

I used two types of conceptual processes in generating the analysis. First, hypothesis testing was central in accounting for specialists' periodic mobilizations. I formulated a great many explanations, examined them in light of available data, and rejected the majority. This aspect of the research process is not obvious in the book's narrative. The text spares readers the many blind alleys I explored before arriving at explanations I judged to be fully compatible with the data.

Second, I employed comparisons to develop more explicitly theoretical formulations. There are several levels of comparison in the book. This chapter has compared pediatrics with other medical specialties, and medical specialties with freestanding professions. Later chapters juxtapose patterns in each stage of pediatric history with those in other phases of the specialty's growth. My aim is to find essential, underlying continuities in social patterns. Arthur Stinchcombe describes theory-generating historical inquiry as a process of identifying deep causal analogies within a class of phenomena. To be successful, these analogies must be made at an appropriate level of conceptual abstraction and rest upon sound historical explanation.[37] I use such comparisons in an attempt to discern occupational dynamics that persist across medical specialties and historical periods.

Chapter 2 presents the results of this comparative analysis. It discusses processes common to various stages in the growth of American pediatrics and explains how these findings build upon and contribute to scholarly literature on professions and medical specialties. The text is relatively abstract and some readers may wish to proceed directly to the historical narrative and return to this discussion after exposure to descriptive material.

Chapter Two

Professionalization as Historical Process

When the history of pediatrics is surveyed in its entirety, certain patterns and processes are especially striking. They are noteworthy both because they reoccur in the specialty's development and because they are seldom identified in sociological treatments of professionalization. This chapter presents four analytic themes that are derived from the book's historical account and discusses the significance of each to the sociological literature. The first theme is the importance of changing work patterns to the birth of pediatrics and its continued development. The second is the influence of surrounding occupational structures on the pace with which pediatrics evolves and the shape it adopts. A third dynamic is the persistent salience of organizational innovation as a generative factor in the specialty's long-term growth. The fourth is a recurrent interplay between professional segments and professional organizations: born within hospitals and medical colleges, specialties then affect the shape that these organizations assume.

Work Patterns and Collective Action

The cornerstone of the book's analysis is an account of social processes underlying professional evolution. Key elements of this process are the emergence of new work patterns, the formation (and periodic reconstitution) of professional collectivities, and the construction of occupational institutions. Actual, historically grounded

18

work contingencies are at the center of this historical dynamic. A nascent specialty is, in the first instance, a heretofore nonexistent division of labor. Collectivities form in response to new configurations of labor and new occupational career tracks. As specialties evolve, they redefine themselves and their objectives in reaction to shifts in the content, context, and social organization of labor. A constellation of factors affect practitioners' work patterns: developments in medical science and technology, innovations brought by social reform movements, growth in demand for professional services, changes in the organization of hospital and medical schools. These may be considered causal variables in the emergence of medical specialties. But new patterns of labor are not the passive product of social change; they are actively forged by practitioners striving to improve their competitive position amid shifting technical, institutional, and market conditions.

Collectivities are a group response to new career contingencies and to the search for improved status and advantageous work arrangements. Practitioners with similar work patterns define themselves as a collective entity and move to establish a distinct occupational unit. They construct a professional ethos which defines the unique tasks and purposes of the field and justifies its stated missions. Professional culture solidifies group identity and gives shape, content, and continuity to incipient work roles. Specialty groups develop and systematize an intellectual basis for practice and consolidate markets for new services. They negotiate with the broader professional and social communities, seeking legitimacy and professional privileges. They mobilize to affect work organizations so that career opportunities are maximized and sustained. Collectivities build occupational institutions including—at different points in a specialty's history—professional associations, training programs, and certifying boards. These institutions establish the specialty as a continuous and legitimate entity outside of work organization.[1] All such efforts stabilize emerging work patterns and assert collective control over the division of labor. Professionalization is, at least in part, a codification of emerging patterns of labor.

This interpretation of professional processes has its roots in the empirical record documenting medical specialty evolution. A repeating sequence of events occurs in the development of pediatrics and its subspecialties: new patterns of labor appear; practitioners coalesce into a new collectivity; as a collectivity they construct occupational institutions and shape work organizations. This sequence takes place three times during the formation of pediatrics. It recurs in an accelerated and modified form in the evolution of several pediatric subspecialties. The first sequence begins in the second half of the nineteenth century. Pediatrics coalesces in the 1880s when a number of elite physicians build careers as partial specialists through work in newly established clinics, hospitals, and asylums for children. These practitioners create the first pediatric associations, formulate an initial professional ethos, and work to expand opportunities for child specialists within contemporary hospitals and medical colleges.

Another cycle of events takes place in the early 1900s. A second generation of pediatricians establishes fully specialized work patterns by combining hospital work, teaching posts, and private consulting practices. They draw private patients on the basis of personal reputations for specialized expertise built through years of institutional appointments. This group creates another professional society and substantially reformulates the pediatric ideology. It also launches an ultimately successful campaign to secure autonomous pediatric departments within American medical schools.

A third round occurs in the 1920s and 1930s. A social-reform movement ushers in a new preventive child-health service and stimulates demand for its use. With a growing market for child-health supervision, pediatricians no longer rely upon hospital and teaching posts to attract private patients. The numbers of pediatricians soar and private office-based pediatric practice is viable as a full-time endeavor. Specialists establish yet another association and again recast the pediatric ethos. They move to consolidate the burgeoning market for their services, establishing a certifying board and standardizing residency training. Additional cycles occur in subsequent decades as pediatric subspecialties emerge through analogous processes. In each of these sequences, significant changes in work patterns precede the mobilization of an occupational collectivity. In each, practitioners' efforts stabilize emerging work patterns and exert collective control over the organization of labor.

While grounded in the historical record, my interpretation of professional processes has antecedents in the sociological literature. Everett Hughes was first to emphasize career lines and everyday work activities and to liken developing professions to struggling collectives or social movements. He viewed the claims of these collectives as a negotiating stance. Professions claim certain attributes in the interest of gaining credibility and higher status.[2] Hughes' perspective is further developed by a number of sociologists. Rue Bucher and Anselm Strauss compare professional segments within medicine to dynamic collective movements.[3] Strauss et al. and later Bucher and Joan Stelling depict professional organizations as negotiated orders where practitioners actively participate in defining professional roles and work rules.[4]

While drawing on this perspective, my own account takes a direction not developed by Hughes' followers. I argue that the evolution of professions is not only a matter of negotiation. Collectivities build institutions which are durable social structures. These institutions give continuity to professional work patterns. They establish professions as stable and legitimate entities outside of work organizations and in doing so greatly aid practitioners in their efforts to secure desired arrangements within work organization. I concur with Bucher and Strauss that collectivities are dynamic, shifting over time in their composition and primary objectives. They form and then realign, articulate goals and then formulate new ones. Segments within established specialties move to establish their own collectivities and articulate more highly differentiated occupational interests. But while collectivities are protean, professional institutions, once established, are not prone to rapid change.[5] These structures endure and their presence affects the possibilities for later segments to emerge.

My approach also has roots in another tradition within sociology. I see professionalization as continuous with more general historical trends toward occupational specialization and societal complexity. Social theorists have been grappling with these phenomena since before the founding of social science disciplines. Émile Durkheim addressed social aspects of the division of labor in an essay written during the late 1800s. Adam Smith examined economic roots of specialization in the work place over a century earlier.[6] Among present-day sociologists, Neil Smelser studies mechanisms leading to greater societal complexity and more highly specialized social structures. Building on nineteenth-century social theories and the work of Talcott Parsons, Smelser proposes a general model of structural differentiation.[7] The present study shares with Smelser's work a focus on historical dynamics producing more highly differentiated social structures. I draw from this tradition the concept of social structure and a concern with social processes underlying its transformation. At the same time, I depart from two premises generally associated with functionalist theories. First, the basic functionalist model assumes a social system at equilibrium and locates impulses for new structures in disturbances to it. I do not assume a system at equilibrium but explain social change in terms of the contingencies facing historical actors, their interests, and understandings of contemporary events. Second, I am not convinced of the utility of seeking a universal model of social change. Such formulations are of necessity so abstract as to be of limited use in generating research questions. My own referent is not change in general but the emergence of professions as a class of occupations.

The perspective of structural differentiation has much to add to the study of professional processes. It links professionalization to progressive specialization in work roles and occupational structures. It underscores that professionalization very often involves the emergence of a new occupational unit. Placing the inception of professions within the orbit of professionalization is not an entirely novel idea, but it is absent from what have been dominant approaches to the study of professions.[8] In much sociological literature, professionalization is conceived of as a process through which a preexisting occupation transforms itself into a profession. This formulation is especially apparent in the ahistorical treatments of professions that predominated in the literature during the 1950s and 1960s. Sociologists were preoccupied with creating a generic definition of *profession* and in distinguishing recognized professions from occupations aspiring to but not fully achieving professional status. Some proposed the notion of an occupational continuum with ideal-typical professions at one end, nonprofessions at the other, and aspiring occupations—now called semiprofessions—somewhere in the middle. Professionalization involved moving farther toward the professional end of the continuum.[9] Even some apparently historical treatments of professionalization presupposed, rather than scrutinized, the inception of the occupations in question. Theodore Caplow and later Harold Wilensky posit temporal steps in the acquisition of professional institutions. In Caplow's account, a professional association is followed by a change in title, a code of ethics, and struggle for legal support of occupational barriers. Wilensky's version starts with the existence of a full-time occupation and proceeds with the establishment of training schools, the founding of a professional association, agitation for legal protection, and a formal code of ethics.[10]

Caplow and Wilensky contribute to the literature by underscoring the importance of professional institutions. But like writers who propose a continuum of occupations, they divorce the acquisition of traits and structures from changes in labor patterns and work contingencies which impel professionalization. Such formulations overlook the fact that nascent occupations most often build professional structures. Professions as we know them emerged in America during the late nineteenth and early twentieth centuries. This period saw both the modernization of professional institutions and the rapid proliferation of new professions. The majority of professions in existence today emerged after the mid-nineteenth century and, for them, coming into being and the construction of professional institutions were contemporaneous and interrelated. For older professions like medicine and law, the second half of the nineteenth century was a time of reorganization. Practitioners recast occupational institutions, building structures appropriate to the new social and economic order. Yet even here, changing labor patterns mediate professional processes. Practitioners were responding to changes in work contingencies accompanying the social transformation of the industrial revolution. Professionalization is best understood when viewed in terms of ongoing changes in the content, context, and social organization of labor.

Isomorphism and Occupational Environments

Professional collectivities design and construct occupational institutions. In doing so, they are strongly influenced by the structures established by earlier professional segments and by the overall organization that specialization takes. Collectivities emulate more legitimate and more fully-established professional segments. They emerge into occupational environments populated with professional institutions and these institutions affect both the pace with which newcomers develop and the shape they adopt.

Isomorphism and institutional environments are well-developed themes in the field of organizational sociology. The impact of environments on the functioning and structure of organizations has been a major focus in this area since the early 1970s.[11] Isomorphism refers to the tendency for organizations to become increasingly similar to others in scope, goals, and internal arrangements. They do so in response to forces in their environment including conditions created by the surrounding organizations. While professions also adopt strikingly uniform institutional forms and are greatly influenced by contemporaneous professions, there is relatively little explicit discussion of these phenomena in the literature on professions. Noteworthy exceptions are found in discussions of professions whose terrain impinges upon the domain of others. The occupational environment is invoked when there is obvious competition among professions and when the efforts of one to achieve autonomy and improved status are blocked by a superordinate profession. Goode alludes to interdependence among professions when commenting on the fate of semi-professions. Eliot Freidson discusses obstacles to the professionalization of ancillary health professions created by medicine's superior standing.[12] But sociologists have not systematically explored the impact of occupational environments on emerging professions nor have they fully examined the tendency for professions to adopt uniform occupational structures. This may be due in part to the definition of professionalization that dominated the literature during the 1950s and 1960s. As already discussed, many conceived of professionalization as the transformation of an occupation into a profession, the latter defined as a set of ideal-typical traits or institutions. This formulation embeds the isomorphic character of professions within the definition of professionalization, obscuring the importance and pervasiveness of imitation as an actual historical phenomenon accessible to empirical study. Scrutiny of evolving medical specialties suggests several points relevant to isomorphism and occupational environments.

The first point was introduced earlier: emerging specialties imitate older, more fully established professional segments. The histories of pediatrics and its subspecialties provide numerous examples of this pattern. Child specialists repeatedly emulate the institutions created by earlier entrants into the occupational field. They modeled the first independent pediatric association—the American Pediatric Society founded in 1888—after specialty associations established in the preceding two decades. They conformed to a pattern widely adopted among contemporary specialties when establishing the pediatric certifying board in 1933 and standardizing residency training in the years which followed. During the 1960s and 1970s, pediatric subspecialists utilized institutional designs created by subspecialties of internal medicine several decades earlier. The historical record indicates that emulation was purposeful. Pediatricians were fully aware of contemporary structures and self-conscious in their imitation. Furthermore, isomorphism is pervasive outside pediatrics among both social-problem based and scientifically grounded specialties.

Imitation is not the only force which might encourage homogeneity in occupational structures. Professional segments are undoubtedly influenced directly by features in their common social and economic environments.[13] At the same time, the nature of the professional enterprise makes it likely that emulation is a powerful contributor. Organizational sociologists argue that uncertainty and the need for legitimacy are among the principal factors impelling imitation.[14] The importance of legitimacy in securing professional privileges seems to render professions especially prone to isomorphism. Mimetic tendencies may be particularly strong among social-problem based fields due to their relatively low social status. But whatever the relative strength of emulation among various professional segments, the overall result of imitations is clear. In an attempt to gain prestige and legitimacy, newly emerging specialties model themselves after older, more established ones. As a consequence, specialties of diverse origin and nature assume remarkably similar organizational forms.

Second, early professional structures not only provide models of occupational design, they actually stimulate the founding of later institutions.[15] The generative impact of established structures helps to explain temporal patterns in the founding of specialty institutions. As mentioned in chapter 1, the history of medical specialties is characterized by waves in the creation of occupational structures.[16] Specialty societies proliferated during the final third of the nineteenth century. The first national medical specialty association in the United States was the American Ophthalmological

Society established in 1864. By the early 1900s, physicians had founded national associations for fourteen of today's primary medical specialties.[17] Certifying boards multiplied between the two world wars. The first specialty boards were created in 1917 and 1924 with thirteen additional boards incorporated in the decade of 1930. Of the twenty-one primary boards now in existence, sixteen were established by 1940.[18] There is another noteworthy temporal pattern in the history of specialization. Segments which emerge relatively late evolve more rapidly than early segments. Pediatric subspecialties developed much more quickly than pediatrics itself. The handful of primary specialties which consolidated after World War II matured in a fraction of the time taken by specialties which originated in the nineteenth century.

While there are many forces which influence the pace at which professional segments develop, structures in the occupational environment are an important determinant. Stinchcombe makes essentially the same point when discussing temporal patterns in the founding of organizations. "Organizations, he suggests, "are themselves aspects of the social structure determining the rate of formation of new organizations."[19] Among medical segments, the impact of established structures may be exemplary or coercive.[20] Models of occupational design allow latecomers to progress with greater speed. But in some cases, emulation of older professional institutions may be defensive. Events surrounding the consolidation of pediatric endocrinology illustrate how structures created by one specialty can influence the development of another segment. Pediatric endocrinology emerged as a discrete research field and academic career track during the 1950s. Through the 1970s, subspecialists met at the conventions of several general research societies but had no separate professional association. Pediatric endocrinologists moved to establish an autonomous society (founded in 1972) and a subspecialty certification mechanism (approved in 1974) following the creation in 1970 of an endocrine certifying committee within the American Board of Internal Medicine. Intraprofessional memos indicate that the actions of "adult" endocrinologists were a major catalyst in the consolidation of pediatric endocrinology. Pediatric subspecialists expressed fears that they would be squeezed out or viewed as less legitimate if they failed to follow the precedent of endocrinologists within internal medicine.[21] The formal organization of pediatric endocrinology was a defensive maneuver in response to the actions of a neighboring segment.

Third, occupational forms are themselves institutionalized over time. Once a professional structure becomes well established, new segments have little choice but to follow the mold. Failure to establish the full range of institutions would jeopardize a segment's standing and members' future economic prerogatives. Medical segments created the original certifying boards before third-party reimbursements were an issue. Today the existence of a board enables specialists to secure higher reimbursement rates from insurance agencies. Specialty leaders are well aware of these dynamics. They view the creation of the standard professional structures as necessary to protect status and economic opportunities.

Finally, the timing of a specialty's development, relative to that of other specialties, has consequences for its eventual outcome. Professional institutions established by one collectivity are part of the occupational environment of segments which follow. Over time, the occupational field becomes more densely populated with professional structures. The number of specialties grows and new varieties of professional institutions accumulate. Late entrants have clear models for occupational design but they may face constraints not encountered by earlier segments. The former must contend with claims made by more established specialties over important arenas of professional activities. Latecomers may also encounter explicitly protective action on the part of older segments. This point is illustrated by actions taken by medical segments in the 1930s and 1940s. During these years, established specialties moved to protect their markets by obstructing the further proliferation of specialty boards. Their vehicle was the Advisory Board for Medical Specialties, a coalition of specialty groups (and representatives of the National Board of Medical Examiners) established in the mid-1930s. The Advisory Board and the AMA Council on Medical Education set up a formal mechanism to approve certifying boards. In 1942 the Advisory Board announced that no new primary boards would be approved and that future medical segments would be accommodated as subspecialties under the sponsorship of existing boards.[22] When compared to early specialties, segments which coalesced after 1940 had a harder time establishing certification mechanisms except as subunits within previously established boards. Whether a segment is currently institutionalized as an autonomous specialty or as a subspecialty is determined largely by the timing of its development. New entrants are at a disadvantage when confronted with the claims and requirements of established fields. As neophytes they are unlikely to win outright struggles against more fully institutionalized segments.

Organizational Innovation as a Generative Factor

Virtually all accounts of the inception of professions identify scientific advance and market forces as catalysts. Many take the importance of science to be axiomatic; specialized intellectual techniques are core characteristics of professions as a class of occupations and it is intellectual advance upon which new professional services are based.[23] Others place equivalent or greater stress upon market forces. Modern industrial capitalism and attending societal reorganization produce demand for a broad range of expert services. This demand stimulates both the proliferation of new professions and, among older professions, the construction of modern occupational institutions. In Larson's account, demand actually triggers the accumulation of knowledge. Practitioners move to enhance and systematize the intellectual foundations of practice in response to an expanded market for professional services.[24]

The present analysis does not challenge the causal role of science and market forces. Both are operative in development of medical specialties. Even in the evolution of a social-problem based field like pediatrics, scientific progress and systematization of knowledge are vital to professional consolidation. I do suggest that organizational innovation is more important to the emergence of medical specialties than accounts by sociologists would indicate. Furthermore, such innovation is operative in ways unanticipated by prevailing treatments of professionalization.

Sociologists have not entirely ignored the role of organizational change. But most grant it major significance in the consolidation of only certain types of professions. As discussed in chapter 1, scholars distinguish professions generated by scientific advance from those stimulated by the demands of social organization. According to Carr-Saunders and Wilson, the latter are engendered by an organizational revolution which accompanies industrialization.[25] Larson identifies a class of professions which arise from expansion in the functions of the state and from "the concentration of administrative and managerial functions under corporate capitalism."[26] Professions of this type usually perform their work within large-scale organizations and are subject to forms of bureaucratic authority. Institutional change is clearly instrumental in the development of such professions. But sociologists have not seen organizational innovation as central to the emergence of so-called free professions in which members engage in private practice and exercise a high degree of autonomy from and within work organizations.

Patterns in the development of medical specialties are surprising in this context. Organizational innovation repeatedly operated as a generative factor in the evolution of pediatrics and its subfields. Specialized hospitals, wards, and clinics for children stimulated the initial consolidation of pediatrics in the 1880s and spurred its continued growth through the early 1900s. Infant-welfare centers established in the 1910s and 1920s were crucial in generating demand for child-health services. Specialized divisions within academic departments and teaching hospitals were critical to the evolution of pediatric subspecialties during the middle part of the twentieth century. This general pattern is not limited to pediatrics or social-problem based specialties. Secondary historical sources indicate a similar dynamic in the development of organ and technology-based specialties. Interestingly, medical and social historians have been more sensitive to the role of organizational change in professional evolution than have sociologists. George Rosen was first to link medical specialization to the appearance of new organizational arrangements. He argues that specialized hospitals and clinics created during the middle third of the nineteenth century stimulated the founding of specialty associations in the decades which followed. Rosen provides evidence for this pattern of events in the development of ophthalmology, otolaryngology, orthopedics, and urology.[27]

Precisely how do specialized hospitals and clinics promote occupational differentiation in medicine? Several dynamics operate. First, separate organizational units facilitate growth in the scientific foundations of specialty practice. Specialized dispensaries of the nineteenth century encouraged medical research by offering concentrated clinical material necessary for systematic investigation. They assisted the systematization of professional services by providing centers where practitioners could acquire new skills and exchange knowledge and information.[28] Specialized units within twentieth-century teaching hospitals served parallel functions in the development of medical subspecialties.

Second, organizations constitute the initial market for specialized medical care. When physicians first begin cultivating a new arena of practice, there is little demand for office-based services. Specialized clinics and hospitals are initial locales for the pursuit of focused areas of medicine. As such, organizations provide the original basis for new increments in the division of labor. Specialized work patterns then stimulate the formation of collectivities and the construction of professional institutions. Third, hospitals and clinics directly promote the consolidation of emerging segments. In Rosen's words, "the hospital is a place where physicians working in a special field can develop a sense of identity leading to formal organization."[29]

The preceding discussion suggests that factors generating medical specialties are highly interrelated. Take for example scientific advance and organizational innovation. Specialized clinical units greatly facilitate the growth of specialized knowledge. Yet there is an initial scientific impetus for organizational differentiation. The concept of localized pathology developed by French clinical researchers in the first third of the nineteenth century challenged the prevailing notion of a unitary disease and provided a rationale for concentrating on the disorders of particular organs. These scientific developments were known to the American medical elite and they provided impetus for organizational innovation. But the idea of localized pathology did not itself constitute the substantive basis for specialized medicine. Practicing specialists themselves built the substantive foundations for specialized services and they did so largely within contemporary medical organizations. The underlying dynamic may be stated as follows. Medical research leads to a new paradigm of disease or to the perception of new scientific possibilities. Such notions justify the creation of specialized organizational units. These units and accompanying work roles speed the accumulation of specialized knowledge.[30] Causal factors are highly interdependent in the evolution of medical specialties with organizational innovation spurred by and in turn mediating scientific and market forces.

Control over Markets and Organizational Arrangements

If organizational innovation is vital to the emergence of new specialties, these segments in turn exert an impressive influence over the evolving shape of hospitals and medical schools. Interplay between medical segment and medical organization is pervasive in the history of pediatrics, particularly during the course of market consolidation. Two market processes are especially noteworthy. First, pediatricians repeatedly use appointments in children's institutions to build fee-for-service specialty practices. In doing so, they employ work organizations to constitute extra-organizational markets for professional services. Second, once demand for private services is generated, specialists mobilize to affect hospitals and medical schools so that favorable market conditions are perpetuated. Pediatrics and other medical segments in the United States succeeded in influencing arrangements within professional organizations so that private specialized practices were permanently maintained.

The first market dynamic is evident in at least two different periods in the specialty's history. Late nineteenth-century pediatric consultants built reputations for expertise in children's disease and infant feeding through appointments in foundling homes, children's hospitals, and medical colleges. They used their reputations to attract private patients. In the 1920s and 1930s, primary-care specialists consolidated a market for child-health supervision with the aid of infant-welfare clinics and a contemporary child-hygiene movement. They invented the well-child conference within welfare centers and then transferred its delivery into fee-for-service practice.

Pediatricians were not alone in their use of hospital and clinic posts to build private specialized practices. Work by both Rosen and Rosenberg indicates that physicians in organ-based specialties were pursuing this strategy during the nineteenth century before the appearance of pediatrics.[31] Practitioners were motivated by the status and financial rewards associated with hospital work and specialization. Institutional appointments were not in themselves highly remunerative. Physicians often donated their time, and salaries, where provided, were modest. But private practices built with the aid of specialized institutional posts were prestigious and lucrative.[32] As early as the mid-nineteenth century, physicians obtained higher fees as specialists than as medical generalists. Dispensary and hospital work provided contacts with established clinicians and lay philanthropists that allowed aspiring specialists to attract affluent clients.[33] At their hospital posts, nineteenth and early twentieth-century specialists treated poor and working-class patients. In their private offices, specialists treated members of the upper and middle classes.[34] Physicians were advancing their own careers by using institutional posts to build private specialized practices. Yet in the process, they were channeling a growing but undifferentiated demand for medical care into markets for specific varieties of medical services. They were generating new professional markets.

The second dynamic closely follows the first in temporal order. While the initial creation of demand is driven by the entrepreneurialism of individual practitioners, safeguarding specialty markets is the task of organized segments. In both the early 1900s and after World War I, pediatricians mobilized to ensure that favorable market conditions were regularized and sustained. In both periods, they permanently influence arrangements within professional organizations.

Early twentieth-century child specialists struggled for and won autonomous pediatric departments within American medical colleges. Pediatricians sought independent departments for a number of reasons. Departmental autonomy enhanced the segment's legitimacy, helped assure the continued development of the specialty's knowledge base, and opened a full range of opportunities for pediatricians within academic medicine. The market for office-based services was a consideration as well. Contemporary pediatricians still relied upon institutional posts to build specialized practices and they drew a large portion of their incomes from these practices. With the ongoing reform of American medical schools, universities were asserting control over appointments at major children's hospitals. As a result, medical schools were replacing hospitals as the key institution in pediatric careers. Autonomous departments maximized specialists' control over the clinical posts on which lucrative practices were based.[35]

Pediatricians again affected medical organizations during the 1930s, this time by participating in a movement of contemporary medical segments that produced sixteen certifying boards by 1940. The certification system allowed medical segments to shape graduate professional education and to structure it around the needs of specialty markets. The boards prescribed training requisite to certification and triggered the standardization of residency programs. Specialty leaders designed board requirements so that graduate training prepared physicians for specialized practice rather than careers in teaching and research as some medical educators had envisioned. Residency programs were located in hospitals—many without university affiliation—and oriented toward clinical skills rather than investigatory capabilities.[36] The certification system had the effect of institutionalizing specialties as divisions of the overall market for medical services. It also gave medical segments permanent leverage over the hospitals where graduate training was located. Specialty associations control the boards which in turn influence residency programs and sponsoring hospitals.[37]

Other sociologists have pointed out that emerging professions influence unfolding arrangements within professional organizations. Discussions of this phenomenon often focus on the issues of professional autonomy and freedom from bureaucratic constraints. For example, Richard Hall comments that the most highly autonomous professions work in the least bureaucratic organizations. He suggests that in the evolution of these organizations, professionals import standards to which the organizations adjust.[38] My discussion suggests that technical autonomy is only one among several goals when practitioners move to shape work organizations. Professionals may have the additional aim of enhancing their control over service markets. Specialties within American medicine secured highly favorable market arrangements and their ability to affect educational institutions accounts, in large measure, for this success.[39]

Analysis and Historical Narrative

The next five chapters present descriptive material on which the preceding analysis is based. In them, I endeavor to capture the multiple and interrelated forces that impel professionalization. I also grapple with the interface of structural change and collective action. Occupational segments are both the products and agents of social change. To clarify this duality, the narrative examines social-structural developments and the viewpoints of contemporary practitioners.

Chapter Three

The Inception of a
Medical Specialty

American pediatrics came into being in the decade of 1880. Two professional associations marked its birth: the AMA Section on Diseases of Children established in the 1880 and the independent American Pediatric Society (APS) founded in 1888. The specialty's inception involved more than formal associations. Late nineteenth-century pediatricians formulated a professional ethos that defined the specialty's mission, justified its pursuit, and elicited members' identification. At the start of the 1880s, pediatrics was a collection of physicians with shared work contingencies and substantive interests. By the late 1890s, leaders were transforming this loosely connected aggregate into a self-conscious professional segment.

The birth of pediatrics raises questions about the dynamics of occupational consolidation. Why do new professional segments arise; what factors contribute to their emergence? How do segments coalesce and why do they adopt particular institutional forms? This chapter addresses such questions as it examines the origins of pediatrics within nineteenth-century American society.

I argue that two sets of generative forces contributed importantly to the specialty's birth. One involves social meliorism, organizational innovation and their impact on patterns of professional labor. In the middle third of the century, social activists created special institutions for children including orphanages, infant asylums, hospitals, and dispensaries. Founders were motivated by a desire to rehabilitate and uplift children of the urban poor. Like

35

other hospitals and asylums of the day, children's hospitals were charities staffed by elite physicians who donated a portion of their time to medical philanthropy. This work in children's institutions was the basis for a new type of medical career. By the 1870s, a group of physicians was practicing as partial specialists in children's disorders and infant feeding. While not restricting their practices to children, these men—no women were among them—cultivated a special concentration in pediatrics by pursuing appointments in children's hospitals, dispensaries, and asylums. A new pattern of labor preceded and spurred the consolidation of pediatrics as a medical segment.

Developments in specialists' occupational environments were another catalyst for the creation of pediatrics associations. Between the mid-1860s and 1880, American physicians established national professional societies for a number of clinical fields including ophthalmology, otology (concerning ear disorders), neurology, gynecology, dermatology, laryngology, and surgery. Elite practitioners founded these associations in large part to reassert their professional standing. Both laymen and professionals linked specialization with advances in medical research, and proximity to the forefront of scientific medicine was becoming a new basis for gradients of occupational status. Founders were encouraged also by the spread of specialized hospitals and dispensaries during the middle third of the century and the growing prevalence of partially specialized work patterns in organ-based fields. Contemporary professional societies stimulated the organizational consolidation of pediatrics and affected the form that pediatrics assumed. Child specialists modeled their associations after existing specialty and scientific societies.

APS leaders took pains to associate pediatrics with the profession's upper strata and the movement for scientific medicine. The association restricted its membership to well-connected East-Coast physicians and promoted the study of children's disorders. Leaders further advanced the specialty's cause by constructing a professional ideology that defined the scope and purpose of pediatrics and justified its cultivation as a division of clinical medicine. This ethos delineated a professional role for child specialists and helped to stabilize emerging patterns of labor. It also worked to engender occupational cohesion by eliciting members' identification and commitment.

Childhood and Social Meliorism

Childhood became a focus of normative and social reform in America during the first half of the nineteenth century. Popular treatises on domestic relations appeared in growing numbers during the 1820s and 1830s and these tracts placed new importance on the early stages of life. The association of childhood with original sin, pervasive in eighteenth-century Calvinist thought, gave way to "a new and clement attitude toward child nature."[1] Contemporary literature depicted children as precious, malleable, and in need of adult protection and guidance. Early nineteenth-century texts were still premodern in character. Authors couched their prescriptions in religious or moral philosophy and they placed considerable stress on the merits of discipline and obedience. Norms governing childhood continued to evolve during the second part of the century. In that period, science replaced theology as the principal authority invoked in domestic tracts. Later writers adopted a progressively more lenient stance toward children.[2] They also had more highly differentiated notions of the life course. By the early twentieth century, the emerging science of child development depicted childhood as a sequence of discrete stages each with its own behavioral expectations.[3]

Yet normative change was clearly underway in the early nineteenth century. It was evident in religious tracts which constituted a large portion of the domestic literature during the antebellum period. Anne Kuhn maintains that romantic notions about children's innocence from outside the church were eroding the notion of infant depravity. Furthermore, "Christian nurture" was challenging church philosophy from within. Proponents of the latter view equivocated on the issue of original sin but emphasized the child's susceptibility to spiritual guidance. "Whether the infant was innocent or corrupt, its early years were most important. Purity, if there at birth, had to be preserved, and sin, if originally present, had to be weeded out."[4] Writers of both religious and secular texts agreed that the early years were highly consequential for the individual's character and eventual standing in society.[5]

New ideas about childhood were part of a broader set of normative changes affecting family life in America. Victorian domestic tracts reconstructed not only the child but also gender roles and marital relations. The literature designated separate spheres of influence for husband and wife. It excluded the woman from labor outside the household while appointing her moral and affective leader within the home. Motherhood acquired unprecedented importance. Domestic writers applauded women as nurturers and educators of the young and discussed mother-child relationships with new reverence. They granted women and children elevated status within the household.[6] Advocates of Victorian family norms came from the middle and upper strata of society. But they sought to reform American society by extending the new domestic ideal to the immigrant and native-born working classes.

There has been a great deal of speculation as to why new conceptions of childhood and family relations arose during the early nineteenth century. Some scholars locate the sources of change in contemporary ideological currents. Carl Degler points to the growing prevalence of individualism. Kuhn underscores shifts internal to Calvinist religious thought and developments in European social philosophy.[7] Child health and welfare movements emerged in Britain and Europe during the second half of the eighteenth century and their presence may have influenced the authors of American domestic tracts. Other scholars link changing ideas about childhood to demographic patterns. Birth rates declined during the nineteenth century and this trend may have altered the social status of children. Richard Shryock speculates that falling birth rates engendered child health and welfare movements in Europe and America.[8] But it is unclear whether lowered fertility was a cause or a result of new attitudes toward childhood.[9] Several writers attribute growing sentimentality about children to declines in infant mortality, arguing that parents were willing to become emotionally invested in their youngsters only when the chances of losing a child were minimal.[10] But this argument apparently does not hold for the United States; data suggest that in America infant mortality rose, at least within major urban centers, during portions of the nineteenth century.[11]

Still other scholars link normative innovations to social structural change and the consolidation of a new type of domestic unit. With the advent of industrialization, economic production was removed from the household leaving affective relationships and child rearing as the family's principal functions. Neil Smelser and Sydney Halpern argue that the Victorian domestic ideal was a response to the new structural characteristics of American families. The separation of economic production and domestic life was altering the basis of family cohesion. It also changed the position of children in the household, work place, and community. Moral entrepreneurs re-acted to these developments by recasting domestic norms and rede-fining childhood as a social category. They also identified social problems associated with children and worked to remedy these problems by constructing institutions for the young. These institu-tions would extend essential societal norms to children of the poor and working classes. [12]

Whatever the precise origins of heightened interest in the young, children were the object of meliorism in antebellum soci-ety. New ideas about childhood and family life were part of more general concern with moral and social order. During the middle third of the century, the country witnessed urbanization and immi-gration as well as onset of industrialization. Reformers portrayed America as a nation in turmoil but they espoused confidence in the ameliorative powers of moral renewal and institutional reform. They also saw the dissemination of middle-class family norms as a means for restoring social order. Advocates of the Victorian domes-tic ideal included clergymen, educators, abolitionists, social femi-nists, and members of the budding temperance movement. Kuhn remarks that these groups sought "to control society by reforming the family."[13] Children of the poor were an especially appealing focus for meliorism because, in the prevailing view, their age ren-dered them highly susceptible to uplift and rehabilitation. Activists believed that institutions for the young would transmit core social values to the lower classes and, by doing so, eliminate poverty, vice, and disorder. [14]

Nineteenth-century social reformers established an array of insti-tutions for children including schools, reformatories, orphanages, foundling homes, and asylums. The common school crusade of the second quarter of the century substantially expanded publicly sup-ported primary education.[15] Infant-school advocates of the same period promoted school attendance for youngsters two through four, particularly those from the poorer classes.[16] Between 1920 and 1950, philanthropists established more than sixty orphanages and an un-counted number of reformatories for disobedient youths.[17] The

founders of these diverse institutions shared two principal motiva-
tions: humanitarianism and the desire to impose firmer controls on
disruptive elements within society. Among common school advocates, the integration of disadvantaged children into the larger social
order was one of the principal rationales for publicly supported education.[18] Promoters of infant education and managers of children's
asylums spoke in dramatic terms about removing youngsters from
the contagion of vice and poverty.[19] It was in this climate of institutional innovation and moral renewal that Americans built hospitals
and dispensaries for children in the nation's cities.

Hospitals for the Young

The first children's hospitals in America were established in the
mid 1850s: Nursery and Child's Hospital in New York City in 1854,
and Children's Hospital of Philadelphia in 1855. At least three
additional institutions appeared in the decade of 1860: Chicago
Hospital for Women and Children in 1865, Boston Children's Hospital in 1869, and the New York Foundling Asylum in 1869. During
the 1870s, philanthropists created more than a dozen additional
medical facilities for children. Most of these were concentrated in
eastern urban centers. Several were in New York City. Others
were located in Philadelphia; Lawrence, Mass.; Radnor, Pa.; Atlan-
tic City, N.J.; Washington, D.C.; and Albany, N.Y. There were
also a few in midwestern cities including Detroit, Cincinnati, and
St. Louis.[20]

Coalitions of charitably inclined laymen and elite physicians established the early children's hospitals. Like the founders of other
institutions for the young, hospital organizers sought to uplift children from the lower classes. Mid-nineteenth century children's
hospitals were charities for the poor. Their purpose was to treat not
only physical ailments but also moral afflictions. Francis Brown,
physician founder of Children's Hospital in Boston, maintained
that an unhealthy moral life within lower-class families rendered
children especially vulnerable to disease. "Children of the poorer
classes," he wrote,

from their insufficient and poor food, the want of care for their cleanliness,
and protection from the weather, their unsanitary abodes, the want of air
and sunshine, and, perhaps, equally the want of healthy moral tone in the

family, of kindness and affection, develop a condition of depressed vitality which renders them easily the prey of disease. To this consideration is to be added the thought of every farseeing philanthropist, that these children are the future members of society, and that the sound mind of the coming citizen depends largely on a sound body.[21]

For hospital managers, sickness provided an opportunity for spiritual reform.

Historian Morris Vogel examined Annual Reports published by Boston's Children's Hospital during the 1870s and 1880s and found abundant evidence of the institution's moral agenda. Trustees spoke of patients who came "from the very lowest; from abodes of drunkenness, and vice in almost every form, where the most depressing and corrupting influences were acting both on the body and the mind." In the hospital, children were "carefully taught cleanliness of habit, purity of thought and word."[22] They received the kind of "moral training as can be found in any cultivated family."[23] Francis Brown describes the hospital's program of uplift and renewal.

It has been the constant aim of managers, while endeavoring to cure or alleviate disease, and give a tone to their general health, to bring the patients under the influence of order, purity and kindness . . . and by means of intelligent and tender nursing, by attractive books, pictures and toys, and by the visits and attentions of the kind and cultivated, to do something toward beguiling their hours of suffering, quickening their intellects, refining their manners, and softening and encouraging their hearts. . . . The managers . . . recall with satisfaction the fact that [these principles] have had an important effect in humanizing and elevating those under their charge.[24]

There were rationales for establishing children's hospitals apart from the social control of lower class families. Elite physicians believed that hospitals for the young would facilitate the study of children's disease. As models, they had clinics and hospitals for children established in Britain, France, and Austria during the first half of the nineteenth century. European hospitals stimulated the investigation of childhood illnesses and there was a modest literature on the subject by the mid-1800s.[25] Practitioners from the upper strata of American medicine typically studied abroad early in their careers and they brought back news of European develop-

ments. Physician organizers of Boston Children's Hospital allude to
these influences in a statement they distributed in 1868.

There is a want in our community, long felt in our medical schools, though
provided for in foreign cities, namely, an opportunity to study infantile
diseases . . . which furnish a distinct branch of medical science, the importance of which can hardly be sufficiently recognized.[26]

Founders of children's hospitals did not have to look to Europe for
examples of institutions that promoted the study of specific types of
disease. American physicians began establishing hospitals and dispensaries for the treatment of organ-specific disorders during the
1820s and 1830s.[27] Scientific work conducted in Paris during the
early 1800s helped to spur the creation of these specialized facilities.
Research by French pathologists granted new significance and legitimacy to circumscribed problem areas within clinical medicine.[28] By
mid-century there was a pervasive movement to establish specialized medical facilities in American cities. With support from lay
contributors, physicians organized specialized dispensaries and specialized departments within general dispensaries. When the Brook-
lyn Dispensary opened in 1847, its managers divided patients
among the following categories: women and children, heart, throat
and lungs, skin and vaccination, head and digestive system, eye and
ear, surgery and unclassified disorders.[29] The trend continued during the final third of the century with the spread of special-purpose
hospitals and special departments within general hospitals.[30] This
proliferation of specialized medical facilities in American cities was
an additional factor encouraging the founding of children's hospitals.

Hospitals for the young resembled contemporary medical facilities in organizational design. The children's hospital of the 1860s
and early 1870s was typically a private institution with twenty or so
beds, housed in a converted family residence. Its managers included a board of lay trustees which provided financial backing, a
board of visiting ladies, and a panel of attending physicians. More
than likely it operated on a shoestring budget. The Children's Hospital in Washington, D.C. ran on little over $5,000 in 1871, the first
year that it opened. Nursery and Child's Hospital of New York, a
relatively well-established and affluent institution, reported expenditures of $45,000 in its seventeenth annual report published in
1871. Some children's hospitals of this period had full-time matrons

but most custodial care of patients was handled by volunteer lady visitors. As the institutions evolved during the late 1870s and 1880s, they added paid nursing staff, boards of consulting physicians, and salaried resident physicians.[31]

Physicians accrued little direct financial gain from work within children's institutions or other specialized medical facilities. Virtually all hospitals and dispensaries of this period were charities for the poor and dependent upon lay and medical philanthropy. Many hospital appointments were uncompensated and the salaries that existed were modest. Nonetheless, institutional posts were crucial in the careers of upper-strata physicians. Charles Rosenberg comments that hospital posts were the single most important criterion for membership in the urban medical elite.[32] For the practitioners who donated time to dispensaries and hospitals—and for the laymen who financed them—stewardship was an expression of social status. Furthermore, nineteenth-century dispensaries and hospitals were centers for the acquisition of clinical skills and the focal points of colleague networks. Institutional posts allowed ambitious young practitioners to establish contacts and reputations that would enable them to build their practices. The physicians who founded and staffed children's hospitals were pursuing a then widespread career-building strategy.

Children's hospitals and asylums contributed to the emergence of pediatrics in a number of different ways. They provided a concentration of case material needed for the investigation of children's disorders. Early pediatricians remarked on "the abundant opportunity for the study of diseases of children afforded by the college clinics, the asylums, and dispensaries" within late nineteenth-century American cities.[33] Hospitals and foundling homes served as training centers where practitioners gained experience in the treatment of children's diseases. Finally, and most important for the organizational consolidation of pediatrics, medical facilities for the young were the basis for a new pattern of labor among a segment of elite physicians.

Pediatric Careers

The physicians who founded pediatric associations in the 1880s were well acquainted with contemporary hospitals, dispensaries, and asylums for children. These men donated time to institutions for the young and by doing so forged careers as partial specialists in childhood disorders. There were no women within nineteenth or early twentieth-century pediatric societies. Women were prominent among the lay sponsors of children's hospitals.[34] But female doctors—a small fraction of all contemporary physicians—were excluded from specialty associations and from hospitals and dispensaries where specialized skills could be learned.[35] Early pediatricians were male physicians with good connections and access to the institutional appointments upon which prestigious careers were built. Like others among the American medical elite, they combined private practice, hospital posts, and medical school teaching. While functioning as general clinicians in their private offices, they concentrated upon children's diseases in their hospital work and teaching appointments. By the late 1870s there were several dozen physicians in New York and other northeastern cities who were semi-specialists in the field of childhood diseases. This pattern of partial specialization preceded and stimulated the consolidation of pediatrics as an organized professional segment.

The work history of Job Lewis Smith exemplifies career patterns among first-generation child specialists. Smith was one of several physicians who founded the American Pediatric Society in 1888.[36] By that time, he had been working in children's hospitals and asylums for more than twenty-five years. Smith began his medical career in New York City after completing a professional degree at the College of Physicians and Surgeons (Columbia University Medical School) in 1853. During the late 1850s, he served as curator to Nursery and Child's Hospital, physician to a children's clinic at Northwestern Dispensary, and attending physician in charge of infants and children at the Charity Hospitals of New York. (The latter were municipal hospitals on Blackwell's Island.) In the 1860s, 1870s, and 1880s, Smith was affiliated with, among other institutions, the New York Foundling Asylum, the New York Infant Asylum (established in 1865), and Infant's Hospital on Randall's Island (created in 1866 as an adjunct to the Blackwell's Island hospitals). Smith also held an appointment as Clinical Professor of Diseases of Children at Bellevue Hospital Medical College, where he started teaching pediatrics in the outpatient department during the 1870s.[37]

Abraham Jacobi, first president of the APS and founder of the

AMA Section on Diseases of Children, also held a series of specialized hospital and teaching posts prior to the 1880s. Jacobi received a medical degree from the university in Bonn in the late 1840s. He emigrated from Germany shortly thereafter, embarking on a medical career in New York City during the mid-1850s. Jacobi served as attending physician at Nursery and Child's Hospital in the decade of 1860. In addition to hospital posts, he ran special teaching clinics on the diseases of children at the New York Medical College during the early 1860s, at the University Medical College during the second half of that decade, and at the College of Physicians and Surgeons beginning in 1870.[38]

Among the other founding members of the APS, Louis Starr was attending physician at the Philadelphia Children's Hospital from 1879. Charles Putnam of Boston was physician to the Massachusetts Infant's Asylum and involved in numerous other charity organizations for the aid of women and children. Samuel Busey—an early member of the APS and instrumental in the creation of the AMA Section—was physician in charge of diseases of children in the outpatient department of Columbia Hospital in Washington, D.C. and attending physician at the Washington, D.C. Children's Hospital. Busey was one of the organizers of the latter institution.[39] Founding members of the APS were, virtually without exception, from cities with well-established medical facilities for children. Of the forty-three physicians on the original roster of the American Pediatric Society, twenty-one were from New York City where children's institutions were especially numerous.[40] The great majority of early APS members were spending a portion of their professional time specializing in diseases of children by virtue of work within hospitals and asylums for the young.[41]

The problems these physicians encountered within children's facilities shaped their professional activities as pediatricians. A central preoccupation of first-generation child specialists was keeping foundlings alive within institutional settings. Abandoned infants were a sizable portion of the inmates within some children's hospitals and nearly all children's asylums during the final third of the century.[42] The Medical Board of Infant's Hospital on Randall's Island in New York estimated in 1871 that there were between three and four thousand foundlings per year in that city. Infant's Hospital alone was admitting 1,200 to 1,400 per year.[43] Mortality among

babies housed in late nineteenth-century institutions was staggering. Smith writes that, during the first year of the New York Infant
Asylum's operation in 1865, the death rate among babies (most
under two months of age) was virtually 100 percent. Mortality at
the public Infant's Hospital during the late 1860s was nearly as
high.[44] Jacobi calculated that in 1870 mortality among babies admitted to Nursery and Child's Hospital was well over 50 percent.[45]
Early pediatricians struggled to alleviate these conditions. Smith
worked to introduce wet nurses into infant asylums, reasoning that
breast-fed babies would thrive better than bottle-fed infants.[46]
Jacobi strongly opposed placing babies in institutions, whatever the
method of feeding. In the early 1870s, Jacobi launched a campaign
to have foundlings boarded out to individual families rather than
housed in large facilities. He brought mortality rates among institutionalized babies to the attention of contemporary professional associations and took his case against foundling homes as far as the New
York State Medical Society. Jacobi's efforts deterred the creation of
infant asylums in other American cities.[47]

Their work within children's facilities also influenced the scientific concerns of nineteenth-century pediatricians. The bulk of papers written by early child specialists were clinical studies of cases
encountered in hospital work.[48] During the 1880s and 1890s, methods of artificial infant feeding became a major topic of discussion in
the pediatric literature. This research focus was an outgrowth of
attempts to reduce mortality among babies housed in asylums and
hospitals.[49]

At the time the original pediatric associations were organized,
child specialists were not restricting their medical work to children.
Smith was publishing articles on obstetrics and general medicine up
to his death in the late 1890s. Jacobi states that he continued to see
adult patients through the end of his career.[50] He declared in 1880
that any physician attempting to practice pediatrics on a full-time
basis "would make himself ridiculous."[51] Whether limitations on the
extent of specialization were due more to inclination or to necessity
is not entirely clear. Demand for the services of child specialists
outside medical institutions was extremely limited during this period. But it was also the case that pediatricians of the 1870s and 1880s
had principled objections to full-scale specialization. Whatever the
precise combination of reasons, the first generation of pediatricians

were part-time specialists, pursuing a special interest in children's disorders as an adjunct to general medical practice.

Pathways to Formal Organization

New work patterns were one factor encouraging the consolidation of pediatrics during the 1880s. Another was the recent formation of numerous specialty associations combined with organizational ferment in American medicine. Elite physicians had initiated at least seven specialty societies by 1880: the American Ophthalmological Association in 1864, the American Otological Society in 1867, and associations of neurologists, dermatologists, gynecologists, laryngologists, and surgeons between 1875 and 1880. Several additional specialty societies appeared in the decade of 1880: the American Climatological Association (concerned with climatic treatment of respiratory diseases), the American Orthopedic Association, and the American Association of Obstetricians and Gynecologists.[52] Specialized dispensaries and work patterns helped spur the formation of these professional associations. By the mid-nineteenth century, partial specialization in ophthalmology, otology, and other organ-based fields was common among the medical elites of major northeastern cities.[53] Upper-strata physicians established specialty and scientific associations both to promote new clinical fields and to differentiate themselves from the rank and file.

The late nineteenth-century medical elite had interests quite distinct from those of middle-strata physicians. The latter were working through the AMA to improve the standing of the profession as a whole by raising entrance requirements and defeating irregular medical sects. Elite practitioners had less to gain from the upgrading of medicine. Their professional standing originated more from their class background and the status of their clients than from the prestige of medicine as an occupation.[54] Elite physicians were among the AMA's leadership but their participation embroiled them in political conflicts. Most AMA members were general practitioners openly hostile to specialization—which they viewed as a source of pernicious economic competition—and the organization's meetings were dominated by procedural and ethical disputes.[55]

Specialty associations allowed elite physicians to advance their unique professional interests and to cultivate scientific concerns unencumbered by battles over ethical conformity and professional politics. The societies also had status-maintenance functions. Efforts by the AMA to reorganize and upgrade medicine as a whole threatened to undermine existing status differentials between middle and upper-strata physicians. Specialization provided a new basis for gradients of occupational prestige because of its perceived link to progress in medical research and the growing legitimacy of scientific medicine. Opposition to specialism was long-standing within medicine and it lingered, following the widespread acceptance of scientific rationales for the pursuit of circumscribed fields. Even upper-strata physicians were ambivalent about specialization. Some distinguished specialization in research from that in practice and considered the latter a threat to the unity of medicine.[56] Nevertheless by the 1870s, specialty and scientific associations were a means for elite practitioners to reassert their professional standing. Early specialty societies admitted members by election and they kept their ranks free of lower-status practitioners.[57]

American physicians established many scientific and professional organizations during the nineteenth century apart from specialty associations. These included both local and national societies.[58] In 1886, a group of laboratory-minded practitioners founded the Association of American Physicians, an exclusive scientific society for general clinicians. Two years later, specialty leaders formed the Congress of American Physicians and Surgeons, a federation of existing specialty associations. Through the Congress, specialists attempted to maintain elite membership standards and prevent encroachment from duplicate or marginal societies. To gain entrance into the Congress, a new association had to be unanimously elected by the organization's eleven member-societies.[59]

The physicians who initiated the American Pediatric Society were familiar with contemporary scientific and specialty societies. Six men on the original APS roster were founders of the Association of American Physicians; fourteen belonged to both organizations.[60] Most charter members of the APS were active in a range of medical associations. Jacobi, for example, was an officer of the New York Pathological Society and the New York Obstetric Society and was a founding member of both the Association of American Physicians and the American Climatological Society.[61] Child specialists used skills they acquired through participation in these professional societies to establish pediatrics as a legitimate division of medicine. They modeled pediatrics societies after existing elite professional associations, constituting a professional segment that would enhance the status of its members.

Advancing the Field of Pediatrics

APS founders pursued a number of strategies to promote the standing of pediatrics. Like other elite societies, the association instituted a policy of admission by election through which it excluded physicians from the middle and lower strata of medicine. Organizers drew several eminent physicians into the association's ranks who, while not practicing as partial specialists, were interested in children's disorders and endorsed the development of pediatrics. These included William Osler, physician-in-chief at Johns Hopkins Hospital from 1889, and Victor Vaughan, who became dean of medicine at the University of Michigan in 1891.[62] APS leaders secured membership for their society in the Congress of American Physicians and Surgeons. They claimed publicly to have modeled the APS after the prestigious Association of American Physicians. These measures were designed to link pediatrics with the upper strata of American medicine and justified the segment's claim to elite status.

Establishing pediatrics as a credible division of medical science was a dominant concern of early child specialists. The official goal of both the AMA Section and the APS was to foster the study of children's diseases and these organizations devoted the bulk of their meeting time to scientific papers. Thomas Morgan Rotch, assistant professor of pediatrics at Harvard, articulated the scientific aims of the APS. "What our society was needed for," he declared, "what it was formed for, what it intends to do, is to place the study of pediatrics on the same elevated plane that has been established for adult life."[63] Contemporary child specialists founded a number of pediatric journals. The first periodical devoted exclusively to children's disorders was *Archives of Pediatrics* established in 1884. Other journals and annuals initiated before the end of the century included the *Transactions of the American Pediatric Soci-*

ety (first published in 1889) and *Pediatrics* established in 1896. The AMA Section began publishing its transactions in a separate volume during the late 1890s.[64]

At the same time, specialists endeavored to expand opportunities for work in the area of children's disorders. They advocated the creation of new children's facilities and the expansion of the pediatric curriculum within American medical schools. In his presidential address to the APS in 1889, Jacobi called upon his colleagues to press for improvements in pediatric instruction and to solicit funds actively for new children's hospitals—as distinct from infant asylums—and for the expansion of existing hospitals.[65] While delivering a speech at the *Festschrift* held in his honor in 1900, Jacobi exclaimed:

Unknown Donor! More unknown or known donors are wanted. A single half million dollars will suffice to build and endow a children's hospital of fifty beds. . . . The race of Vanderbilts, Carnegies, Sloanes . . . and Pierpont Morgans cannot possibly be extinct.[66]

The APS as an organization did not launch campaigns for hospital endowments or specialized teaching posts, but Jacobi was clearly urging its members to do so. The existence of a formally constituted specialty added legitimacy to efforts by individual practitioners to open new positions for pediatricians within medical organizations.

Especially important at this stage of the segment's development, leaders constructed a professional ideology that defined the core tasks of pediatrics and justified its cultivation to both the specialists themselves and the profession at large. This ethos worked to generate a sense of common mission and group identity among contemporary pediatricians. It was Abraham Jacobi who assumed the task of articulating professional norms and values. More than any of his contemporaries, Jacobi served as the ideological leader of nineteenth-century pediatrics.[67]

Professional Ethos of the Partial Specialists

Jacobi delineated the content and scope of pediatrics in a series of papers delivered during the 1880s and 1890s. He included the full range of children's disorders within the field's domain but his conception of pediatrics extended well beyond pathological conditions.

From the outset, Jacobi argued that the pediatrician should be concerned with infant feeding, child hygiene, and the prevention of disease. This position is clear in his inaugural address to the AMA Section on Diseases of Children in 1880.

A special section on the pathology of children will . . . not only give its attention to the sick, but to the well child. The questions of how to nurse and how to feed, both naturally and artificially, cannot claim to be fully answered to the satisfaction of all. We need not wonder at the uncertainty in these important points amongst the public when, though much has been settled, so much is left to doubt, uncertainty, or even ignorance in the profession. Nothing is more vital to the raising of the baby than its hygiene, which comprises more than feeding alone, and has to pay attention to dress, air, sleep, bath and exercise, both physical and mental. Every one of these topics requires repeated discussion.[68]

Jacobi envisioned the pediatrician as a political being, involved in formulating social policy as it affected the young. Specialists would provide expert advice on public hygiene, the design of primary education, and school preparedness of children.[69]

Because pediatrics is in some ways an anomalous medical field, arguing for its legitimacy presented strategic problems. Nineteenth-century child specialists acknowledged that pediatrics was a peculiar division of clinical medicine. Jacobi remarked more than once that pediatrics was not a specialty in the common use of the term because it dealt with an entire organism rather than a discrete organ.[70] He discussed the relation of pediatrics to other clinical fields in several papers and emphasized the absence of clear boundaries dividing it from organ-based specialties. "Indeed," Jacobi stated, "if all the teaching obtained from pedology and pediatrics could be disjointed from those branches, these latter would be stripped of their best material."[71] Borden Veeder, an early twentieth-century child specialist, offered an especially incisive statement on the unique features of pediatrics. Veeder remarked that

pediatrics occupies a unique position among clinical specialties in that it has an entirely different basis for its separation. Neurology, ophthalmology, dermatology, etc., have their basis in the study of the diseases of some particular anatomical part or system, while pediatrics is a division or separation based entirely on age and in a broad sense embraces all fields of clinical medicine.[72]

He continued:

The pediatrician is, . . . so far as his medical work is concerned, a general practitioner limiting his work to an age group.[73]

Specialties that coalesced during the nineteenth century were, almost without exception, rooted in the study of a particular organ system or in the development of specialized technologies. They were outgrowths of the notion of localized pathology and they implied a limited set of foci for research and clinical practice. Pediatrics had an entirely different conceptual basis and it traversed the domains of virtually all existing divisions of clinical medicine. How to justify the existence of this anomalous field to the broader professional community was a problem confronting the nineteenth-century pediatric leadership. Jacobi constructed a case for the legitimacy of pediatrics by developing three distinct lines of argument.

First, while acknowledging that pediatrics cut across other specialties, Jacobi maintained that the physiology and pathology of children were sufficiently different from those of adults to merit classification as a special branch of clinical medicine. This was a central theme in several of Jacobi's papers, including his presidential address to the APS in 1889. On this occasion Jacobi declared:

Pediatrics does not deal with miniature men and women, with reduced doses and the same class of diseases in smaller bodies, but . . . it has its own independent range and horizon. . . . There is scarcely a tissue or an organ which behaves exactly alike in the different periods of life. . . . There are anomalies and diseases which are encountered in the infant and child only. There are those which are mostly found in children, or with a symptomatology and course peculiar to them.[74]

Second, Jacobi appealed to dominant social norms regarding the importance of childhood as a life stage and the need to socialize children from the immigrant and native-born working classes. He argued that pediatricians' input into the care and education of children was crucial to the preservation of America's institutions and core social values. Jacobi expounded:

If there is a country in the world with a great destiny and grave responsibility, it is ours. Its self-assumed destiny is to raise humanitarian and social development to a higher plane by amalgamating, humanizing, and civilizing the scum of all the inferior races and nationalities which are congregating under the folds of our flag. Unless the education and training of the young is carried on according to the principles of sound and scientific physical and mental hygiene, neither the aim of our political institutions will ever be reached nor the United States fulfil its true manifest destiny.[75]

Finally, Jacobi and his colleagues argued that pediatrics was legitimate precisely because it failed to designate a highly restricted arena of professional practice. Here they were appealing to ambivalence toward specialization prevalent among late nineteenth-century physicians, even those within the upper strata of medicine. William Osler's sentiments about specialization were typical of the contemporary medical elite. He commented upon the subject in an address to the American Pediatric Society in 1892. Osler discussed advantages of specialization for the conduct of medical research. But he added that

specialization is not . . . without many disadvantages. . . . In the cultivation of a specialty as an *art* [that is, in medical practice as distinct from medical science] there is a tendency to develop a narrow and pedantic spirit.[76]

While adopting the organizational form of contemporary medical segments, first-generation pediatricians had mixed feelings about specialization. Jacobi repeatedly disavowed "the exaggerated specializing tendencies of the times."[77] In his address to the AMA Section in 1880, Jacobi presented a satirical account of contemporary specialism in which organs and appendages were "conquered as special property" by segments within the profession.[78] In a later speech he exhorted:

During my . . . life . . . I had to observe, first in Europe, then with us, the tendency to exaggerated specialization, which has contributed much to narrow the scientific, mental and moral horizon of many a young man who means to become a wealthy and famous specialist without ever having been a physician.[79]

Child specialists argued that pediatrics avoided the narrowness to which other specialties were prone. They claimed the field was not a specialty at all but, rather, a branch of general medicine.[80] By this they meant that pediatrics was more important and more fundamental to the practice of medicine than fields like ophthalmology or neurology which involved the treatment of a more circumscribed set of medical problems. Pediatrics avoided the shortcomings of these fields because it implied an extremely broad range of therapeutic foci and because it was indivisible from clinical medicine as a whole. On the latter point, Jacobi was resolute. "As far as practice is concerned," he wrote, "my belief is this: that the diseases of children must never be torn away from general medicine." And again, "to study and practice a specialty should not mean to cut loose from medicine."[81] Pediatrics was a field consistent with the outlook and professional commitments of the general medical practitioner. It was the generalist's specialty.

Pediatric leaders directed their ideological formulations both to external audiences and to the collectivity itself. On the one hand, they endeavored to persuade members of the profession at large that pediatrics was a legitimate and honorable division of clinical medicine. Their repudiation of exaggerated specialization was an appeal to prevailing values within medical culture. On the other hand, leaders sought to affect the emerging community of pediatricians.[82] Nineteenth-century professional ideology had three analytically distinct functions for the nascent specialty. First, it supported career building on the part of individual practitioners. Child specialists were now contributing to a broader mission and were endorsed by an elite association when they pressed for more prerogatives within medical organizations. Second, the ethos helped stabilize contemporary work patterns by delineating a coherent occupational role. Statements about the nature and purpose of the field defined what activities and commitments were appropriate to a member of the specialty. The nineteenth-century pediatrician was a medical generalist with a special interest in children's diseases and infant hygiene. He promoted pediatrics and pursued work in the field without relinquishing his tie with general medicine or his membership in other specialty societies. Finally, the ethos formulated by early pediatricians helped to bind specialists to a common set of goals and commitments at a time when there were few formal structures generating solidarity. Occupational ideology stimulated members' identification and, through its agency, leaders began to transform pediatrics into a cohesive professional segment.

Dynamics of Occupational Inception

Pediatrics came into being during the late nineteenth century through the convergence of diverse social forces. My account emphasizes two sets of generative factors. The first line of argument details a sequence of developments including social meliorism directed toward children of the poor, the founding of children's hospitals and asylums, and the emergence of new work patterns among a segment of elite physicians. Children's institutions provided the basis for semi-specialized medical careers which, in turn, stimulated the consolidation of pediatrics as a medical segment.

My second line of argument concerns the impact of recently founded specialty societies. These associations provided further impetus for the consolidation of pediatrics and models for how a medical segment might be conceived and organized. Children's disorders were an unusual focus within nineteenth-century medicine. Other fields that coalesced during the 1860s, 1870s, and 1880s had their roots in the notion of localized pathology or in technological innovations. Even with the appearance of partially specialized work patterns in children's disorders, it seems unlikely that pediatricians would have mobilized when they did had no other medical specialties already been constituted.

Pediatricians were motivated to build specialized careers and to establish professional associations because these work patterns and occupational societies augmented physicians' status and gave them competitive advantages. Both lay and medical communities linked specialization with scientific medicine, and confidence in the profession's scientific capabilities rose significantly during the second half of the nineteenth century. Membership in an organized specialty conferred prestige at a time when the ongoing reform of medicine was eroding older bases of intra-professional status. The elite physicians who founded specialty associations during the nineteenth century did so in large part to reaffirm their professional standing.

Another set of processes accompanying the inception of pediatrics merits comment. These concern science as a causal factor in the specialty's birth. My analysis suggests that scientific factors contribute to the emergence of pediatrics in several ways. A new paradigm of disease forged in Paris during the early part of the century encouraged specialization in general by granting significance and legitimacy to circumscribed problem areas. Medical research stimulated pediatrics indirectly through the emergence of organ-based fields and directly by providing additional rationale for the creation of hospitals for the young. Perhaps most remarkable about the science as a generative factor is how closely it is tied to contemporary organizational arrangements. Children's hospitals founded in the second half of the century facilitated the growth of literature on children's disorders. Jacobi remarked that, between 1850 and the early 1900s, publications on diseases of children multiplied more than tenfold.[83] Scrutiny of nineteenth-century pediatric journals indicates that the scientific preoccupations of contemporary specialists were a direct outgrowth of the problems they confronted within children's institutions. Normative currents combined with the perception of scientific possibilities spurred the formation of children's hospitals. These organizations, in turn, promoted investigation in focused arenas of clinical medicine.

Chapter Four

Autonomy within American Medical Schools

In the early 1900s, pediatricians dramatically recast their ethos and embarked on a new mobilization. The notion of the pediatrician as partial specialist and the conception of pediatrics as a division of general medicine, fundamental to nineteenth-century professional beliefs, gave way to a new ideology. A younger generation of physicians promoted pediatrics as an independent arena of medical work. Their goals were to establish the legitimacy of pediatrics as a discrete specialty and to win autonomous pediatric departments within American medical schools. The new segment was highly successful in meeting its aims. By the end of World War I, it had institutionalized pediatrics as a consulting specialty and secured a favorable position within academic medicine.

Changing attitudes toward specialization undoubtedly contributed to the reorientation of pediatricians' goals and ideology. Scientific medicine was highly legitimate in the cultural climate of early twentieth-century America; both the profession and public linked specialization to advances in medical research and treatment. Opposition to specialization from within the profession, intense during the nineteenth century, abated somewhat in the 1900s and middle-class clientele found specialized services increasingly attractive. But other forces were operating as well. Specialists were responding to alterations in the content and organizational context of their labor.

Two developments were central to the professional mobilization of the early twentieth century. The first involved changes in specialists' work patterns. By the turn of the century, a group of physicians was limiting its professional activities entirely to pediatrics. These full-scale specialists combined hospital posts, teaching appointments, and specialized private practices. Their work patterns were an artifact, in part, of an expanding range of opportunities within medical organizations. During the 1880s and 1890s, children's hospitals grew in size and number and medical colleges introduced teaching appointments in the diseases of children. Pediatricians used institutional appointments to build specialized practices, attracting clients through reputations for exceptional expertise gained through years of hospital and teaching posts. With new attitudes toward specialization and with the increase in teaching and hospital posts, a broader range of physicians were pursuing careers in pediatrics.

The second development was a shift in the balance of power among professional organizations which rendered medical schools increasingly important to specialists' careers. In the late nineteenth century, hospitals were key institutions for the medical specialists. Even teaching appointments were obtained on the basis of hospital connections. But by the early twentieth century, university control over facilities used for clinical instruction was a pivotal issue in educational reform. Medical schools were bringing teaching hospitals within their domain, securing arrangements whereby academic departments controlled hospital appointments. This shift in the locus of power was highly consequential for pediatricians. Demand for office-based services was still very limited and institutional positions were crucial to contemporary work patterns. Child specialists sought independent departments both to protect existing career opportunities and to ensure the continued development of the specialty.

Pediatricians drew upon a contemporary child health and welfare movement in promoting their cause. They argued that autonomous departments and full-scale specialization would reduce infant mortality and improve child health. The creation of separate pediatric departments, spokesmen insisted, was one of the university's responsibilities in the area of public health. These arguments were very effective with the vanguard of scientific medicine, a group sympathetic to progressive social reform. Despite criticisms of pediatrics in the area of scientific research, the academic leadership of the profession promoted the establishment of pediatrics as a major division of clinical medicine. It was through the agency of this emerging professional elite that pediatricians obtained modern, autonomous academic departments.

Expanding Institutional Arenas

The founding of special institutions and departments for children, begun in the 1850s, continued in the final two decades of the nineteenth century. Philanthropists established new children's hospitals in New York City; Boston; Chicago; St. Louis; Detroit; San Francisco; Baltimore; Syracuse; Buffalo; Milwaukee; and Columbus, Ohio.[1] Separate departments for children within general dispensaries and hospitals became more numerous also. By the 1890s, cities without a children's hospital were likely to have special units within municipal facilities. In Cleveland, the Babies' and Children's Hospital was not founded until 1906. But directors of Cleveland City Hospital established a ward for children in 1876 and it was housed in a separate cottage on the hospital grounds from the mid-1880s. Children's wards multiplied even where well-established children's hospitals existed. In Chicago, which had two children's hospitals in the mid-1880s, managers of several general hospitals created special departments for children during the two final decades of the century.[2] By 1900, virtually every major American city had at least one, and often several, inpatient facilities for children.

Meanwhile, existing institutions grew in size and internal complexity. Children's hospitals started out in the 1870s as small, informally managed operations on modest budgets. By the end of the century, hospital boards were securing stable sources of income, erecting new buildings, and restructuring their medical and custodial staffs. Managers allocated the day-to-day care of patients—originally the work of unpaid matrons and associations of lady visitors—to salaried, professionally trained employees. As the hospitals grew, so did the number of their medical personnel and the range of opportunities afforded staff physicians.

Changes within the Children's Hospital in Washington, D.C. during the final decades of the century illustrate patterns of growth among contemporary children's hospitals. When it opened in 1870, the District of Columbia hospital consisted of a dozen beds and a dispensary in a rented house. A voluntary staff of four attending physicians (the hospital's founders), a matron, and a board of lady visitors provided all medical and custodial care. By the mid-1890s, the institution had relocated to a newly constructed, permanent building with three wards and a hundred beds. The staff included a matron and several nurses, all professionally trained and salaried. The hospital had begun a nursing school and student nurses assisted the paid employees. There were also changes in the institution's medical staff. The original group of attending physicians was supplemented with five consulting physicians, several resident physicians (at least one of whom received a salary), and a number of student residents.[3]

A similar expansion in medical personnel took place at the children's hospital in Boston. When the institution was founded in 1869, its medical staff consisted of two physicians and two surgeons. Before the turn of the century, the hospital added a board of consulting physicians, numerous assistant surgeons and physicians, several house officers, and a separate medical staff for an outpatient department.[4]

At the same time, new positions were opening for child specialists within American medical colleges. During most of the nineteenth century, there were no separate appointments for pediatric instructors. The field was subsumed under midwifery or taught with gynecology as the diseases of women and children. At the University of Pennsylvania Medical School during mid-century, a professor of midwifery handled the present-day subjects of obstetrics, gynecology, and pediatrics; in 1875 the college added another professorship and obstetrics was separated from the diseases of women and children.[5] By the late 1800s, medical schools were expanding their curriculum on children's diseases and introducing teaching posts in pediatrics. A handful of schools created positions in the 1860s and 1870s. During these decades, Abraham Jacobi held newly established chairs in pediatrics at New York Medical College and University Medical College; he was also Clinical Professor of Diseases of Children at the College of Physicians and Surgeons (Columbia University). Job Lewis Smith accepted a special clinical professorship at Bellevue Hospital and Medical College in New York City and Samuel Busey assumed the position of Professor of Diseases of Infancy and Childhood at Georgetown University in Washington, D.C.[6] But it was during the final two decades of the century that professorships in diseases of children became widespread. The University of Pennsylvania introduced a clinical professorship in diseases of children in 1884. Harvard named Thomas Morgan Rotch Assistant Professor of Diseases of Children in 1888 and promoted him to full professor five years later.[7] The Chicago Medical College (Northwestern University) initiated a pediatric appointment in the early 1880s.[8] Johns Hopkins, Rush Medical College (affiliated with the University of Chicago during the early 1900s), and Western Reserve established separate professorships during the 1890s.[9]

A survey of medical colleges conducted in 1898 by J. P. Crozer Griffith reveals how pervasive pediatric teaching appointments were at the turn of the century. When he conducted the survey, Griffith was clinical professor of pediatrics at the University of Pennsylvania and chairman of the AMA Section on Diseases of Children. He obtained data from the catalogs and announcements of 117 (out of a total of 130) regular medical colleges in the United States. Griffith found that 64 schools (55 percent) had a separate position in pediatrics, many with the title of professor of pediatrics or professor of diseases of children. Others were called clinical or assistant professorships.[10] Thus by 1900, the majority of American medical colleges had separate posts in the diseases of children. This development and the proliferation of children's hospitals and wards greatly expanded the opportunities available to aspiring specialists. Careers in pediatrics become possible not only in the northeastern cities where specialization began but in a large number of urban centers. Practitioners choosing to specialize found a broader range of institutional openings.

Turn-of-the-Century Work Patterns

During the late 1800s, pediatricians began restricting their medical work entirely to children. They did so by combining hospital and medical school posts with specialized private practices. Full-scale specialists were a new generation of pediatric practitioners, considerably younger than the men who founded the first pediatric societies during the 1880s.[11] While their ranks were small at the turn of the century, these pediatric consultants became more numerous in the early 1900s.

The professional biography of Luther Emmett Holt, one of the better known of the second-generation pediatricians, illustrates the career patterns of early twentieth-century child specialists. Holt began his medical career in New York City about thirty years later than Jacobi and Smith. He obtained his medical degree at the College of Physicians and Surgeons, completed an internship at Bellevue, and opened an office for the practice of general medicine in the early 1880s. Holt had decided to cultivate pediatrics as a special area, but as a young physician without reputation, he was in no position to build a specialized practice. Like other young physicians of the contemporary medical elite, Holt established himself through a series of hospital appointments. During the 1880s and 1890s, he held positions at more than half a dozen children's hospitals and asylums in the New York City area. Holt directed medical services at a county branch of the New York Infant Asylum for eight years and served as chief physician at the Babies' Hospital in New York City for several decades.

On the basis of his hospital experience, Holt published a series of clinical papers and secured a reputation as a rising young authority on children's disorders. In 1890, he obtained his first teaching appointment, a professorship of pediatrics at the New York Polyclinic Hospital and Medical School. He left this post in 1901 to succeed Jacobi as professor of pediatrics at the College of Pediatrics and Surgeons. By then he had produced a long list of publications including a textbook on pediatrics (1897) and an extremely popular infant-hygiene manual, *The Care and Feeding of Children* (1894). Meanwhile, his private practice was thriving. In the early 1890s he stopped accepting new adult patients and by mid-decade was limiting his practice entirely to children.[12]

Holt's work history underscores the centrality of institutional posts in the professional lives of contemporary specialists. Hospital and teaching appointments were important in part because they generated income for young physicians. While hospitals did not ordinarily pay consulting physicians, assistant and resident physicians received modest salaries.[13] Many, though not all, teaching appointments provided some remuneration. Of twenty-four pediatric professors surveyed in the mid-1890s, fourteen were receiving financial compensation.[14] But even more important, hospital posts were a means to acquire experience and a reputation for specialized expertise. Teaching appointments, which often followed, added to the specialist's professional standing. Reputations built through institutional appointments enabled pediatricians to establish specialized practices. One result was that "men [fell] over one another to get hospital and college appointments."[15] As a physician moved into more prestigious institutional posts, his practice became increasingly lucrative.

There are relatively few published sources on the type of services pediatricians provided in their hospital work or private offices. Child specialists did not begin conducting studies of the content of pediatric practice until the late 1920s. But the records of pediatric societies and the content of specialty journals give ample evidence of pediatricians' scientific preoccupations. Apart from children's diseases, infant feeding was one of the principal foci of pediatric studies. Between 1900 and 1915, APS members delivered ninety papers on the subject at annual scientific meetings.[16] Interest in artificial feeding originated in the late nineteenth century, an outgrowth of pediatricians' efforts to keep babies alive within institutional settings. By the mid-1890s, pediatricians had constructed an intricate technology for bottle-feeding babies known as the percentage method.

Thomas Rotch, professor of pediatrics at Harvard University, introduced the percentage method. It was based upon the notion that artificial feeding of infants would be more successful if cows' milk was altered to more closely approximate the chemical composition of mothers' milk. Specialists considered the casein in cows' milk to be the cause of indigestibility and reducing its level was a principal objective of the percentage method. These simple, though unfounded, assumptions led to the creation of elaborate formulas for modifying cows' milk. Suggested procedures became increasingly complicated until, in the words of one physician, "some of the articles [published by adherents] seemed terrifyingly like treatises on mathematics or higher astronomy."[17]

There was never unanimity among pediatricians about the percentage method. Jacobi and several other APS members stoutly rejected it even during the height of its popularity. Jacobi voiced some of his criticism in an address to the AMA Section called, satirically, "The Gospel of the Top Milk." His title alludes to the fact that many of the mixtures produced with the percentage method were dilutions of cream which, in unhomogenized milk, collects at the top of the bottle. Cream was used in an effort to reduce protein levels. Jacobi objected both to the high fat content of these mixtures and to the prevailing orientation toward infant feeding. His irritation with his colleagues is evident in Jacobi's remarks:

Cow's milk cannot be changed into woman's milk. . . . The advice to add cow's milk fat to cow's milk in order to make it more nutritious or to make its casein more digestible, is dangerous. . . . Feeding cannot be regulated by mathematics so well as by brains, and by the wants of the individual baby.[18]

Nonetheless, percentage feeding was widely adopted by turn-of-the-century pediatricians and taught in detail at leading medical schools. Holt was one of its proponents and the subject took up a large portion of his lecture course at the College of Physicians and Surgeons. Edwards A. Park, who went on to become chairman of pediatrics at both Yale and Johns Hopkins, studied under Holt and describes his instruction.

Holt taught us in this period (1903 to 1905) percentage feeding in the greatest detail, and . . . enveloped the subject with an esoteric aura. Indeed it appeared the very Eden of Pediatrics, where skill was most needed and the pediatricians reigned alone and supreme. . . . Although percentage feeding has now only the importance of a historic curiosity, . . . it was actually an important factor in the development of pediatrics as a specialty. Its build-up into a system of great complexity, the feeding difficulties it created, the attitude toward it akin to mysticism, and finally its grip on pediatric thought, all united to make infant feeding a subject which only the specialist of specialists could tackle.[19]

The percentage method began to lose favor around 1915 and by the 1920s and 1930s had become an embarrassment.[20] The latter sentiment is evident in an anecdote told by Joseph Brennemann, a pediatric leader between the two world wars. In a 1933 address, Brennemann quipped: "A surgeon once asked me: 'What are you feeding babies *today?*' And I could not logically resent the implication."[21] But whatever its aftermath, the percentage method was very much in vogue during the first decade of the twentieth century. The existence of this complex and apparently scientific procedure contributed, for a time, to the prestige of the specialty and its members. The technology lent pediatrics a scientific aura that helped justify specialists' claim to unique expertise. Historian Kathleen Jones argues that, with percentage feeding, Holt and his contemporaries generated a small market for pediatric services among highly affluent mothers.[22] In this way, "scientific" infant feeding may have facilitated the development of fully specialized practices.

Whatever the contribution of the percentage method, pediatricians were drawing private patients and restricting their professional activities to children. Just how many full-scale specialists there were at the turn of the century is difficult to estimate.[23] A survey conducted by Samuel W. Kelley, professor of pediatrics at the College of Physicians and Surgeons in Cleveland, located about a dozen in the mid-1890s.[24] But the numbers may have been considerably higher. At that time, sentiment within the American Pediatric Society (APS) was weighted against considering pediatrics an autonomous field, and members limiting their work to the specialty were not likely to announce the fact. APS historians Harold Faber and Rustin McIntosh claim that by World War I, most of the society's members were restricting their professional activities to pediatrics.[25] An AMA survey conducted in 1914 found 138 men who confined their medical practices to children.[26] But the trend was in evidence by 1900. With the help of institutional posts, a complex technology, and changing social attitudes toward medical science, pediatricians were forging careers as full-scale specialists.

Transformation of American Medical Colleges

While pediatricians worked to expand their specialized practices, American medical schools were undergoing a profound transformation. Mid-ninteenth-century medical colleges were proprietary institutions. Even those formally linked to universities were managed by and in the interest of local medical elites. Between the 1870s and 1920s, university presidents, along with the leadership of scientific medicine, restructured medical colleges into modern professional schools that functioned as academic units within institutions of higher education.[27] Changes within late-nineteenth-century medical schools were numerous and far-reaching. University administrators ended the long-standing practice among medical professors of splitting proceeds from student fees; colleges initiated salaries at considerable loss of income to faculty.[28] Schools raised entrance requirements and upgraded programs of instruction by strengthening examination policies, lengthening training, expanding curricula, and introducing sequenced course offerings. Of particular relevance for the emerging specialties were moves to incorporate practical clinical training into academic curricula. This trend led to fundamental alterations in the management of teaching hospitals and had significant implications for pediatric careers.

At mid-century, the typical medical schools offered courses in nine or so subjects including anatomy, physiology and pathology, chemistry, *materia medica*, surgery, medicine and obstetrics, and the diseases of women and children.[29] Training consisted almost entirely of classroom instruction; even courses in the clinical fields (medicine, surgery, and midwifery) took place in the lecture hall. Medical colleges offered almost no bedside instruction. Physicians obtained clinical experience early in their careers as apprentices or as resident or assistant physicians at dispensaries and hospitals.

In the latter part of the nineteenth century, schools broadened their course offerings and introduced teaching positions in specialized clinical fields. The spread of professorships in the diseases of children during the 1870s and 1880s was not an isolated phenomenon. When Bellevue appointed Job Lewis Smith clinical professor of pediatrics, the school retained instructors in nine special subjects including dermatology, psychological medicine, and orthopedic surgery. The faculty at College of Physicians and Surgeons in the mid-1870s included appointees in dermatology, diseases of the eye and ear, laryngology, and diseases of the mind and nervous system.[30] Harvard created posts in ophthalmology, dermatology, and hygiene in 1871 and positions in laryngology, gynecology, otology, and neurology during the 1890s. The pattern was repeated at many other medical colleges.[31]

The addition of teaching appointments in clinical specialties was part of the more general trend toward practical, bedside instruction. At a number of schools, the creation of new professorships coincided with the opening of college hospitals or dispensaries. The University of Pennsylvania added posts in ophthalmology, otology, and diseases of women and children when the University Hospital was established in 1874.[32] At the College of Physicians and Surgeons, professors in the clinical fields taught at the outpatient department run by the school during the 1870s and 1880s.[33] Other colleges initiated specialized appointments to establish ties with hospitals where bedside instruction took place. Physicians chosen for professorships in the clinical specialties were, almost without exception, well entrenched within local hospitals and dispensaries. They were men who would have little difficulty making wards accessible for instruction of medical students.

Competition among medical schools fueled their attempts to establish hospital connections. During the late nineteenth century, clinical instruction became important to the prestige of colleges and their ability to attract students. By the early 1900s, links with hospitals were so crucial to the relative status of medical colleges that, according to educator Abraham Flexner, "schools in the same community vied with one another in capturing hospital facilities by giving school appointments freely to physicians and surgeons already holding hospital posts."[34] (One of Flexner's aims, in his famous report of 1910 for the Carnegie Foundation, was to curtail the influence of hospital physicians on American medical colleges.)

The situation with pediatric appointments was consistent with this general picture. In fact, the existence of separate clinical facilities for children may have been a decisive factor in the initial creation of pediatric professorships. It is certain that professorships in diseases of children went to physicians with good positions in children's hospitals. Prior to his appointment as assistant professor at Harvard, Rotch had access to the contagious disease wards at Boston City Hospital and the Boston Dispensary and held posts at both the Children's and Infant's hospitals. Holt was in charge of a major children's hospital in New York City, and affiliated with half a dozen others, when Physicians and Surgeons named him pediatric professor. Both men routinely used clinical facilities for teaching purposes. Rotch's courses at Harvard included regularly scheduled clinical demonstrations and exercises at children's wards in Boston, while Holt conducted informal clinics at Babies' Hospital for students at the College of Physicians and Surgeons.[35]

Most of this instruction on hospital wards took place in the absence of formal arrangements that would make "teaching" hospitals university-affiliated.[36] In the late nineteenth century, the majority of schools were dependent upon hospital appointees for the provision of clinical instruction. What this meant for medical colleges was that local professional elites controlling hospital posts wielded tremendous influence over teaching appointments.[37] What it meant for specialists was that hospitals were the key institutions; positions there were the route to professorships.

Medical school reform of the early 1900s fundamentally altered this relationship between hospital and teaching appointments. Leading schools established agreements with hospitals whereby academic departments controlled hospital posts. At issue was not only who made the appointments but the basis upon which they were made. When medical elites prevailed, the principal criterion for selection was the incumbent's position within local medical hierarchies.[38] Academic leaders sought to have choices based on physicians' contributions to medical research. This group objected to the use of academic appointments to build private practices and was working to create discrete career tracks in medical teaching and research.[39]

Shifts in control over hospital posts were part of broader structural and normative changes bringing medical colleges more fully into the university's domain. By the second decade of the twentieth century, medical school deans were building modern academic departments, introducing full-time salaried appointments for clinical faculty, and promoting the assimilation of scientific norms within clinical departments. The practicing branch of the medical profession opposed many of these reforms, particularly full-time clinical appointments. Nonetheless, advocates of university control made substantial progress in the early part of the twentieth century.[40]

These developments were highly consequential for pediatric consultants. Hospital and teaching appointments remained critical to pediatricians' livelihoods. It was still reputations built upon institutional posts that enabled specialists to attract private clients. Like other facilities used for undergraduate clinical teaching, children's hospitals were becoming university-affiliated. Medical schools began establishing formal arrangements with children's hospitals in 1910, but the trend toward university control was evident by 1900.[41] With access to leading children's hospitals shifting to teaching institutions, pediatricians became increasingly concerned about the status of the specialty within medical colleges.

Their concern was heightened by the fact that medical education was a prominent issue among major professional associations. In the mid-1890s, the Association of American Medical Colleges (AAMC) began publishing recommendations regarding hours to be allotted clinical specialties in college curricula.[42] The AMA's Council on Medical Education began developing policies on undergraduate curricula during the 1900s. The profession's leadership was making decisions about the organization and content of medical training which would have implications for the standing of clinical departments in years to follow.

Specialists sought to ensure that pediatrics was institutionalized within medical schools on a par with other clinical fields. The initial appearance of faculty appointments in diseases of children did not guarantee that autonomous clinical departments would follow. A pediatric professorship of the 1880s or 1890s was a very different position than that title implied in the 1920s and 1930s. The early posts were part-time; some were unsalaried. Many of the original professors were not granted full faculty membership. Of twenty-eight pediatric appointees surveyed in the mid-1890s, nine were denied voting rights within medical faculties.[43] At stake in the early 1900s was the specialty's transition into a modern clinical department. Such departments were necessary for the protection of both existing pediatric careers and the continued development of the specialty.

Professional Program Reformulated

In the first decade of the century, child specialists articulated a radically new vision of pediatrics. The initial statement of the new professional ethos came in 1905 at the AMA Section on Diseases of Children. John Lovett Morse, an instructor in Rotch's department at Harvard, introduced the revised ideology. Morse was delivering his chairman's address to the Section, a paper describing the pediatric curriculum at Harvard, when he turned to two sensitive and consequential issues. The first was the matter of full-scale specialization. Breaking entirely with the professional beliefs of first-generation pediatricians, Morse declared that only full-scale specialists were sufficiently knowledgeable to teach pediatrics.

No man is competent to appreciate how much there is to be known about pediatrics and how little there is known about it, even by the best men in other lines, except the man who makes it a specialty. . . . No one who does not make a specialty of pediatrics is, moreover, competent to teach it as it should be taught.[44]

The second matter was the position of pediatric departments within medical schools. Again deviating from the precedent set by the nineteenth-century professional leadership, Morse argued strongly for departmental autonomy.

Pediatrics can never be satisfactorily taught unless it is a separate department. If it is made a part of the department of obstetrics or of gynecology, as in some schools, it is certain to be neglected and to be improperly taught. It is too important a subject even to form a part of the department of internal medicine. When it is in that department, as it is in some schools which in other ways are most progressive, it is sure to be insufficiently and imperfectly taught, as it is in them.[45]

The twin issues of full-scale specialization and departmental autonomy became cornerstones of a new ethos and a new professional mobilization.

The American Pediatric Society did not guide the movement for autonomous departments and specialty status. Morse was an APS member at the time he delivered his address to the AMA Section and it is probable that others in the APS shared Morse's convictions. But older physicians in the APS continued to espouse a nineteenth-century vision of pediatrics. These men were decrying narrow specialism and insisting that pediatrics was part of general medicine well into the decade of 1910.

The Association of American Teachers of the Diseases of Children (AATDC), established in 1907, directed the early twentieth-century mobilization. This organization was an outgrowth of the AMA Section on Diseases of Children.[46] Its founders differed in social origins from physicians in the APS. The latter society was still composed of upper-crust, East Coast physicians who were graduates from and professors at elite medical schools. In 1907, thirty-eight of its fifty-seven members were from New York City, Philadelphia, or Boston.[47] The Society's policy of admission by election perpetuated its homogeneous composition. In contrast, of the approximately thirty specialists who established the AATDC, two-thirds were from the midwestern or southern United States.[48] While all were pediatric professors, the majority taught at, and had obtained degrees from, less prestigious medical schools.

At AATDC meetings, specialists elaborated the new professional ideology. Speakers declared that the pediatrician of the 1900s was a combination of teacher, investigator, and consultant, "able to aid the family physician in serious cases."[49] They retained parts of the older pediatric ethos. Full-scale specialists did not substantially alter notions about the field's intellectual scope and substantive content. But they reshaped prescribed work roles and recast the specialty's relationship to general medicine. AATDC members repeatedly underscored the advantages of full-scale specialization and the merits of considering pediatrics an autonomous field of medicine. Immediately following its creation, the AATDC spearheaded a drive to improve the specialty's position within American medical schools. In 1908 its leaders established a Committee on Pediatric Training mandated to define the proper scope of pediatric instruction and advance the cause of pediatric instruction through negotiation with other medical societies. During the following year, the AATDC adopted a resolution that "every medical college should have a chair of pediatrics. It should be a full professorship, quite independent; i.e., not subordinate to any other chair."[50] The AMA Section passed a similar statement.[51]

In addition to autonomous faculty appointments, the AATDC sought improved hospital and outpatient facilities for pediatric instruction, broader pediatric course offerings, and an increase in the time allocated pediatrics in undergraduate medical curricula. AATDC representatives met with the AMA's Council on Medical Education and the AAMC's Committee on Curriculum for the Clinical Years. In 1910, Samuel Kelley, head of the Committee on Pediatric Teaching, announced that he had persuaded the AAMC to increase its recommended minimum hours of pediatric instruction from 100 to 150. While this fell short of the 190 hours (10 percent of the third and fourth years) that the AATDC had proposed, Kelley considered it a significant improvement.[52] In 1916 the Association began a campaign to ensure that newborn clinics were placed under the jurisdiction of pediatric rather than obstetric departments. A contemporary child-health organization endorsed this effort.[53]

Social Movement and Professional Ethos

When pediatricians began to campaign for autonomous departments, appointments in diseases of children were similar to those in most of the other clinical specialties. During the early 1900s, professorships in ophthalmology, neurology, dermatology, and the like were also part-time.[54] Information on the relative independence of faculty posts is extremely difficult to obtain but it is clear that, at many schools, initial appointees were subordinate to professors of medicine or surgery.[55] American medical colleges did not have clinical departments in the modern sense of the term until the decades of 1910 and 1920. At the turn of the century, clinical specialties other than general medicine and surgery faced a common set of problems regarding their institutionalization as bona fide departments within university-controlled medical colleges.

But pediatrics confronted some problems which few other specialties shared. Many physicians—indeed, a good number of pediatricians—remained unconvinced that pediatrics should be considered a discrete specialty. They questioned whether the intellectual basis of pediatrics was sufficiently distinct from that of other fields to merit its classification as a separate division of clinical medicine. Rudolf Matas, professor of surgery at Tulane University, articulated contemporary reservations about the status of pediatrics as a medical specialty. In 1896 Matas wrote:

My personal impression is that the specialties of medicine and surgery will encroach in the future as they do at present upon the domain of pediatrics to the extent of reducing the specialty subordinate to other specialties. There will always be men who will be more skillful in the management of the diseases of children in all communities, but it is extremely doubtful that pediatrics will ever rank as a distinct specialty like oculistry, otology, or laryngology or orthopaedics. The simple reason for this lies in the fact that a special knowledge of the diseases of children is largely a synthesis of the other specialties, and that what is not included in the other specialties will be of such a general character that the "general practitioner" must claim it as a part of his special province.[56]

Opinions of this type were a potential obstacle to the creation of autonomous pediatric departments. At the turn of the century, there was a very real possibility that pediatrics would be established as a subordinate division within departments of internal medicine.

Even physicians supporting autonomous pediatric departments faulted the specialty for its performance in research and teaching. David Edsall, addressing the APS in 1910, admonished the group for failing to keep up with developments in scientific medicine. Edsall, who became dean of the Harvard Medical School in 1918, was deeply involved in the movement to upgrade clinical instruction and research within American medical colleges. He acknowledged that research and teaching in all clinical fields were inferior to those in the laboratory specialties. But, he asserted, "criticism is better justified when directed at pediatrics" than at other clinical fields.[57]

So far as I can see, the propriety of studying pediatrics as a special subject rather than as a mere part of general medicine is based essentially upon the fact that the infant and young child differ from adults enormously in degree and almost equally in kind, in susceptibility to infections, and especially in liability to derangements of nutrition. . . . In spite of the fact that these subjects [infection, immunity, and the physiology and pathology of nutrition] are simply teeming with points that are of the most intense interest in acquiring sound and broad methods of practice, there are certainly scarcely any places where an attempt is made to bring out systematically and thoroughly their relation to clinical pediatrics. So far as these subjects are at all broadly dwelt upon by clinical teachers, it is almost entirely in courses on general medicine not in pediatrics. . . . It is no wonder that in the eyes of many of the best students pediatrics becomes the tail to the general medical kite.[58]

If the quality of pediatrics research was in question, developments outside of medicine lent the specialty a different legitimacy. A child health and welfare movement greatly aided pediatricians in achieving their goals. Like other social reform movements in the United States, the child-health movement gained momentum in the political climate of the early 1900s. The Progressive Era brought a new level of organizational sophistication. Child-welfare work had taken the form of local philanthropy during the 1800s. In the early twentieth century, activists established effective national organizations and won federal recognition for the problems of childhood. A national child-health organization was formed in 1910: the American Association for Study and Prevention of Infant Mortality (AASPIM).[59] This society was a coalition of lay and physician child-health activists. Among the physician members, some (but not all) were pediatricians. Meanwhile, the first in a series of White House conferences on children and youth was held in 1909. The meeting resulted in legislation that established the U.S. Children's Bureau in 1912. Infant mortality was one of the Bureau's initial programmatic foci. Through the efforts of the new organizations and agencies, child health became a social issue receiving nationwide attention.

In arguing for autonomous departments, specialty leaders did not make claims about pediatrics as a division of medical knowledge. Rather, they asserted that independent departments would contribute to improvements in child health and to the well-being of society at large. Spokesmen linked the goals of their professional segment to the aims of the child-health movement. The meetings of child-health associations were occasions to consolidate support for the specialty's programmatic aims. Some pediatricians even claimed that autonomous departments were a necessary condition for lowering infant mortality rates. Ira Wile, a physician-activist from New York City, spoke at the inaugural meeting of AASPIM on the subject, "Do medical schools adequately train students for the prevention of infant mortality?" He declared that "the possibility of reducing the infant death rate is retarded as long as preventive work remains untaught in a *special department* of pediatrics."[60] At the majority of schools, he complained, pediatrics is a part of general medicine. Wile continued:

Are the best medical schools of this country to be regarded as overlooking their responsibility in the matter of preventing disease? . . . Let the medical schools recognize their responsibility for the poor results that their graduates have shown in the reach of diseases of infancy. Let independent departments be organized for giving instruction and training in the hygiene of infancy and the treatment of the diseases of infancy.[61]

Borden Veeder, professor of pediatrics at Washington University in St. Louis, offered a somewhat different rationale for independent departments. In his view there were two principal reasons why the specialty merited administrative autonomy. The first was that the special needs of children required that their hospital wards be entirely separate from those for adults. In his words:

The best results from every standpoint are obtained when the children's work is either in a distinct but affiliated institution, or in a separate building when part of a general hospital. . . . the technic of handling children, of nursing, the food supply, the difference in the character of equipment, the unavoidable noise of a children's ward, all are factors that cannot be solved in a general hospital. Moreover, I have never seen a children's ward in a general hospital which did not get the "short end of the stick"—so to speak—when it came to nursing and hospital service. . . . before we can have a successful children's service, we must have a separate physical unit in the hospital equipment of the medical school.[62]

With clinical departments of medical schools being built around university-controlled hospital facilities, it was a relatively short step from separate children's hospitals to autonomous academic departments.

Veeder's second line of defense was to underscore the university's responsibilities in the areas of preventive medicine and public health. Having noted that physicians trained in child hygiene were already contributing to a reduction in infant mortality, Veeder declared:

A university to fulfill its proper function must be a living factor in the life of the community, and a department of pediatrics has an unusual opportunity to be a connecting link between the two, as so many social problems center about the child. . . . We are often criticized for the failure of pediatricians in this country to do "scientific work." It has seemed to me that the explanation lay in the way sociological-medical work has offered the bigger opening, and the opportunity for obtaining the greatest results in the shortest time.[63]

Response of the Scientific Elite

Arguments of the type developed by Veeder were highly effective with the vanguard of scientific medicine in America. This group was leading the reform of clinical instruction during the early 1900s. Its goals included the creation of full-time salaried professorships and the ascendancy of university research norms within clinical departments. Its members were also strongly committed to preventive medicine, public health, and progressive social reform.

How medicine's scientific leadership reacted to pediatrics is illustrated by the sentiments of David Edsall. While criticizing the specialty's scientific output, Edsall considered pediatrics to be a major division of clinical medicine and fully endorsed its institutionalization. In his opinion, "the dignity of any of the intellectual pursuits" rests not only on research accomplishments but also on "the extent to which those who follow that pursuit engage in matters that favorably affect the welfare . . . of the public at large."[64] Edsall urged pediatricians both to strengthen their research and teaching and to become more involved in child-welfare work.

William Welch, professor of pathology and dean at Johns Hopkins Medical School, held a similar constellation of sympathies. Welch was a central figure in the reform of American medical schools.[65] In addition to promoting scientific medicine, he participated in a wide array of public health efforts and was a member of innumerable public health associations.[66] His support extended to the child-welfare movement. Speaking at the first meeting of AASPIM, Welch declared that the association was initiating "one of the most important campaigns in preventive medicine in this country."[67] On improvements in pediatric instruction, Welch remarked that "there is no question but that the great need of medical schools in this country is the establishment of satisfactory training in preventive medicine and public hygiene."[68]

Commitments to both scientific medicine and public health fit the political ideology dominant in early twentieth-century America. Social historians have written a good deal about Progressives' faith that science could alleviate social problems associated with industrialization and urbanization.[69] These beliefs facilitated the ascendancy of scientific norms within American universities and their medical schools. The push to professionalize medical school faculty may be considered a reform movement in its own right with scientific norms justified for the social benefit they would yield.

The result for pediatrics was that physicians most likely to fault the specialty's scientific performance favored its establishment as a major division of clinical teaching and research. The scientific elite supported the creation of modern pediatric departments and, with the aid of this influential group, contemporary specialists went far in achieving their aims. A survey of forty-two class A medical colleges conducted in 1917 revealed that half had independent pediatric departments.[70] By the early 1920s, 62 percent of class A colleges (forty-two out of sixty-eight) had separate departments of pediatrics.[71]

Furthermore, when medical colleges obtained endowments for the salaries of clinical faculty, pediatric departments were among the first to receive full-time professorships. Johns Hopkins created a full-time position in pediatrics in 1913; the only other clinical departments allocated full-time faculty at that time were medicine and surgery. At Yale and Washington Universities, pediatrics, along with medicine, surgery, and obstetrics, were the first full-time departments.[72] At least ten medical schools created full-time salaried posts in diseases of children by 1923.[73] Medical colleges not only established autonomous pediatric departments; consistent with the goals of men like Edsall and Welch, the institutions were also upgrading pediatrics into a division of modern medical research.

Dynamics of Professionalization

Organizational innovation and changing patterns of labor were central to professional processes within early twentieth-century pediatrics. These same factors had been crucial to the initial consolidation of the specialty during the 1880s. They came into play again at the turn of the century, stimulating a redefinition of pediatricians' goals and ethos. Pediatric consultants were responding both to new labor patterns and significant developments in the organizations where they worked. The impact of these factors on the pediatric collectivity was multifaceted. My explanation for the mobilization of the early twentieth century has three analytically distinct components.

First, with the proliferation of children's hospitals and teaching posts, aspiring specialists found it easier to focus on pediatrics. They used institutional posts to build specialized practices and began restricting their professional activities entirely to children. Full-scale specialization rendered nineteenth-century professional beliefs obsolete. Pediatricians reorganized and formulated an ethos that would rationalize and promote emerging work roles. In the new ideology, pediatrics was not simply a part-time interest but an independent division of medical practice.

Second, and closely related, the spread of teaching and hospital posts opened opportunities for pediatric careers to a broader range of medical practitioners. Specialization was no longer limited to the upper strata of physicians in major northeastern cities. Doctors who spearheaded the new mobilization were a very different group than the pediatric leadership of the 1880s. APS founders were graduates of Ivy League colleges and members of the medical elites of New York, Boston, and Philadelphia. The practitioners who established and ran the AATDC were from a younger cohort of child specialists; most were midwesterners who had obtained degrees and taught at less prestigious medical schools. They mobilized to promote the interests of pediatricians excluded from the APS. For these men, advancing full-scale specialization was a vehicle for upward mobility within the profession and for entry into a new type of American medical elite.

Finally, pediatricians were responding to a shift in the balance of power among medical organizations. With the modernization of medical education, the specialty's position within training institutions became more crucial to specialists' careers. Administrative autonomy for pediatric departments, the chief programmatic aim of the new mobilization, had both symbolic and real value.[74] On the one hand, it acknowledged the importance and dignity of the field and its acceptance by the medical profession as a bona fide specialty. It had, on the other hand, practical implications. Without administrative independence, pediatricians would be at a disadvantage in competing for resources within medical colleges. Concerns of this nature were voiced at AATDC meetings. Julius Hess, pediatric professor and division head at the University of Illinois Medical School, reported in 1922 that pediatrics was "still coupled with the department of medicine" at his institution. Hess complained that, as a result, the field had "second place in the distribution and use of funds."[75] Where the specialty was subordinate to the department of medicine, control over the allocation of pediatric positions might also be at issue. Departmental status for pediatrics would ensure that child specialists had the best chances for mobility and maneuverability within academic institutions.

The multiple forces impinging upon specialists are one noteworthy feature of turn-of-the-century pediatrics. Another is the complex interplay between the emerging segment and developing medical organizations. Expanding opportunities within hospitals and medical colleges helped give rise to full-scale specialists. Yet the new segment was not a passive product of organizational change. Pediatricians actively used hospital and teaching posts to build their practices and establish themselves as full-scale specialists. They then reconstituted themselves outside of work organizations and mobilized to affect the shape these organizations took. Through their agency—and with the help of a social reform movement and the support of academic leaders—pediatric departments became a universal and permanent fixture within American medical colleges. Engendered by changes within hospitals and professional schools, the new collectivity influenced the unfolding structure of these organizations.

Chapter Five

Consolidating the Market for Child-Health Services

Pediatrics entered the third decade of the twentieth century in a much stronger position than it held during the late 1800s. Leading medical schools were introducing full-time salaried pediatric professorships and autonomous pediatric departments. In 1920, the AMA Council on Medical Education set up committees in specialized medical fields to make recommendations concerning undergraduate and graduate professional training. The Council designated pediatrics as one of eleven divisions of clinical medicine.[1] These were major steps toward institutionalizing pediatrics as a modern medical specialty. But the specialty had not assumed its mature form and significant changes occurred in the years that followed.

During the 1920s and 1930s, yet another generation of child specialists coalesced and mobilized to consolidate its market status. Spokesmen again recast the segment's ethos, this time emphasizing the stance of the pediatricians toward youngsters and families. They argued that the specialty's domain included not only childhood diseases and infant feeding but children's normal growth and development as well. Leaders founded the American Academy of Pediatrics in 1930 to represent the interests of office-based specialists. The culmination of their efforts was the American Board of Pediatrics, a national certifying body established in 1933 that examines candidates for specialized competency. The board designated a course of graduate professional training requisite to certification and, through its qualifying exam, formally defined the specialty's knowledge base. These measures initiated the standardization of pediatric residency programs during the 1930s and 1940s. The impact of the board and residency training was to specify a discrete professional commodity and securely establish pediatrics as a market division within American medicine. Why did child specialists build a new tier of occupational structures at this time? What conditions fostered their redefinition of pediatric terrain?

As in earlier stages of the specialty's history, the actions of pediatric leaders are understood best with reference to the contours and context of physicians' labor. Between the two world wars, private pediatric practice became viable as a full-time endeavor. The previous generation of pediatricians had maintained specialized practices but their professional lives revolved around hospital and medical colleges; these turn-of-the-century specialists had attracted private patients through reputations for expertise built through years at institutional posts. Two decades later, growing numbers of pediatricians were drawing fee-for-service patients in the absence of prolonged institutional apprenticeships. Their major professional activity was direct patient care and their principal work place was the private office.

The appearance of this primary-care specialist was an outgrowth of rising demand for pediatric services. By the third decade of the century, Americans were consulting pediatricians for reasons other than advice on artificial infant feeding or medical treatment when youngsters were ill. Parents were seeking counsel on routine child management and training. Practitioners mobilized during the 1920s and 1930s to stabilize emerging work patterns and to structure the burgeoning market for child-health supervision. How demand for primary-care pediatrics arose and how specialists consolidated their market are the foci of this chapter's narrative.

Demand Is Created

Two types of data indicate that demand for pediatric services increased dramatically following World War I. One is observations by contemporary pediatricians and child-health advocates. Both practitioners and lay activists commented that, during the 1920s,

TABLE 1   *Numbers of Pediatric Specialists, 1914–1966*

Year	Practice Limited to Pediatrics	Special Attention to Pediatrics	Total
1914	138	741	879
1921	664	1,798	2,462
1923	689	1,820	2,509
1929	1,333	2,154	3,487
1934	1,734	2,115	3,889
1938	2,205	2,166	4,371
1940	2,416	—	—
1949	4,315	—	—
1955	6,567	—	—
1961	9,836	—	—
1966	12,558	—	—

Sources: Borden S. Veeder, "Trend of Pediatric Education and Practice," *American Journal of Diseases of Children,* 50, 1 (1935): 7; Commission on Graduate Medical Education, *Graduate Medical Education* (Chicago: University of Chicago Press, 1940), p. 261, table 9; U.S. President's Commission on the Health Needs of the Nation, *Building America's Health,* 5 vols. (Washington, D.C.: U.S. Government Printing Office, 1952–53), 3: 160, table 209; Rosemary Stevens, *American Medicine and the Public Interest* (New Haven: Yale University Press, 1971), p. 545, table A4 and p. 162, table 1.

parents began consulting child specialists in unprecedented numbers.[2] Another indication is exponential growth in the ranks of self-identified pediatricians. Table 1 illustrates that in 1914 there were only 138 full-scale child specialists in the country; the figure climbed to 664 in 1921 and to 1,734 in 1934.[3] There was a tenfold increase in full-scale pediatricians between 1914 and 1934 and a threefold increase in part-time child specialists.

Rising demand for specialized medicine in general accounts for a portion of this growth. Middle-class Americans found the services of specialists increasingly attractive during the postwar years. The ongoing reform of American medical colleges and the spread of postgraduate professional training programs during the early decades of the twentieth century bolstered the legitimacy of both scientific medicine and specialized practices. Between 1923 and 1934, the portion of American physicians practicing in specialized

TABLE 2   *Rates of Growth of Full-Scale Specialists, 1923–1934*

Specialty	Number of Full-Scale Specialists 1923	1934	% Increase
All Fields	15,408	26,756	74
Selected Fields:			
Internal Medicine	1,958	4,452	127
Obstetrics & Gynecology	697	1,691	143
Ophthalmology & Otorhinolaryngology	4,703	6,297	34
Pediatrics	689	1,734	152
Psychiatry & Neurology	945	1,601	69
Public Health	315	836	165
Radiology	588	1,169	99
Surgery	3,336	4,787	44

Source: U.S. President's Commission on the Health Needs of the Nation, *Building America's Health*, 5 vols. (Washington, D.C.: U.S. Government Printing Office, 1952–53), 3: 160, table 209.

fields rose from 11 to 17 percent. There were approximately 15,000 specialists in 1923 and nearly 27,000 in 1934.[4]

Yet pediatrics was growing at a rate faster than most other medical segments. Table 2 indicates that in the ten years following 1923, the number of medical specialists rose 74 percent. In the same period, the number of child specialists climbed 152 percent, more than twice the rate for specialists as a whole. Other fields with above-average growth rates during the 1920s and early 1930s include public health and obstetrics-gynecology.[5] These figures suggest that markets for pediatrics and other social-problem specialties arose somewhat later than markets for the first scientifically based specialties like ophthalmology, otolaryngology, and surgery. In the case of pediatrics, growth in demand awaited developments that originated outside the medical profession.

How demand for primary-care pediatrics was generated is one of the most fascinating chapters in the history of the specialty. It involves social activism, the creation—and eventual disappearance—of a social institution, and the invention of a new professional service. During the second and third decades of the century, child-health advocates established a multitude of small, loosely organized centers called infant-welfare clinics. The clinics provided medical surveillance for babies and advice for parents. Physicians and nurses weighed and examined babies and instructed mothers on the care of infants. Medical practitioners quickly structured these activities into a discrete professional service called the well-baby conference. Supported by private philanthropy and municipal funds, the clinics offered services free of charge. Meanwhile, activists unleashed a barrage of propaganda urging parents to obtain periodic medical supervision for their healthy children. The example of the clinics and the accompanying publicity rendered child-health services attractive both to the lower-class women for whom it was originally designed and to middle-class women. American parents began consulting pediatricians in public clinics and, with growing frequency, in private offices. The pediatrician's clientele sought not only treatment when youngsters were sick but also counsel when children were well.

The Infant-Welfare Clinic

Turn-of-the-century child-health activists concentrated their efforts on lowering rates of infant mortality. By the final decades of the nineteenth century, observers considered bacteria within urban milk supplies to be a likely source of infections fatal to infants. Diarrheal diseases were the most common cause of infant deaths. These were more prevalent among bottle than breast-fed babies and were most widespread during the summer months. Child-health activists reasoned that if they made safe milk available in urban communities, particularly in working-class and immigrant neighborhoods where death rates were highest, then infant mortality would decline. Toward this end, they established milk stations that offered sterilized milk at modest cost. Health reformers established the nation's first milk depots in New York City during the early 1890s. Some were located at neighborhood dispensaries, others were set up as booths in the city's tenement districts. The milk distribution program in New York proved successful and the innovation quickly spread to other American cities.[6]

During the second decade of the twentieth century, milk-station sponsors shifted their focus from dispensing milk to instructing mothers on infant feeding and hygiene.[7] There were a number of practical reasons for this change. In some cases, milk distribution had the unintended consequence of encouraging bottle feeding. Welfare activists came to feel that supplying milk had limited value if unaccompanied by educational work. Furthermore, the quality of commercial milk supplies was improving. In addition to such practical considerations, the child-welfare movement as a whole was shifting its focus. By World War I, emphasis on clearly delimited issues like infant mortality and child labor gave way to a much broader interest in child growth and development. Reformers became more professional in orientation and more concerned with norms regarding age-appropriate behavior in children.[8] A principal objective of the movement in the postwar years was to educate parents about these behavioral norms and to disseminate child-rearing techniques. It was in this context that child-welfare centers supplanted the milk stations of the early 1900s.

Infant-welfare clinics—constituted as centers for the diffusion of child-rearing advice—proliferated in America during the second and third decades of the twentieth century. The speed and extent of their spread were extraordinary. Virtually every large and mid-sized city had clinics sponsored by a local child-welfare society or municipal agency. National child-health organizations, the first established in 1910, and the U.S. Children's Bureau, created in 1912, encouraged the activities of local welfare societies. A study of child-health centers conducted in 1930 by the White House Conference on Child Health and Protection found 1,511 clinics operating in American cities.[9] Sponsoring agencies endeavored to establish numerous small, part-time centers in a variety of urban neighborhoods. Chicago had 49 infant-welfare stations in 1923, one in each of the city's districts. The municipal government ran about half and an Infant Welfare Society sponsored an equivalent portion. There were 30 well-baby and preschool centers in Boston by 1924. Minneapolis boasted 8 in 1923. As early as 1911, Cleveland had 13 clinics, then called Babies' Prophylactic Dispensaries. There were 87 centers in New York City by 1926.[10] Table 3 illustrates temporal patterns in the proliferation of urban welfare centers. It shows that the founding of new clinics reached a peak in the early 1920s.

TABLE 3   *Urban Child-Health Centers by Years of Establishment,*
1900–1930

Year Established	Number of Centers	% of Total
Before 1900	20	1
1900–1904	97	6
1905–1909	76	5
1910–1914	258	17
1915–1919	230	15
1920–1924	439	29
1925–1929	359	24
1930	32	2
All Years	1,511	100

Source: White House Conference on Child Health and Protection, Subcommittee on Health Centers, *Child Health Centers: A Survey* (New York: Century, 1932), p. 4, table 1.

Over time, municipal agencies took an increasingly active role in the funding and administration of welfare centers. Child-health work began as an arena for private philanthropy. Voluntary organizations like Cleveland's Milk Fund Association and Minneapolis' Infant Welfare Society initiated child-health centers in most cities. During the second and third decades of the century, municipal health departments expanded their purview, particularly in the area of child health. By 1930, a hundred cities had established special bureaus of maternal and child health and were allocating about a third of their total health department budgets to these divisions.[11] That year, municipal or county health departments ran 52 percent of the clinics located in urban areas. Private charities sponsored the remaining 48 percent.[12]

The more than 1,500 clinics in American cities were only a portion of all welfare centers established by 1930. According to the White House Conference report, rural communities created an additional 2,600 child-health centers with funds provided through the federal Maternity and Infancy Act passed in 1921.[13] Better known as the Sheppard-Towner Act, this legislation provided grants-in-aid to states for maternal and child-health care programs in communities with populations under 10,000. Newly established state bureaus of maternal and child health administered the Sheppard-Towner funds and the U.S. Children's Bureau coordinated the program at the federal level. By the late 1920s, child-health activists had constructed an elaborate set of public and private agencies and an extensive network of small-scale institutions devoted to the professional supervision of healthy children.

Invention of a Professional Service

By 1920, *the well-baby conference* had gained currency as the term for infant-welfare clinic services. By that time also, clinic services offered in various parts of the country were quite uniform. From the outset it was professionals who conducted infant and preschool conferences. Physicians and registered nurses made up the bulk of health clinic personnel and the great majority were paid employees. Nurses most often held full-time positions and physicians usually had part-time appointments.[14] Welfare centers stated that they provided no medical treatment for children's diseases and they instructed mothers to keep sick babies at home. The well-baby conference focused on the development and routine care of the healthy child.

A principal feature of the new service was frequent, periodic medical consultations. The first visit to the clinic typically occurred about three weeks after the child's birth. Nurses weighed and measured the baby and took a history from the mother including information on feeding and daily routine. A physician then examined the child and interviewed the mother. During this consultation, the practitioner dispensed advice about infant feeding, training, and management. Child-health advocates recommended medical visits at regular intervals, weekly during the early months of the infant's life, bi-weekly or monthly until one year, and every three months thereafter. On these occasions, medical personnel again weighed, measured, and examined the baby and offered mothers instruction on nutrition, habit training, and—in the vocabulary of the day—mental hygiene.[15] While this protocol is commonplace today, during the 1920s it was a remarkable innovation. Never before had practicing professionals concerned themselves in a systematic manner with the normal growth and development of individual children. Nor had there existed a discrete and structured service designed for this purpose. The well-baby conference was an entirely new social invention.

It was physicians working at clinics or otherwise involved in child-welfare work who created and refined the well-baby conference. Medical practitioners were among the participants of national child-health organizations. Many, though not all, of these physician-activists considered themselves pediatricians. On numerous occasions, specialists discussed infant and preschool-conference procedures at the meetings of national pediatric societies.[16] The Children's Bureau and national child-health organizations also played a role in systematizing the new service. The Bureau produced educational materials for clinic staff including a pamphlet published in 1917 entitled, "How to Conduct a Children's Health Conference."[17] Both the Bureau and the American Child Health Association had committees of physician consultants that reviewed and disseminated materials on child-health conference techniques.[18] Standardizing the well-baby conference required, among other things, agreed-upon criteria on what constituted normal development. Pediatricians and other professionals devised such standards and national health organizations facilitated their distribution. Specialists sought criteria that were scientifically grounded and they looked to the newly emerging field of child development for guidelines.[19]

The most widely used tool for assessing physical growth was weight-height-age charts. These were tables showing mean weights of same-sex and same-age children of equivalent heights. The practitioner assessed a child's "nutritional condition" by comparing the youngster's weight to the appropriate average. Deviation of more than 10 percent below or 20 percent above the mean was indicative of abnormality.[20] Pediatricians and public-health practitioners constructed weight-height-age tables and the American Child Health Association disseminated the charts along with numerous articles on their use. While child-health procedures remained quite stable during the 1920s and 1930s, standards used to evaluate child development evolved. In the late 1920s, practitioners criticized height and weight charts on a number of grounds. The tables were insensitive to differences in children's skeletal structure and to variations in their growth patterns over time. Some argued that weight and height were inadequate measures of nutrition and their use for that purpose should be discontinued.[21] But such criticism led not to the abandonment of physical measures but to the creation of more complex standards. Tables published in the early 1930s included hip width, chest width and depth, and the girth of arms and calves.[22]

The search for developmental indices was by no means limited to physical growth. Pediatricians and health activists advocated the adoption of psychosocial norms analogous to those used to evaluate biological maturation. Arnold Gesell, who held degrees in both medicine and child psychology, argued that behavioral standards were indispensable to the success of child-health supervision. In 1926 Gesell asserted:

It is important to recognize that such psychological norms are attainable, and that standards of mental health are as legitimate and as feasible as standards of physical status. Even in our present state of comparative ignorance, it is possible to lay down for various ages of infancy and childhood certain concrete minimum essentials of mental health expressed in tangible behavior terms.[23]

Gesell did just that in *Mental Growth of the Preschool Child* published in 1925.[24] Based on the observation of several hundred healthy babies, the book delineates behaviors expected for children in successive stages of development.

The White House Conference committee report on growth and development, a standard reference for pediatricians for many years after its 1932 publication, adopted the same orientation toward assessing children's psychosocial maturation. The report summarized research on intelligence testing, personality formation, language and motor development, and social adjustment. One of the authors' overriding concerns was the identification of developmental indices. They declared that

for every age group . . . there are . . . ascertainable *norms* of behavior which must enter into an estimate of [the child's] mental and physical health. Any full inquiry into the status of his health must give systematic heed to these behavioral conditions and bring them into the scheme of developmental supervision.[25]

Child-health specialists quickly integrated Gesell's norms and others like them into the technology of the well-baby conference. Norms of this sort even made their way into medical record forms. In 1926 the American Child Health Association, with the approval of its Medical Committee, distributed Developmental Record Forms intended to aid physicians in assessing the progress of children one through six. The forms included a listing of behavioral benchmarks considered normal for children in specified age categories.[26] Like the well-child conference itself, materials like Developmental Record forms and weight-height-age tables were new to the decade of 1920.

Child-Health Campaigns

A number of factors helped stimulate demand for the new professional service. First, the sheer prevalence of infant-welfare centers meant that large numbers of parents would be aware of their existence. There were several thousand clinics in existence by 1930; major cities like New York and Chicago had child-health centers in nearly all their districts. According to the White House Conference Report, clinics were operating in 43 percent of the counties in the United States.[27] A second contributing factor was the "educational activities" of municipal public-health departments. In some cities it was routine for the health department to dispatch a nurse to every household for which a recent birth had been registered. Visiting nurses informed mothers about the clinics and urged them to obtain periodic health supervision for their infants either at public centers or at private medical offices. Boston employed this system with the result that, in 1928, half the babies in the city under one year of age were being seen at municipal infant-welfare clinics.[28]

Also instrumental in stirring public demand was a flood of propaganda from the Children's Bureau and national child-health organizations. Some of the material produced by these organizations was directed at teachers and school-age children but most was aimed at the parents of preschool children. In 1918, the Children's Bureau, with the aid of women's clubs, orchestrated a Children's Year Campaign to promote child-health supervision. The focus of the Campaign was a "weighing and measuring test" designed to impress on the public the need for preventive health care for youngsters. The Bureau printed and distributed five million cards for recording and reporting the height and weight of America's children.[29]

In subsequent years, national child-health organizations sponsored educational demonstrations and conferences and published a magazine on child hygiene for mothers. During the mid-1920s, the American Child Health Association launched a drive to have May 1 proclaimed Child Health Day, "devoted to the promotion of every form of activity which protected the life and health of children."[30] According to the *Chicago Journal of Commerce*, "the publicity given to that campaign by magazines and newspapers of this country, was second only to that accorded to such events as the Dempsey-Tunney fight, the Lindbergh flight, and the World Series."[31] By the end of the decade there were radio talk shows on the subject of child health.[32]

Women flocked to the clinics. Infant-welfare centers were so fully utilized during the 1920s that continued expansion of facilities was necessary to accommodate rising demand. At the same time, the clinics and the accompanying publicity stimulated use of private professional services. A number of physicians involved in child-welfare work commented on this trend. The commissioner of health in Cincinnati declared that "in every large city where child health conferences are under way, thousands of mothers seek the advice of their own physicians. The clinics . . . have a tendency to stimulate private practice."[33] Pediatrician Harold Stuart, who coordinated child-health services in Boston, pointed out that many women acquainted themselves with well-child care at the clinics and subsequently sought the same service from office-based practitioners. He observed also that

the whole training given at these conferences makes mothers more observant of their children's health and more ready to seek the advice of their physicians for minor illnesses. Furthermore, innumerable mothers are referred by the conference physicians to their family physicians for conditions detected by the former which would never otherwise reach the latter.[34]

Indeed, physician-activists viewed the public centers as primarily educational: a means of persuading the community at large and mothers in particular of the value of periodic medical exams for healthy children.[35] The clinics certainly familiarized their clientele with the well-child conference as a professional service. By the 1920s, American parents had a perceived need for expert child-rearing advice. Whether the child-welfare movement stimulated this need or merely reflected its presence is open to debate. But it is clear that, within child-welfare clinics, a vague proclivity for scientifically grounded counsel was channeled into concrete expectations regarding a new professional service.

Impact of Demand on the Specialty

The invention of the well-baby conference and soaring demand for its delivery had significant consequences for pediatrics as a specialty. Exponential growth in the specialty's ranks has already been mentioned. The more than tenfold increase in child specialists in the two decades before 1934 yielded a very different professional constituency than had existed earlier. Growth in the market for child-health services had other noteworthy consequences as well. There were changes in pediatricians' career patterns and in the content of their medical practices.

With the advent of child-health supervision after World War I, it is likely that the care of well children constituted a growing portion of pediatricians' activities. Turn-of-the-century child specialists were experts on artificial infant feeding but demand for such services outside of children's asylums and hospitals appears to have been limited.[36] Unfortunately, it is not possible to document shifts in the content of pediatric practice between the late 1800s and the early 1930s. There were no studies of practice composition until the late 1920s. But whatever the relative dominance of well and sick children in the practices of turn-of-the-century pediatricians, it is clear that, for postwar specialists, preventive care was a central activity.

A survey of seventeen pediatricians conducted in the late 1920s found that 39 percent of patient visits were for vaccinations, physical exams, or supervision of infant feeding.[37] C. Anderson Aldrich analyzed the composition of his pediatric practice, located in a suburb of Chicago, during the early 1930s. Aldrich reported that 29 percent of his caseload involved "routine care of infants" and another 10 percent routine examinations and preventive treatment of older children. Visits with well children constituted 39 percent of his practice.[38] Arthur London gives a comparable figure in assessing his pediatric practice within Durham, North Carolina in the mid-1930s. Thirty-nine percent of his patients received routine care, routine examinations, or immunizations.[39] While the relative proportion of well and sick visits undoubtedly varied by geographical location and individual physician, available data suggest that, from the late 1920s on, well-child care constituted from a third to a half of private pediatric practices.[40]

Closely related to the salience of preventive care were alterations in the career patterns of contemporary child specialists. Early twentieth-century pediatricians had combined office-based practices with hospital and teaching appointments. At that time specialized private practices were built very slowly on the basis of individual reputations gained through institutional posts. The situation in the 1930s was quite different. A child specialist no longer had to spend years establishing a name for himself before he could attract private pediatric patients. Pediatricians were being consulted less for personal reputations than for the particular professional service they were prepared to deliver. With the burgeoning demand for preventive child-health care, the private practice of pediatrics was becoming viable and a full-time endeavor.

Specialists' work patterns were not transformed overnight. The 1920s and early 1930s seem to have been a transition period with pediatric practice only partially differentiated from general practice on the one hand and pediatric teaching and research on the other. During these years, child specialists typically worked at infant-welfare clinics on a part-time basis early in their careers. The White House Conference Report on Health Centers indicates that, in 1930, 246 physicians were employed at clinics full-time and 1,261 part-time. Authors of the report suggest that these figures underestimate the actual extent of physician employment.[41] Temporary appointments at health centers very probably assisted pediatricians in building their private practices. But if institutional posts were still prevalent during the 1920s and early 1930s, opportunities in private specialty practice were clearly blossoming. Full-time office-based pediatric practice was emerging as a discrete career track. In subsequent decades, careers in academic pediatrics and pediatric practice would become increasingly distinct.

Market Consolidation

Changes in pediatricians' career patterns triggered a complex set of responses from contemporary specialists. As suggested earlier,

the segment's overriding aims during this period were to organize the expanding market for well-child services and to regularize and protect emerging careers in office-based practice. The
actions of child specialists were multifaceted because organizing
the market was a complicated undertaking. I argue that there
were four distinct aspects to market consolidation in pediatrics.
While analytically discrete, these dynamics took place, to a large
degree, contemporaneously.

First, practitioners systematized the techniques of well-child
care and rendered child-health supervision a recognizable professional service. This aspect of the professional mobilization has already been documented. Physicians working in public clinics developed and standardized the well-baby conference. Both pediatric
societies and child-health associations disseminated the new technology. Constructing a recognizable professional commodity seems
to have been critical both to the initial creation of demand and to
later market stabilization.

Second, specialists brought the new service squarely into the
segment's domain and proclaimed it as a distinctly pediatric commodity. They did so by introducing training in well-baby care into
pediatric curriculum and by formulating a new professional ideology. Specialty leaders articulated a pediatric ethos that redefined
the practitioner's stance toward children and their families. Apart
from general practitioners, pediatricians had no competition in the
area of well-child care and the specialty's jurisdiction over the new
service was easily established.

Third, pediatricians transferred the delivery of child-health supervision from public clinics, where it was provided free of charge,
into private medical practices. The publicity campaigns of child-
health activists and the example of the clinics stimulated the use of
private pediatricians. Nonetheless, child specialists engaged in a
number of maneuvers designed to curtail the delivery of free services. As they succeeded in shifting well-child care into private
offices, there was a change in the clientele. Families attending
welfare centers were predominantly working class; those consulting private pediatricians were largely middle class.

Fourth, in the early 1930s, pediatric leaders established formal
market structures. They founded the American Academy of Pediatrics to represent the new constituency of primary-care providers.

The Academy initiated the American Board of Pediatrics, a national certifying body that delineates the segment's knowledge base and examines candidates for evidence of specialized competency. The board permanently institutionalized pediatrics as a market division within medicine. In creating a qualifying mechanism, child specialists were following a pattern widely adopted by medical segments during the 1930s. The final three of these market dynamics are elaborated below.

Counselors of Health

During the early 1920s, child specialists began a concerted effort to ensure that child-health supervision was brought unambiguously into the domain of pediatrics. By that time, practitioners had already systematized the well-baby conference and it was relatively easy to incorporate the service within the specialty's boundaries. Other medical specialties had little interest in healthy children, and general practitioners, the only group besides pediatricians that delivered well-child care, had no means for establishing jurisdiction over a particular medical service. Pediatricians made their initial claim by integrating child-health conference techniques into pediatric curriculum and by altering pediatric ideology regarding the specialist's orientation toward clients. The new additions to pediatric curriculum included courses on preventive pediatrics and practical clinical training within university-affiliated infant-welfare centers.

In 1920 the American Pediatric Society developed guidelines for instruction on child-welfare techniques and sent copies to ninety American and Canadian medical colleges. A year later the APS polled the schools on whether they offered training in child hygiene. Thirty-seven responded affirmatively.[42] As the decade proceeded, some pediatric departments established cooperative relationships with city-run infant-welfare centers. Boston had what was probably the most thorough coordination of municipal child-health programs and university teaching. In 1925, pediatric leaders created a system whereby all the city's child-health clinics were supervised by faculty from one of Boston's three medical schools.[43] In addition to courses for undergraduate medical students, some university departments initiated "post-graduate" instruction for practicing physicians seeking exposure to child-hygiene procedures. By

1930, thirteen medical schools offered intensive "short courses" in child-health supervision for medical graduates. Fifteen states offered extension courses for physicians through some combination of state universities, state medical societies, and boards of health.[44] These programs were very popular when parents began seeking child-health services from private practitioners.

As pediatricians brought health supervision into the mainstream of specialty, leaders articulated a new professional ideology. Concern with infant mortality and children's diseases that dominated professional rhetoric in the early 1900s gave way to a focus on children's growth and development. In recasting their professional ethos, pediatricians drew liberally from the rhetoric of the child-health movement.

It was Borden Veeder, professor of clinical pediatrics at Washington University, who articulated the new professional ethos most clearly. During the 1920s, Veeder was active in national child-health organizations and was becoming an increasingly visible figure within the specialty. In his chairman's address to the AMA Section in 1923, Veeder insisted that it was not study of childhood diseases that made a pediatrician, it was knowledge of the child.

Child hygiene is at present the most important motif in our work, as it will continue to be in the future, and in child hygiene work it has been the child that has been the topic of consideration—not disease or medicine. . . . The change in conception of the physician from the healer of disease to the counselor of health is the great advance made by the present era of medicine.[45]

What separated the pediatrician from his medical colleagues was knowledge about children's physical growth and mental development.

The idea of the pediatrician as overseer of child development required a complementary notion of the physician's stance toward the parents. The new professional ethos provided this as well. The child specialist was advisor to the family, educating parents on child management. One specialist spoke of pediatricians' " 'bringing up' parents" and stressed "the importance of guiding parents in the proper training of children."[46] Spokesmen differed in the zealousness with which pediatricians were to carry out this task. Aldrich envisioned the physician fostering a natural attitude in parents toward children's growth and developmental problems.[47] Philadelphia pediatrician Charles Fife pictured the specialist assuming a more aggressive posture. In a presidential address to the APS entitled "The Child's Family Advisor," Fife argued that it was the pediatrician's responsibility to "search out . . . the earliest manifestation of biological instability and of behavior difficulties" and teach the child's parents how to handle them. Through such interventions, "an alert pediatrician" could "avert many a physical, mental and moral crash."[48]

The specialty's new domain included nothing short of the normative regulation of childhood. Borden Veeder stated this unambiguously when describing the expanded scope of preventive pediatrics in a book written for general practitioners.

We are interested in the knowledge of the normal growth and development of the child and in methods of preventing disease and deviations from normal development.[49]

Veeder was explicit that the pediatrician's concern with normalcy was not restricted to physical maturation.

No small part of the deviations from normal health and development have their origin not in biochemical or biological causes but in habits, mental reactions, and psychological conflicts. We venture to prophesy that this last field which is on the threshold of being opened up will write the next important chapter in the scientific development of pediatrics.[50]

The normative aspects of the specialist's expertise were central to the emergence of primary-care pediatrics. In Veeder's opinion, it was the specialty's concern with children's growth and development that justified the promotion of pediatrics as a restricted field of medical practice.[51]

The themes introduced into pediatric ideology during the 1920s gave shape and purpose to specialists' professional tasks. They prescribed a new professional role and a new stance toward patients. The ethos also helped to designate child-health supervision as a pediatric service. It was not inevitable that specialists deliver well-child care. General practitioners could do so competently. Child-hygiene techniques were neither arcane nor arduous to acquire. Yet preventive medical care for children came to be identified with pediatrics and, from the 1920s on, a growing portion of American parents took their youngsters to child specialists rather than general practitioners.

From Public Clinic to Private Office

That pediatricians integrated child hygiene into the specialty's domain is not an intuitively unsettling fact. But how was a service initially delivered in free clinics transferred into private offices? According to White House Conference reports, there were more than 4,000 infant-welfare centers in 1930. A decade and a half later, the clinics were restricting their clientele and preventive child-health care was being absorbed into fee-for-service practice. Accompanying this shift in the location of delivery was a change in the clientele receiving pediatric services. Child-health activists designed the well-baby conference for the native-born and immigrant working classes. Women from blue-collar families predominated among welfare-center clientele.[52] But middle-class women constituted the bulk of patrons in private offices.

These transitions were due in large measure to forces external to pediatrics. The example of the clinics and publicity campaigns launched by health activists encouraged parents to consult private pediatricians. Middle-class Americans were utilizing other types of professional services for children by the 1920s and 1930s. The child-welfare movement inaugurated psychiatric care for youngsters through the introduction of child-guidance clinics between the 1890s and World War I. Like the health centers, guidance centers were originally geared toward low-income groups but affluent families were soon patronizing both guidance clinics and office-based psychiatric specialists.[53] The private practices of these professions grew because middle-class parents had acquired a perceived need for scientific child-rearing advice.

At the same time, pediatricians engaged in actions designed to ensure that child-health supervision was transferred from public centers to private offices. Beginning in the early 1920s, they moved to place restrictions on the types of clients eligible for clinic services. Involved here was the issue of "clinic abuse." Welfare centers provided consultations without charge and many physicians objected to the provision of free medical care to families sufficiently comfortable to pay for it. Julius Hess of Chicago was among those who complained about the clinics' middle-class patronage. "We found that twenty-five percent of our patients were rolling up in automobiles and that about as many more were wearing good fur coats."[54] In the early 1920s, he and other physicians attempted to exclude affluent families from Chicago's centers. This precipitated a conflict with the Infant Welfare Society, an organization funding half the city's clinics, which wanted no such restrictions.[55] Meanwhile, debates began at the meetings of pediatric societies and child-welfare associations about the appropriate relation of the clinic to the private physician.

There was never unanimity among pediatricians on the issue of clinic restrictions. By the mid-1920s, welfare centers were integral to the pediatric course curriculum at numerous medical colleges and it was clear that their presence stimulated use of private professional services. Furthermore, the clinics provided financial remuneration, albeit modest, to a great many young specialists.[56] Physicians embarking on pediatric careers used part-time employment at health centers to gain experience in child-health supervision and to help build their practices. Defenders of nonrestrictive policies argued that the clinics were not competitive with the vast majority of medical practitioners. No treatment of sick children was permitted at the centers and, they insisted, few private physicians were trained or interested in providing child-health supervision. Stuart put it this way:

Instances are constantly being encountered of mothers, who with previous children had never consulted a physician except in illness, becoming interested in the possibilities of preventive medicine through a few visits to free conferences, and then placing their children in the hands of private practitioners, hoping to obtain a better and more personal grade of preventive service. Unfortunately not infrequently these same mothers return to the city conferences, complaining that their private physicians had disappointed them, and were obviously disinterested in the well infant or child.[57]

But if most physicians did not offer well-child care, pediatricians did. As the number of pediatric primary-care providers grew, competition between the clinic and the private physician became an increasingly sensitive issue.

There were nonpecuniary reasons for encouraging the use of

office-based practitioners rather than welfare centers. Veeder stressed that clinic services had several weaknesses: the centers were overcrowded, staff changed frequently, and physicians who saw a child only once had scanty knowledge of the family environment. Failure to treat sick children was another shortcoming. Fee-for-service care had none of these limitations and, in Veeder's opinion, the private practitioner was in an ideal position to conduct developmental supervision.[58]

Whatever the justifications, specialists were imposing restrictions on clinic use in some cities by the early 1920s. Pediatrician Edgar J. Huenekens describes changing policies in Minneapolis during this period.

In the beginning when these clinics were established they were open to every one regardless of financial circumstances. I think that was a very good thing. They were educational. Everyone was invited to see what benefits could be developed from these welfare clinics. As those clinics have grown we have gradually cut down more and more on the kind of mothers and the kind of babies that are admitted. . . . [Financial pressures] forced us to cut down on the number of cases we expected to take care of in the infant welfare clinics. Most people thought that was a misfortune. I think it was a very good thing. This year we have been forced to exclude those who could afford to pay for such service. Then the question came up, if they could not get such service free in the welfare clinics where could they get it. There were few [family] physicians in the city who were prepared to give such service. Most of the pediatricians were prepared. I felt and they [other pediatricians] felt for the last few years that free infant welfare work should be cut down after it had a good start; after the people had been educated to demand that sort of thing that it should be cut down and given only to people in poor economic circumstances.[59]

In 1921, 33 percent of all children born in Minneapolis were seen in the city's infant-welfare centers. As a result of new policies, this proportion fell to 17 percent by 1928.[60] Clinic managers advised mothers turned away from the centers on the basis of income to consult private physicians.

Efforts to curtail free health services for children continued during the late 1920s and 1930s. By this time the attitude of pediatric spokesmen toward local and federal funding of well-child services had cooled substantially. In the early 1920s child specialists had enthusiastically supported the Sheppard-Towner Act, a federal bill that helped finance infant-welfare clinics. In fact, the AMA Section on Diseases of Children had publicly endorsed Sheppard-Towner and by doing so had incurred a rebuke from the AMA House of Delegates. But when the legislation came for renewal at the end of the decade in the form of the Jones-Bankhead Act, pediatricians balked. A committee of the newly formed American Academy of Pediatrics recommended that the organization support the bill's passage only if it included a provision forbidding government clinics in competition with fee-for-service practice.[61] The Academy's leadership was divided on whether to endorse Jones-Bankhead and the organization ultimately avoided taking an official position by permanently tabling the issue.[62] In the end, the legislation failed to pass in Congress. The Academy's ambivalence toward federal initiative in the area of child health was evident again in the 1940s when the society's relationship with the U.S. Children's Bureau seriously deteriorated.[63]

Infant-welfare clinics gave birth to primary-care pediatrics but once office-based practice was truly viable, specialists moved to curtail the competition of public clinics. Yet in fairness to pediatricians, protectionist activity was by no means limited to their speciality. Groups within medicine at large were moving to end "abuse of medical charity" in the early decades of the century and, by the 1920s, dispensaries were dying out as independent institutions.[64] The profession moved to the right during the 1930s, a shift encouraged by the arrival of the Great Depression. Charles Rosenberg suggests another reason for the disappearance of freestanding outpatient clinics: with the proliferation of hospital-based residency programs, young physicians no longer found dispensary appointments to be highly attractive.[65] (University outpatient clinics took over some of the care provided earlier by independent dispensaries.) Child-health clinics did not disappear in the 1930s like freestanding dispensaries. But with increasing frequency, well-baby centers imposed income restrictions on their clientele or charged for clinic services.

The transfer of pediatric services from clinic to private office had numerous precedents. Organ-based specialties had their origins in dispensaries that provided charitable services for the indigent. In these fields also, practitioners systematized new services within institutions for the poor and then built office-based practices patronized by the affluent. Furthermore, changing the location of child-health supervision was essential for the practice of pediatrics as we know it today. Had this not taken place, the majority of pediatricians would be employees of public agencies rather than office-based professionals.

Formal Market Structures

By 1930, child specialists had made substantial progress toward organizing the market for primary-care pediatrics. They had systematized a new professional service and incorporated it within the specialty's purview. American parents recognized child-health supervision and considered it a desirable professional commodity. Practitioners were successfully shifting service delivery from clinics to private offices. It remained for favorable market arrangements to be permanently secured. Specialists embarked on this task in the late 1920s and began by establishing the American Academy of Pediatrics.[66] While the Academy would serve many functions in subsequent decades, stabilizing the pediatric market was preeminent at the time of its formation.

Specialists' strategy for consolidating the market was to create a mechanism for setting training requirements and designating qualified specialists. Isaac Abt, the Academy's first president, articulated this objective when addressing his constituency in 1931.

The Academy is interested in establishing qualifications for pediatric practice and eventually in giving an answer to the question: Who shall be considered a pediatrician? . . . It is desirable that some organizations should prescribe the preparation and training of . . . specialized physicians and define the educational attainments that they should achieve. In order to accomplish this purpose and for other reasons . . . the American Academy of Pediatrics is today holding its inaugural session.[67]

Enlisting the participation of older pediatric associations, Academy leaders moved quickly to institute a certifying body. The result of their efforts was the American Board of Pediatrics (ABP) incorporated in 1933. The Board was composed of three members each from the Academy, the American Pediatric Society, and the AMA Section on Diseases of Children. Its mandate was to designate educational standards for entrance into the field and to assess the "proficiency of the individual physician to practice pediatrics as a specialty."[68] Practitioners who completed training requirements and passed a board-administered examination would receive a certificate of competence in pediatrics. The ABP began examining candidates in 1934.[69]

From the outset, the Board had a powerful effect on graduate professional training, influencing both the duration and character of residency programs. Beginning in the mid-1930s, the ABP required that recent medical graduates have one year of internship and two years of pediatric training in an approved residency program prior to examination.[70] Approved programs were those inspected and sanctioned by the AMA Council on Medical Education. During the 1950s, the Board became directly involved in the inspection and approval of residency training programs through participation, along with the AMA Council, in a Pediatric Residency Review Committee.[71] But the Board shaped the content of graduate training from the 1930s. In order to attract high-quality house staff, training directors had to design residency programs with an eye toward the content of certifying exams.

In creating the ABP, pediatricians were adopting an institutional pattern that was becoming universal among contemporary medical segments. Specialty groups established fourteen qualifying boards between 1930 and 1940.[72] Ophthalmologists and otolaryngologists set up the first certifying bodies in 1916 and 1924, respectively. They were followed by obstetricians and gynecologists in 1930 and dermatologists in 1932. Pediatricians modeled the ABP after contemporary qualifying boards.

The proliferation of certifying boards during the 1930s functioned to divide and stabilize the overall market for specialized medical care. While not restricting the professional activities of uncertified M.D.s, boards formally designated discrete professional services and established segments' claims to sectors of the medical market. Certification also regularized boundaries between fields of practice. With the widespread movement toward certification among medical specialties, individual segments felt impelled to follow suit. Pediatric leaders understood the importance of creating a board when the market as a whole was undergoing division. Borden Veeder, chairman of the Academy's Committee on Medical Education, commented in 1932 that a "board for Pediatrics should be established as a matter of self protection. It seems that we have reached a point where such a step will become almost necessary if we are to avoid future troubles."[73] Following the multiplication of boards in the decade of 1930, established segments took measures to prevent unlimited fragmentation of the medical market. In 1942, through the Advisory Board for Medical Specialties, they instituted policies for the approval of new boards that made it more difficult for additional primary certifying bodies to be established.[74]

Several developments stimulated the division of the medical specialty market at this point. One factor was growth in demand for a variety of specialized medical services. In 1923, 15,400 physicians classified themselves as full-time specialists. Twenty-two percent were surgeons and 30 percent were either ophthalmologists or otolaryngologists.[75] These segments were the first to initiate regulatory procedures.[76] Another factor catalyzing market division was a decline in physician-population ratios. George Rosen argues that market consolidation was feasible during the 1930s because, by then, the reform of medical colleges had strengthened the profession's control over entrance into practice.[77]

But perhaps most important to the timing of formal market structures was growing controversy within medicine over graduate professional education. There was no prescribed route for the acquisition of specialized expertise during the 1920s. Undergraduate medical training was being fully integrated into the university through the reform of American medical colleges but graduate medical education was not. Young physicians aspiring to specialized careers had an array of options for post-M.D. training. Several medical schools offered specialty training that closely resembled Ph.D. programs and prepared physicians for careers in medical research and teaching. There was a wide range of hospital-based residencies, varying considerably in length and quality. In some fields, pediatrics among them, "short courses" were available for medical practitioners seeking a brief exposure to specialized techniques.

Medical leaders concurred that order should be brought to this confusing diversity of programs. But they disagreed on how graduate education should be organized and where it should take place. Was specialty training to be based in and controlled by medical colleges or located outside the university in community hospitals? Was it to be training for careers in research and teaching or careers in practice? Should there be licensure for specialty practice as there was for medical practice more generally? Would the AMA play a major role in the design and organization of graduate medical education? All of these were real possibilities during the 1920s.[78] Early in the decade, members of the AMA's Council on Medical Education advocated that specialty training be university based and regulated through state-administered licensing exams. As the market for specialized services grew, pressures to systematize training heightened. By the late 1920s attempts to establish specialty licensing procedures were being initiated within state legislatures.[79] Specialty leaders realized that if they failed to act quickly, the design of graduate education would be permanently removed from their purview.

By establishing qualifying boards in the 1930s, medical segments effectively preempted other groups within the profession and seized control over graduate medical training. They organized post-M.D. education so as to protect and perpetuate existing market sectors. Specialty training would take place not at university medical schools but in hospital-based residency programs strongly influenced by certifying boards and, through the boards, by the needs and interests of specialty associations.[80] It would be training not for careers in teaching and research, as some medical educators had envisioned, but for careers in specialized practice. This system is unique among American professions; with the exception of medicine and health occupations modeled after it, graduate professional education in the United States is designed to prepare candidates for academic careers.[81] Not coincidentally, medicine is the only profession in which specialties developed as organized, market-oriented segments prior to the modernization of graduate professional training. Medical schools exerted increasing influence upon residency training after World War II.[82] But by then, specialties were well established as divisions of the market for professional services.

Events of the 1930s were highly consequential for the ultimate character of American medical practice. The system of hospital-based residency programs and certifying exams included no structural obstacles to unlimited growth of specialized fields. Indeed, graduate training was organized to allow all physicians access to specialty practice. In subsequent decades, incentives were such that a rapidly growing share of medical graduates chose to pursue specialized careers. While this trend expressed itself in the middle decades of the century, its course was built into institutional arrangements established during the 1930s. With the creation of a certifying board, pediatrics, like contemporary medical segments, institutionalized itself as a permanent and expanding division of medical practice. More physicians would join its ranks but the segment's organization would remain essentially stable in the years to follow.

The Pediatrician as Family Advisor

Child-health supervision placed the pediatrician in a new relation to the American family. The specialty's core tasks now included the dissemination of norms regarding parenting and age-appropriate behavior in children. As the segment's patronage grew in subsequent decades, it members dispersed family norms to a growing portion of the American population. Pediatricians were fully aware that medical care for healthy youngsters was a radical social invention. They spoke explicitly of taking over functions served by grandmothers in previous generations.[83] Medical advice on child rearing was not in itself a novelty. American parents were consulting child-training manuals written by physicians during the nineteenth century. But never before had professionals intervened directly into parent-child relationships on a routine and periodic basis. Primary-care pediatrics was an altogether new agency for the social regulation of childhood and family life.

Child specialists played a vital role in establishing child-health supervision. They systematized the well-baby conference, realigned their stance toward families, moved service delivery out of free clinics, and built formal market structures. But they did not create the initial demand for well-child care. A social movement much broader than medicine generated the perceived social need for preventive pediatrics. This movement underwrote the invention of the new service, financed its original delivery, and persuaded parents of its merit. Activists channeled an unfocused interest in scientifically informed child rearing into demand for a specific professional service. Pediatricians capitalized on the child-health movement and eventually coopted it. Yet their new relation to the family rested upon a firm—if essentially middle-class—social mandate.

Preventive pediatrics and the movement that created it had implications for the social construction of childhood as a stage of life. Both professionals and parents sought "scientific" criteria to assess children's developmental progress. One result was increasing specification of the parameters of normal maturation. Pediatrician Joseph Brennemann—known among his colleagues for never following the crowd—offers quasi-satirical commentary on this trend. His account stresses maternal demand for developmental standards while minimizing the undoubted contribution of contemporary professionals. But if biased in this regard, Brennemann's observations are trenchant on the consequences of ongoing trends for the normative regulation of childhood.

Now, as is well known, a normal gain in weight is one of the essential attributes of growth, and is the best, single, comparative, objective measure of normal physical development that can be expressed in figures. Always duly appreciated as such, at least in infancy, it became a sort of fetish when the campaign directed toward weighing and measuring all children came as an aftermath of the World War. . . . The scale and the measuring rod became the sole arbiters of nutrition, and the height and weight charts became as fixed guides as if they too had been handed down on tablets of stone from Mount Sinai. . . . The natural effect on the mother when confronted by a standard was to proceed to standardize her child, to make him weigh what he should according to the chart. . . . She set about characteristically to do her maternal duty by her child, and struggled heroically and futilely, as every pediatrician knows, to make him eat. . . . When his mother tried to coax and finally to force him to eat in order to bring him up to standard, as is done in the majority of homes, he either refused to eat or else vomited or dawdled over his meals for hours. . . . The healthy child who will not eat is, ipso facto, a behavior problem.[84]

Enforcing standards of physical development was producing eating disorders in children. Brennemann warned that the next step would be the creation of other behavioral and developmental problems.

In the campaign of measuring height and weight, mothers attempted to mold their children to a more or less fixed pattern of physical development; is there not at least an equal danger that they will now attempt to mold them to an ideal, more or less fixed, mental and behavioral pattern? Infants are already being matched with Gesell, with resulting gloom or elation; older children are being measured by intelligence quotients and behavioristic yardsticks. The psychologists, psychiatrists, behaviorists, child guiders and parent teachers can say all they may about normal variation, and the rest of us can talk till the cows come home, the psychologically and psychiatrically minded mother is going to hold her child up to an ideal mental and behavioral pattern. In doing so I am afraid that even more than on the former occasion she will encounter [in her child] a normal biologic spirit of rebellion.[85]

Child-health supervision inaugurated heightened social control of childhood and carried with it the seeds of new normative violations.

Continuing Occupational Processes

Dynamics within post-World War I pediatrics are highly distinctive in several ways. They involve exceptionally rapid growth in demand for professional services. They result in a new mechanism for disseminating age norms and for social regulation of childhood. Yet at least three underlying processes operative in this period are continuous with those in other phases of the specialty's history.

First, organizational innovation and changing work patterns are key factors stimulating the mobilization of contemporary specialists. The crucial organization during the 1920s and 1930s is the infant-welfare clinic. Social activists set up several thousand of these facilities and launched publicity campaigns encouraging preventive medical care for children. With growing demand for pediatric services, office-based specialty practice became viable on a full-time basis without years of preparatory institutional appointments. Practitioners moved to consolidate the market for child-health services and thus stabilized the careers of primary-care specialists.

Second, developments in their occupational environment powerfully influence the type of market institutions pediatricians built and the timing of their mobilization. Child specialists modeled the pediatric board after qualifying bodies established in earlier decades and after other boards being constituted in the 1930s. Creation of the pediatric board was part of a broader movement by contemporary segments to divide the overall market for specialized medical care and to secure existing market sectors. Pediatric leaders considered the creation of a certifying procedure at this time crucial for the continued well-being of the specialty.

Third, events of the 1920s and 1930s demonstrate specialists' ability to maneuver within and effect the ultimate form of medical organizations. Pediatricians employed medical facilities to launch markets for office-based services and then mobilized to shape work organizations so that favorable market arrangements were permanently maintained. After World War I, they succeeded in using infant-welfare centers to build primary-care practices and then, with the help of medicine at large, to eliminate competition from the clinics by restricting clinic patronage. Even more dramatic was the impact that specialties had upon graduate medical education. Through the certification system, medical segments seized control over graduate professional training and organized residency programs so as to protect and perpetuate specialty markets.

Chapter Six

Birth of a Scientific Subspecialty:
Pediatric Endocrinology

By World War II, pediatrics and other medical segments of nine-teenth-century origin had built modern occupational institutions. Professional associations, specialized academic units, certifying boards, and residency programs were in place. Existing certifying boards had taken measures to protect specialty markets by restrict-ing the proliferation of new boards. The basic structure of the medical specialty system was complete. Both this system and the internal organization of established specialties would remain quite stable in the years that followed.

Yet segmentation continued. After the war, new groups of physi-cians coalesced, constructed professional institutions, and strug-gled to establish themselves within the medical specialty system. Few of the new segments won autonomous certifying boards. The Advisory Board for Medical Specialties (ABMS) successfully blocked the multiplication of primary boards, approving only four after 1950.[1] But many newcomers secured sub-boards or special examin-ing committees under the sponsorship of established boards.[2] To-day, twenty-one primary boards and two conjoint boards examine candidates in approximately six dozen fields of medical practice. As of 1986, the American Board of Internal Medicine (ABIM) granted special certificates in twelve subspecialty areas: cardiovascular dis-ease, pulmonary disease, gastroenterology, endocrinology and metabolism, hematology, infectious disease, oncology, nephrology, rheumatology, critical care medicine, diagnostic laboratory immunology, and geriatrics. The ABMS approved the first three in 1940; it accepted the next six in the early 1970s, and the final three during the mid-1980s.

Segmentation proceeded within pediatrics also. By 1986, eight special examining bodies operated within the American Board of Pediatrics (ABP). Special pediatric certificates (with dates of ABMS approval) are available in cardiology (1960), hematology and oncology (1973), nephrology (1973), neonatal and perinatal medicine (1974), endocrinology (1976), diagnostic laboratory immunology (1984), critical care medicine (1985), and pulmonary disease (1985).[3]

Subspecialties have many of the organizational features of primary medical specialties. They are institutionalized as separate departmental divisions within teaching hospitals and medical schools. Their leaders initiate journals, create sections within medical societies, and found autonomous professional associations. Like primary boards, the sub-boards specify training requirements and examine individual candidates. The principal difference in the two tiers of qualifying boards is that certification in a primary specialty is a prerequisite for subspecialty certification. Sub-boards delineate market divisions, in this case divisions internal to major specialties.

This chapter examines the development of pediatric subspecialties, focusing on pediatric endocrinology and, to a lesser extent, pediatric cardiology. As in previous sections of the book, the goal here is to identify processes underlying the development of professional segments. Pediatric subfields first emerged as focal areas within medicine during the 1930s and 1940s, more than a half-century after the initial consolidation of pediatrics. The newer entrants emerged in a very different organizational context than their parent specialty. Pediatrics appeared when hospitals and training schools were premodern in character and it coalesced in clinical facilities outside the medical colleges. Pediatric endocrinology grew up within modern academic departments and university-controlled hospitals. The conceptual foundations of subspecialties are dissimilar as well. While pediatrics is a social-problem based segment spurred largely by health-related social movements, pediatric subfields have their roots in scientific and technical innovation. Despite these differences, some of the dynamics operative in the rise of pediatric subspecialties are remarkably similar to those found in the emergence of pediatrics and other specialties of nineteenth-century origin.

Scientific Possibilities and Specialized Clinics

A combination of scientific and organizational factors stimulated the initial development of pediatric endocrinology. On the scientific side were advances in the study of hormonal processes. In the early 1920s, investigators discovered that insulin relieves the symptoms of diabetes, and the finding intensified ongoing experimental efforts. Researchers extracted the products of the thyroid, adrenal, and parathyroid glands and administered them to animals and, in some cases, to patients with endocrine imbalances. Newly developed bioassay techniques allowed scientists to analyze hormonal secretions for clinical purposes and to diagnose endocrine disorders with greater certainty. Meanwhile anatomists and physiologists were clarifying the functioning of the body's endocrine system. Research-oriented physicians considered endocrinology an exciting field. With progress in basic research and some dramatic breakthroughs in the clinical management of adult disorders, the treatment of endocrine problems in children could now be imagined.[4]

The segment had compelling organizational antecedents as well. During the early twentieth century, American universities were struggling to integrate scientific norms into their medical schools and to create distinct professional roles for academic physicians. Two organizational innovations provided a foundation for scientifically oriented academic careers: full-time salaried professorships and specialized research units. Elite medical schools introduced both into their basic science departments during the late nineteenth century. By the early twentieth century, clinical departments were following suit. The result was dedicated academic tracks for faculty who combined specialized clinical instruction and applied medical research.[5]

Pediatric department chairs initiated subspecialty clinics during the 1920s and 1930s. By then, specialized laboratories and service divisions were becoming widespread among the clinical departments of prestigious medical colleges. Pediatric endocrinology is one of a number of pediatric subfields that grew up within specialized clinical units. It began during the 1930s as a part-time research endeavor and quickly evolved into a full-time academic career.

The spread of pediatric clinics is difficult to document. Histories of medical schools and hospitals provide only scanty information on departmental organization. But published addresses of contemporary pediatricians indicate that, by the mid-1930s, subspecialty clinics were common within the pediatric departments of leading medical schools. Children's Memorial Hospital in Chicago (affiliated then with the University of Chicago) and the Children's Hospital in Boston (affiliated with Harvard Medical School) had specialized units in the mid-1920s.[6] Boston's hospital ran clinics in the fields of cardiology, syphilis, neurology, and allergy.[7] There were also specialized outpatient units operating within the pediatric department of Yale Medical School during the early 1920s. These included specialized clinics in syphilis, heart disease, allergy, and tuberculosis.[8] The Johns Hopkins pediatric department initiated specialized clinics during the late 1920s and by the mid-1930s had outpatient units in congenital syphilis, epilepsy, cardiology, pulmonary disease, and endocrinology.[9]

Events surrounding the creation of pediatric clinics at Johns Hopkins illustrate both the assumptions underlying their introduction and the consequences for scientific developments. Edwards A. Park established subspecialty clinics at Hopkins upon assuming the chairmanship of the pediatric department in 1927. Park succeeded John Howland who in 1913 had become the first full-time salaried pediatric chairman in the country. Howland's chairmanship inaugurated scientific pediatrics at Johns Hopkins. Howland organized the department around a new, university-controlled pediatric hospital called the Harriet Lane Home. He assembled a group of young clinicians and researchers to staff the department and set out to build the foundations for modern pediatric research.[10] Howland ran the Harriet Lane Home on the German model.[11] He kept the department small and highly centralized, allowing his subordinates little autonomy. Howland's focus was upon wet-bench research—a colloquial term for laboratory investigation—and he granted minimal importance to clinical investigation. There was a clear distinc-

tion between clinical staff and laboratory researchers; the former
were discouraged from engaging in research while the latter were
excluded from the hospital wards. Park, who served as outpatient
director under his predecessor, describes Howland's regime.

If there ever was a "one man department" it was pediatrics under
Howland at the Harriet Lane Home. He took sole care of the children on
the wards. He also took charge personally of all the private patients. He
used to do certainly two-thirds of the teaching and of course all the administration. . . . There was a sharp division between the clinical staff on the
wards and the laboratory men. Howland did not want his resident staff to
have any duties except the care of the children and always demanded that
at all times they be at his beck and call. . . . The research staff were
allowed to work in the dispensary but were not given ward privileges.
[One laboratory man] . . . had the greatest difficulty in obtaining consent
even to work in the dispensary. . . . I used to think that Howland's
method of organization of the department was not the best for its fullest
fruition. We underlings were never allowed experiences essential for the
developments of ideas and we had no opportunity to carry out the ideas
which we did have. With the exception of a clinic for the treatment of
congenital syphilis, Howland would not allow any special clinics or the
formation of any subdepartments. But the organization had great advantages, particularly for him. His policy kept the department small and
completely under his immediate control. He was able to spend every
afternoon in the laboratory.[12]

When he assumed the chairmanship, Park set out to remedy
what he considered the shortcomings of Howland's administration
and bring pediatrics in line with the medical school's commitment
to clinical research.[13] The subspecialty clinics were among his innovations. He insisted on their creation as a matter of policy despite
opposition from some members of the department who argued that
organizational divisions would weaken the dispensary.[14] Park had
three rationales for establishing subspecialty clinics. First, the
units provided a basis for distributing departmental tasks that gave
young academic staff autonomy and latitude in which to develop
clinical and investigatory skills while providing direction to their
efforts. Subspecialty clinics were an instrument for fostering the
research skills of physicians showing academic promise.[15] Second,
Park thought the units would hasten improvements in managing
serious but poorly understood childhood disorders. They would

help generate new treatment modalities by attracting a much larger number of unusual cases than would ordinarily be encountered in medical practice.

Finally, like others among the scientific leadership of American medicine, Park envisioned the dispensary units as an ideal organizational design for promoting systematic clinical investigation. Under Howland's chairmanship the scientific work conducted at the Harriet Lane Home was almost exclusively laboratory research. Path-breaking studies conducted during his chairmanship were in the areas of nutrition, metabolism, and electrolyte balance. Clinical work at the Harriet Lane Home was integrated with departmental teaching but divorced from research; the distinction Howland maintained between clinical and research staff was indicative of this fact. Park extended the institution's scientific norms to encompass research on the clinical treatment of disease. The result was two pediatric research roles: the basic scientist who conducted wet-bench research and the clinical investigator. For the latter, the laboratory was the clinic itself.

Park initiated the endocrine clinic in 1935, appointing Lawson Wilkins as director. At that time, knowledge of hormonal disorders in children was virtually nonexistent. Wilkins reports that when Park first asked him to head the endocrine clinic, he responded, "Do you wish to make me a charlatan?"[16] But the chairman persisted. Park was astute in perceiving possibilities for clinical investigation and thought endocrine research was on the verge of significant discoveries.[17] In Park's words,

it was plainly evident in 1935 that great advances were about to be made in endocrinology. Scientific knowledge had developed just enough to stimulate speculation and not enough to control it. . . . endocrinologists were making diagnoses of complex endocrine disturbances from little more than conjecture and remarkable results from the administration of various hormone preparations by mouth were being reported.[18]

Park also had several existing research units as models. At the time he initiated the pediatric endocrine clinic at Johns Hopkins, endocrine programs for adult patients were operating at the Mayo Clinic and at Massachusetts General Hospital, affiliated with Harvard Medical School.[19]

As Park predicted, the endocrine outpatient clinic attracted substantial numbers of children with hormonal disorders, providing a pool large enough for systematic research. His expectations of significant advances in clinical treatment were also realized. During the first decade of the clinic's operation, Wilkins focused his scientific work on thyroid disorders, and by 1945 made contributions to the understanding of infantile hypothyroidism and its treatment. He then expanded his investigations to other endocrine disorders. Meanwhile, a group at Harvard's Massachusetts General Hospital was making strides in the clinical study of children's metabolic and endocrine disorders. Both Wilkins and the Boston group successfully treated a variety of pseudohermaphroditism with the adrenocortical hormone, cortisone, during the late 1940s.[20] By midcentury, researchers at Hopkins and Harvard had established the intellectual underpinnings of a new clinical field.[21]

There was an interrelationship between scientific and organizational factors in the inception of pediatric endocrinology. Early research created a conceptual, but not substantive, basis for the new medical field. Institutional leaders responded to the perception of scientific possibilities by introducing organizational arrangements they believed would promote clinical investigation. With the backing of medicine's scientific elite, department chairmen initiated clinical research units and specialized work roles. These organizational innovations in fact spurred the growth of knowledge. Practicing subspecialists working in dedicated research divisions forged new treatment modalities and created the substantive basis for a new arena of clinical practice. This sequence is comparable to one found in the emergence of organ-based specialties during the nineteenth century. At that time, a new model of disease granted heightened importance to localized pathology and legitimized the founding of specialized dispensaries and hospitals. The latter, in turn, facilitated the accumulation of substantive bodies of knowledge.

Emerging Careers and Initial Professional Structures

As scientific advances proceeded, subspecialists were building new careers within academic medicine. During the 1930s, pediatric endocrinology was a part-time investigatory focus for a handful of faculty at elite medical schools. By the 1950s, researchers were pursuing the study of endocrine disorders on a full-time basis at leading pediatric departments. Three interrelated trends supported new career tracks within academic medicine: progressive expansion of medical school faculties, the continued spread of clinical research units, and, following World War II, the availability of research and training grants from the National Institutes of Health (NIH).

The number of full-time pediatric professorships grew substantially during the second quarter of the century. In 1922, only ten medical schools in the country had full-time salaried posts in pediatrics; there were fewer than 40 full-time pediatric instructors—a figure that included resident staff—and more than half of these worked in one of three academic departments.[22] In 1947, forty-six schools had at least one full-time professor of pediatrics and the total number of pediatric faculty stood at 239.[23] At this point, full-time professorships were still concentrated at elite medical schools. By 1959, American medical colleges had 700 full-time pediatric professors.[24]

Meanwhile existing clinical research units were producing a new generation of pediatric subspecialists. Most of the clinics functioned as de facto training programs for young pediatricians in the early stages of academic careers. The clinics offered research opportunities in exciting and rapidly evolving arenas of medical science. After work in an established research unit, many young investigators moved on to other academic departments where they set up their own subspecialty programs. The availability of trained subspecialists and new full-time equivalents encouraged the spread of programs to a growing number of teaching hospitals. By mid-century, the top dozen pediatric departments in the country were staffed by full-time salaried pediatric subspecialists. This was a dramatic change from the 1930s when even elite departments were composed of pediatric generalists and part-time faculty. Subspecialty careers received a further boost in the 1950s when the NIH gave out increasing numbers of research and training grants for subspecialty programs within clinical departments.[25]

What these organizational patterns meant for emerging careers is illustrated by examining Lawson Wilkins' work history and those of second-generation subspecialists. Most striking about Wilkins' career is that he spent most of it as a general pediatric practitioner.

Wilkins completed his medical degree and pediatric residency at Hopkins and in 1922 opened a private practice in the city of Baltimore. He maintained ties with the Hopkins department, publishing several papers with colleagues there during early years of his practice. In the late 1920s, he took a part-time and unsalaried post in the epilepsy clinic, one of the first special divisions established within the pediatric dispensary. It was through this appointment that Edwards Park became aware of Wilkins' research abilities. When Wilkins became head of the newly created endocrine clinic in 1935, he had no special training or expertise in hormonal disorders and minimal knowledge of the biochemistry relevant to endocrine functioning. His appointment was part-time and unsalaried and remained so for the first decade of the clinic's operation. Wilkins earned his living from private practice and he performed many of his clinic duties during evenings and weekends.[26]

Pediatric endocrinologists who launched careers in the 1950s had markedly different work histories. These physicians obtained training in endocrinology early in their careers at one of the established clinical research units. Furthermore, pediatric endocrinology was no longer a part-time or uncompensated activity. Subspecialists moved into academic posts that provided full-time salaries for work in their subfield.

Between the mid-1930s and mid-1950s, similar shifts occurred within other pediatric subspecialties. For the first-generation subspecialists, clinical research was an adjunct to either private practice or more general academic duties. Some of the early subspecialists held academic posts for which they were compensated, but research and teaching in their subfield was combined with other departmental activities. By mid-century, pediatric endocrinology and a number of other fields were well along in becoming distinct, full-time academic career tracks.[27]

As in the emergence of primary medical segments, new work patterns stimulated the formation of collectivities and the construction of occupational institutions. Pediatric subspecialists built initial professional structures during the late 1950s when they moved to create subspecialty sections within general pediatric research associations. At mid-century, the joint meetings of the American Pediatric Society (APS) and the Society for Pediatric Research (SPR) were the principal national forum for academic pediatricians. A group of young scientific investigators founded the SPR in 1929 during the period when the number of salaried professorships began climbing.[28] The SPR established subspecialty sections in 1959, responding to pressure from a growing contingent of subspecialists within its ranks. That year there were seven sections in all, including those in endocrinology, metabolism, hematology, and cardiovascular disease.[29] The American Academy of Pediatrics initiated scientific sections around the same time; by the late 1950s it was holding special sessions in cardiology, pulmonary disease, allergy, and surgery.[30]

Scientific sections were not the only meeting places for groups of pediatric subspecialists. In some fields there were professional or scientific societies that included physicians other than child specialists. Pediatric endocrinologists regularly attended sessions of The Endocrine Society (founded in 1917), an association with both laboratory researchers and clinicians among its members. Pediatric endocrinologists had another forum as well. After Lawson Wilkins' death in 1963, his students established a biannual lecture and symposium at Johns Hopkins in his honor. Its meetings were a precursor to the autonomous professional society founded in the decade which followed.

From Scientific to Market Structures

Pediatric endocrinologists had established initial professional structures by the early 1960s. There were symposia and special sections within pediatric associations where practitioners discussed research and professional issues of mutual interest. The aims and functions of these forums were primarily scientific and affiliative. Subspecialty sections made no effort to standardize training or construct occupational boundaries. They generated little professional ideology. Nor did members launch collective efforts to improve organizational arrangements affecting specialists' work lives. Programmatic activities of this sort were unnecessary in part because subspecialization was highly legitimate within American medical schools. Universities were a protected environment for the emergence of subspecialty career tracks. The status of pediatric departments was greatly enhanced by the presence of highly specialized research faculty and department chairs were eager to add as many full-time slots as possible. Academic norms functioned to maintain the quality of clinical and scientific work without externally generated standards. Through the 1960s, pediatric endocrinology was as much a discipline as an occupational unit and the character of early professional institutions reflected this fact.

During the early 1970s, pediatric endocrinologists built occupational structures of a different sort. They established an autonomous society and created formal market boundaries by initiating a certifying procedure. Senior men began discussing a separate association in the late 1960s and in 1972 they formed the Lawson Wilkins Pediatric Endocrine Society (LWPES). The new association moved quickly to establish a certifying mechanism, submitting a formal application for a pediatric sub-board in 1974. The American Board for Medical Specialties approved a special certificate in 1976 and two years later the endocrinology subcommittee began examining candidates. Pediatric endocrinology was no longer a loosely organized aggregate of research-oriented physicians. With the creation of a qualifying mechanism, it was a fully constituted professional unit.

Several factors encourage an emerging subspecialty to construct market boundaries. In the history of pediatric endocrinology, the introduction of certification by a potentially competing segment was the determinative factor. But leaders were responding also to modest growth in demand for services and accompanying changes in career patterns. Four analytically distinct developments precede a subspecialty's move to establish formal market structures. The initial three were evident in pediatric endocrinology in a rudimentary form.

First, the number of subspecialists begins to climb. There were about 20 pediatric endocrinologists in 1950; between 40 and 75 in 1960. LWPES membership stood at 160 in 1972. By 1975, leaders estimated that there were 270 pediatric endocrinologists.[31] Continued growth of medical school faculties helped fuel expansion in the ranks of pediatric subspecialties. During the 1950s and 1960s, federal research support flowed into American medical colleges and clinical departments used these funds to add faculty appointments.[32] Table 4 illustrates increases in full-time pediatric faculty during the postwar years. The number of pediatric professorships more than doubled every decade: there were 700 in 1959; 1,883

TABLE 4   *Full-Time Faculty Appointments within American Medical Schools, 1923–1979*

Year	Total Appointments	Appointments in All Clinical Departments	Appointments in Pediatric Departments
1947	—	—	239
1951	3,993	2,276	—
1959	10,350	6,504	700
1969	23,014	15,916	1,883
1979	46,598	33,913	4,052

Sources: American Academy of Pediatrics, *Child Health Services and Pediatrics Education* (New York: Commonwealth Fund, 1949), p. 171; Association of American Medical Colleges, "Full Time Medical School Faculty," *Datagrams,* 7, 4 (1966): 1; American Medical Association, Walter S. Wiggins et al., "Medical Education in the United States and Canada," *Journal of the American Medical Association,* 171, 11 (1959): 1528; American Medical Association, "Medical Education in the United States," *Journal of the American Medical Association,* 210, 8 (1969): 1477; American Medical Association, "Medical Education in the United States," *Journal of the American Medical Association,* 243, 9 (1980): 849.

in 1969; and 4,052 in 1979.[33] Subspecialists occupied most of the newly created academic posts.

Second, subspecialists migrate into a broadening range of medical settings. During the 1950s, specialized clinical researchers were concentrated in the pediatric departments of a dozen or so elite medical schools. By the 1960s, many other medical schools added clinical investigators to their staffs. The proliferation of fellowship programs and the graduation of increasing numbers of trainees encouraged the spread of subspecialists to a progressively wider circle of medical facilities. In some fields, diffusion proceeded beyond academic medicine, with subspecialists initiating practices in community hospitals without (or with only loose) university affiliations.[34] This trend has been less pronounced in pediatric endocrinology than in neonatology and some of the subspecialties of internal medicine. Movement into community hospitals is especially likely when clinical research yields treatment modalities applicable to reasonably large populations of patients. As subspecialists disperse, they carry technologies learned at university training centers into new treatment settings.[35]

Third, when experimental treatment methods are accepted as standard medical practice and subspecialists move into community settings, careers in subspecialty practice become increasingly differentiated from those in teaching and research. A group of subspecialists begins functioning as customary patient-care providers. Few of the pediatric subspecialties have generated extensive patient-care markets and most community practitioners spend a good part of their time providing general pediatric services. They draw subspecialty patients largely through colleague referrals. In case of pediatric endocrinology, the majority of conditions treated are sufficiently rare that practice is viable only in the context of a large medical facility. Pediatric cardiology and neonatal medicine are hosptial-centered owing to the severity of the conditions treated and the nature of the technologies used.

Fourth, the leaders of emerging subspecialties are strongly influenced by developments in their occupational environment. As mentioned earlier, the formal consolidation of a potentially competing segment was the crucial event spurring pediatric endocrinologists to create an autonomous association and a certifying body. In the late 1960s a segment of "adult" endocrinologists moved to establish a certifying mechanism within the American Board of Internal Medicine and in 1970 won approval for an endocrine and metabolism examining committee within the ABIM. Child specialists feared that without their own examining procedure, they would lose prestige, and be squeezed out by the ABIM group. Pediatric endocrinologists also were concerned about establishing a favorable fee scale for third-party reimbursements. They encountered no resistance from within the specialty at large. The American Board of Pediatrics favored the creation of an endocrine certificate. In fact, the ABP initiated discussions with pediatric endocrinologists on the subject during the early 1970s. At the time the certifying committee was established, the practice of pediatric endocrinology outside of research institutions was very limited. But leaders felt that the possibilities for increased demand existed and, with the pressure created by a certifying procedure within the ABIM, they moved to protect this potential market.[36]

The consolidation of pediatric cardiology involved the same basic constellation of factors. This segment coalesced somewhat earlier than pediatric endocrinology with leaders initiating a pediatric cardiology sub-board in 1960. The development of pediatric cardiology followed a familiar pattern. Department chairs established pediatric cardiology clinics during the 1930s and clinical researchers forged significant technical advances in subsequent decades. Cardiac catheterization and angiography techniques, developed during the 1940s, greatly facilitated the diagnosis of rheumatic and congenital heart diseases in children. In the mid-1940s, Helen Taussig, head of the pediatric cardiology clinic at Johns Hopkins, designed a procedure to correct a congenital heart condition called tetralogy of Fallot. Alfred Blalock, chairman of the Hopkins surgery department, successfully performed the operation. Open-heart surgery techniques developed during the early 1950s enabled specialists to correct other cardiac abnormalities. The availability of reliable diagnostic techniques combined with several successful ameliorative procedures stimulated widespread interest in pediatric cardiology. A growing number of hospitals undertook the treatment of children with cardiac disorders and a variety of medical and surgical specialists began moving into the field.

This situation was cause for concern among pediatric cardiologists. At Hopkins, a regularized division of labor had been established between pediatric cardiologists and cardiovascular surgeons. The former conducted all diagnostic work-ups and decided which patients were suitable for surgery. While not performing operations, pediatric cardiologists played a major role in patient management. With the spread of cardiac surgery on children, this role was threatened. Alexander Nadas, a pediatric cardiologist at the Harvard-affiliated Children's Hospital in Boston, commented on the proliferation of service units.

Any thoracic surgeon, any pediatrician or internist, and any hospital, could theoretically undertake the management of [children with heart disease]. As a matter of fact the number of "centers" attempting to do this kind of work, amounting to several hundred, according to the rather sketchy information available, already seems higher than is indicated for the best interests of patients. It is not unusual to have five to seven institutions competing for the relatively small patient material in one metropolitan area.[37]

Pediatric subspecialists were especially concerned about encroachment from medical cardiologists who had established a sub-board within the ABIM in 1940. According to Nadas, that group's "knowledge of cardiology, reinforced with the prestige of their Cardiology Sub-board, gave them considerable advantage over their pediatric colleagues in being designated as the experts in heart disease of children."[38] Competition was heightened by the availability of federal funding for patient care and clinical research through the U.S. Crippled Children's Service. What type of cardiology programs would receive Crippled Children's funds was at issue.

Pediatric cardiologists moved to establish a certifying mechanism in response to these market conditions. At the time, the number of trained pediatric cardiologists was still relatively small. By 1955, about forty fellows had trained at the Hopkins pediatric cardiology clinic under Taussig and this group was the core of a new collectivity.[39] Pediatric cardiologists established a section within the American Academy of Pediatrics in 1959 and a sub-board shortly thereafter. This certifying body strengthened their position in the delivery of cardiac services to children. It designated pediatric subspecialists as the preferred providers of cardiac care for children and gave them leverage over competitors in obtaining patient referrals, research funding, and reimbursements from third-party payers.

Pediatric endocrinology and pediatric cardiology began as clinical research foci and evolved into formally constituted professional segments. Not all research fields develop in this manner. Some remain loosely organized arenas of clinical investigation. The present analysis suggests that subspecialists initiate certification in response to new market conditions: the development of treatment modalities applicable to reasonably large populations of patients, growth in demand for services outside university research centers, the movement of subspecialists into community settings, and the creation of market structures by competing segments. Certifying boards function to consolidate segments' claims over expanding or potential patient-care markets.

The transition from scientific to market structures can stir controversy within a segment. Sentiment among pediatric endocrinologists about certification was divided. Some expressed concern that board requirements would take precedence over scientific creativity within fellowship programs and that the quality of these programs would decline as a result. Program directors feared that certification might jeopardize funding from federal agencies mandated to support training for careers in basis research. These leaders considered the creation of an examining body to be a move away from scientific norms toward a stronger emphasis on clinical practice.[40]

Segmentation in Postwar Pediatrics

In at least four ways, the development of pediatric endocrinology parallels the earlier rise of pediatrics. First, changes in labor patterns mediate the consolidation of both professional segments. There are discernible generations of pediatric endocrinologists and a trend toward increasing specialization. Yet again, practitioners with shared work patterns and interests form collectivities and build occupational structures. Second, like specialists, subspecialists are strongly influenced by developments in their occupational environment. Pediatric endocrinologists establish a qualifying mechanism in direct response to the creation of an endocrine certificate by the American Board of Internal Medicine. They act to protect their future market position and forestall encroachment by a neighboring segment. Third, organizational innovation is a key generative factor in the histories of pediatrics and its clinical subspecialties. For pediatric endocrinology, the crucial organizational change occurs within academic departments and university-controlled hospitals. Full-time faculty posts and subspecialty clinics encourage the segment's growth by promoting new career patterns. Fourth, a familiar interaction between scientific and organizational factors occurs in the development of pediatric endocrinology. Investigatory breakthroughs during the early decades of the twentieth century support the perception of new scientific possibilities and provide rationales for introducing dedicated research units and more highly differentiated work roles. Organizational change in turn stimulates the growth of a substantive body of specialized knowledge. This dynamic is comparable to the interplay of intellectual and organizational factors in the emergence of medical specialties during the nineteenth century.

Yet patterns in the rise of pediatric endocrinology are not a simple reproduction of those in the history of pediatrics. Discontinuities occur in the settings where segmentation takes place and in underlying occupational processes. Pediatrics and its clinical subspecialties emerged within very different contexts. The former appeared when there were few professional institutions structuring specialization and only a handful of medical segments. The latter evolved when the specialty system was fully developed and numerous segments were already well established. Hospitals and medical schools were undergoing radical changes during the decades that pediatrics coalesced. By the time pediatric subspecialties appeared, these organizations had assumed their near modern forms. Pediatrics emerged within children's hospitals and dispensaries before these facilities were university affiliated. Pediatric endocrinology grew up within academic departments and university-controlled hospitals.

Practice patterns among the early members of these segments are also dissimilar. The initial generations of pediatricians held institutional posts but office-based medical practice was always central. Early pediatric endocrinologists were forging full-time academic careers.[41] Other discontinuities in practice patterns arise from differences in demand for specialized care and from the nature of service markets. The conditions that pediatric endocrinologists treat are fairly rare. Even when demand for these subspecialists expands beyond university-based research clinics, markets are limited. General pediatricians draw upon widespread public demand for child-health services and they obtain many of their clients from lay referrals. Pediatric endocrinologists and pediatric cardiologists rely almost exclusively on colleague referrals and they must situate themselves at large medical centers to attract even modest numbers of clients needing subspecialized care.

Several differences in occupational dynamics are noteworthy as well. Pediatric subspecialties matured more quickly than had general pediatrics. In the history of the latter segment, eight decades elapsed between the creation of the first children's hospitals and the incorporation of a certifying board. Pediatric endocrinologists introduced certification four decades after the initial subspecialty clinic was established. Increments in the division of labor proceeded very rapidly during the evolution of pediatric endocrinology. Lawson Wilkins began his work as a partial subspecialist during the mid-1930s. A decade later he moved into a salaried professorship that enabled him to function as a near full-time subspecialist. In the development of pediatrics, changes in work patterns took place more slowly and successive generations of specialists are more highly distinct. Finally, pediatric endocrinologists and pediatric cardiologists established market structures in the absence of widespread demand for their professional services. They did so in response to competitive pressures generated by contemporary medical segments.

Chapter Seven

Resurgence of the Generalist: Psychosocial Pediatrics

While pediatric subspecialists were building occupational structures, another major development was unfolding. During the late 1950s, a group of academically based specialists began pushing for renewed emphasis on psychosocial issues in pediatric teaching, research, and practice. Its leaders referred to this movement by a number of terms: "the new pediatrics," ambulatory pediatrics, and psychosocial or behavioral pediatrics. They claimed that pediatric residency programs provided inadequate training in the behavioral and developmental problems encountered in office-based practice. The group argued that social and psychological phenomena were appropriate subjects for pediatric research and initiated investigatory efforts in these areas.

The term *new pediatrics* is a misleading label. The psychosocial movement is, in fact, consistent with the specialty's long-standing missions. Abraham Jacobi portrayed pediatrics as vitally concerned with the mental hygiene of children in papers delivered during the 1880s. In the 1920s and 1930s, leaders institutionalized office-based pediatrics and placed at its center the care of well babies and supervision of normal child development. The pediatric ethos of this period stressed the practitioner's advice-giving role and its importance for the prevention of behavioral problems in youngsters. Benjamin Spock's *Baby and Child Care*, published in 1946, exemplified this advice-giving stance for a later generation of parents. Spock popularized psychoanalytically informed child-rearing practices while embodying the concerned, supportive, counsel-imparting pediatrician.[1] Meanwhile, articles on growth and development appeared in specialty journals during the second quarter of the century and some pediatric faculty made psychosocial issues their principal focus.[2] All of this predated the psychosocial movement of the late 1950s.

But in certain respects, mid-century behavioral pediatrics was new. For the first time there were discrete segments within the specialty committed to advancing the study and treatment of psychosocial problems. The earliest of these groups coalesced in the mid-1950s and created the Ambulatory Pediatric Association (APA) in 1960. The organization's founders were directors of university-based outpatient clinics who shared work patterns and common problems within academic medicine. Over time, interest in general ambulatory care gave way to more highly focused problem areas. By the 1970s, there were full-time academics in the fields of adolescent medicine, developmental disabilities, and behavioral pediatrics. These specialists concentrated their research and teaching on psychosocial issues including a host of recently identified behavioral disorders. "The new pediatrics" has involved three new phenomena: discrete academic career tracks, dedicated professional segments, and a shift in emphasis from preventive care of well children to the treatment of behavioral syndromes and developmental pathologies.

Several conditions helped to foster psychosocial pediatrics. Medicine as a whole was placing greater emphasis on social phenomena during the postwar years. This trend took many forms including exploration of the organizational and interpersonal dimensions of medical delivery, concern with primary care and the "whole patient," and examination of social and psychological variables in the etiology of physical disease.[3] A growing disparity between pediatric education and practice undoubtedly contributed as well. This disparity was inevitable granted the organizational form pediatrics had assumed and its nature as a division of clinical medicine. Nineteenth-century child specialists recognized that pediatrics implied a much broader range of concerns than organ-based specialties; they conceived of office-based pediatrics as general practice on a particular age group. When specialists made well-child care a mainstay of community pediatrics during the 1920s, they reinforced the breadth of office-based practice. Meanwhile, pediatric leaders continued to build occupational structures comparable to those established by organ-based segments. This included hospital-based residency programs constituted during the 1930s and 1940s. By mid-century, rotations through inpatient units and subspecialty clinics dominated pediatric training. Residencies prepared specialists to treat serious diseases. Yet office-based pediatrics remained a combination of general practice on children and well-baby care. Concerned about the discontinuity between education and practice, academic leaders facilitated the growth of ambulatory and psychosocial pediatrics in an effort to bridge the gap.

I argue that the immediate catalyst for psychosocial pediatrics was the appearance of new career tracks within academic medicine. During the 1950s, pediatric department chairs began allocating regular faculty slots to the directors of university-affiliated outpatient clinics. The directors of these clinics formed a new collectivity, established the APA, and mobilized to restore the prestige that ambulatory care had lost with the eclipse of the child-health movement during the 1930s, and the rise of scientifically-grounded pediatric subspecialties during the 1940s and 1950s. Training grants in behavioral medicine, available in growing numbers during the 1950s and 1960s, supported the emergence of more highly differentiated academic tracks and the consolidation of new psychosocial specialties. These segments have emulated established subspecialties. Leaders promote research, establish professional associations and, in some cases, advocate certification for psychosocial specialists.

Trends in Community Practice as Generative Factors

My explanation for the rise of "the new pediatrics" differs from another account in the sociological literature. Dorothy Pawluch locates the origins of the psychosocial movement in the composition of community practice and threats to the market for office-based pediatrics. She argues that declines in child mortality and in some morbidities during the first half of the twentieth century undercut demand for "curative pediatrics" and, as a result, "prevention gradually displaced treatment as the pediatrician's primary task."[4] The author claims that community pediatricians also faced increasing competition from family practitioners who moved to constitute a formal specialty after World War II. These trends, she writes, "threatened to destroy the largest segment of the specialty," office-based pediatricians.[5] Pawluch continues:

Worried about their declining status and possible disappearance as primary care specialists, pediatricians sought a new mission in ministering to the psycho-social and behavioral needs of children. . . . After 1950, they increasingly defined their specialty not in traditional terms of childhood illness, its treatment, and prevention, but in broader terms of the active promotion of child health in all its aspects.[6]

That changes in community practice helped to generate the psychosocial movement is a reasonable hypothesis and Pawluch's explanation appears highly plausible. But there are at least three serious flaws in her argument. First, while inferences about content of pediatric practice made from mortality and morbidity rates are intuitively satisfying, they involve several logical fallacies. For one, they rest on the unwarranted assumption that death and disease rates are positively correlated with rates of clinical intervention. For another, they assume that declines in the incidence of certain infectious diseases imply declines in overall treated morbidity. In fact, as rates of some disorders fall, other diseases become more prevalent or are brought under more systematic medical treatment.[7] Furthermore, rates of treated morbidity among children could decline without altering the mix of curative and preventive care delivered by pediatricians because, until very recently, it was general practitioners who provided the bulk of medical services for children. Pediatricians took over a progressively larger share of the medical treatment of children during this century as the proportion of physicians in general practice fell and the number of child specialists climbed. But when the psychosocial movement emerged in the 1950s, child specialists were still providing only a fraction of these services. A survey conducted in New York City in 1962 indicates that pediatricians handled only 25 percent of the medical care given children under six years of age; the remaining 75 percent was provided by general practitioners (61 percent) and other specialists (14 percent).[8] The proportion of services delivered by pediatricians in earlier decades was even lower.[9] Equally important, pediatricians have always seen higher ratios of well to sick children than either general practitioners or other specialists treating children.[10] With GPs providing more care of sick youngsters than pediatricians, treated morbidity among children could very easily have fallen without eroding pediatricians' curative activities.

Second, data on the content of pediatric practice fail to support Pawluch's contention that there was a shift from curative to preventive care during the second and third quarters of the century. Child specialists have conducted numerous surveys of pediatric practice and Pawluch cites some of the studies in support of her argument.[11] Use of these surveys to assess trends over time is problematic because diagnostic categories have changed over the years and researchers use different units to measure the content of care. Some report the distribution of patient diagnoses or physician interventions while others give estimates of the overall allocation of time. Putting aside issues of comparability, this body of research does not corroborate Pawluch's depiction of a shift from curative to preventive care. Three studies conducted during the late 1920s through the 1930s suggest that preventive services constituted about 40 percent of contemporary specialists' professional activities.[12] One group of researchers estimates that, in the twenty years between 1934 and 1953, health supervision remained a stable portion (about 40 percent) of pediatricians' work load.[13] Six studies of pediatric practice conducted between 1948 and 1975 reveal no consistent temporal patterns; well-child care ranged from an average of 30 to 54 percent of pediatricians' work activities with a great deal of variation among contemporary practitioners.[14] Health supervision has been a mainstay of primary-care pediatrics since this variety of practice was institutionalized during the first quarter of the twentieth century. Like most present-day commentators, Pawluch is unaware of the original basis of office-based pediatrics and underestimated the centrality of well-child care before World War II.

Third, the timing of events precludes the possibility that competition from family practice was a factor in the genesis of behavioral pediatrics. The psychosocial movement arose during the late 1950s. The newly consolidated specialty of family practice began producing trained graduates in the decade of 1970.[15] In fact, during the third quarter of the century, pediatricians were benefiting from declining competition. Tables 5 and 6 show that the combined numbers of general and family practitioners fell steadily from the 1960s through

TABLE 5   *Numbers of Family Practitioners, General Practitioners, and Pediatricians, 1965–1985*

Medical Field	1965	1970	1975	1980	1985
Family Practice	—	—	12,183	27,530	40,021
General Practice	—	—	42,374	32,519	27,030
Combined Family & General Practice	71,366	57,948	54,557	60,049	67,051
Pediatrics	15,665	17,941	21,746	28,342	35,617

Source: American Medical Association, Department of Data Release Services, Division of Survey and Data Resources, *Physician Characteristics and Distribution in the U.S.*, 1986 ed. (Chicago: American Medical Association, 1986), p. 19, table A-2.

Note: The AMA classified general and family practice together (under general practice) for 1976 and prior to 1975. Field-of-practice designations are based on physician self-report and many of those identifying themselves as family practitioners have not completed family practice residencies. These figures are for active, federal and nonfederal physicians.

the mid-1970s.[16] Even with rapid growth in the numbers of practicing pediatricians, the ratio of primary-care providers per child decreased through the late 1960s.[17]

During the mid-1970s, pediatricians did encounter increased competition. The combined number of general and family practitioners began to climb. Probably more important is a trend not mentioned by Pawluch: a drop in the birth rate that resulted in small cohorts of young children.[18] Such unfavorable market conditions may encourage the diffusion of new forms of psychosocial care from academic settings where they originated into community practice. Later in the chapter, I discuss evidence bearing on whether such diffusion is taking place and identify forces that would promote or impede its progress. But whatever the impact of market forces after 1970, pediatricians experienced no attenuation of demand when the psychosocial movement arose in the 1950s. As late as 1968, pediatric leaders declared that there were "staggering deficits" in the number of primary-care physicians serving children.[19]

But Pawluch is right that mid-century leaders were concerned about the prestige of office-based pediatrics. Articles in professional journals suggested that many young specialists were dissatisfied with community practice. These practitioners were having no problem keeping their offices crowded. Their grievances had to do with the rewards and perceived worth of general pediatric care.

TABLE 6   *Numbers of Family Practitioners, General Practitioners,*
and Pediatricians, 1970–1980

Medical Field	1970	1972	1974	1976	1978	1980
Family Practice	—	—	—	—	21,611	27,530
General Practice	—	—	—	—	34,586	32,519
Combined Family & General Practice	57,948	55,348	53,997	55,479	56,197	60,049
Pediatrics	17,941	19,610	20,682	22,481	24,545	28,342

Source: American Medical Association, Department of Data Release Services, Division of Survey and Data Resources.

Note: The AMA classified general and family practice together (under general practice) for 1976 and prior to 1975. Field-of-practice designations are based on physician self-report and many of those identifying themselves as family practitioners have not completed family practice residencies. These figures are for active, federal and nonfederal physicians.

Authors reported complaints of boredom, drudgery, and low professional status; primary-care pediatrics was physically and emotionally exhausting yet intellectually unstimulating.[20] Routinization of community practice may have contributed to these perceptions. While there is no evidence that pediatricians were seeing higher ratios of well to sick children, it may be that, of the sick children they treated, a higher proportion had non-life-threatening, self-limiting, and chronic diseases. Changes in the context of practice undoubtedly contributed also. With the demise of the child-welfare movement in the 1930s, health supervision was a less prestigious activity. Perhaps most consequential, pediatric residency training was increasingly dominated by inpatient rotations and highly specialized care. Well-baby clinics, a focal point for pediatric education during the 1930s, had been supplanted by hospital wards and subspecialty clinics. It is not surprising that a portion of young specialists would find general pediatric practice unsatisfying. It was a disappointing aftermath to residency training filled with serious illness and heroic interventions.

Trends in primary-care pediatrics may have fostered the psychosocial movement in two different ways: by exacerbating the discontinuity between education and practice during the 1950s and by encouraging the diffusion into community settings of new approaches to behavioral care beginning in the 1970s. But contrary to

Pawluch's claim, the psychosocial movement originated among academic specialists, not community practitioners. A segment of pediatric faculty spearheaded "the new pediatrics" and they mobilized in response to new career patterns within academic medicine.

The Academic Origins of Psychosocial Pediatrics

By the mid-1950s, there was a small but growing number of pediatric faculty whose principal task was directing outpatient clinics in university-affiliated hospitals. Many of the OPD directors of this period held part-time academic appointments which they combined with other institutional posts or private practice. At some institutions, the director of outpatient services was a full-time professor who carried other major academic duties. But with increasing frequency, department chairs were creating separate salaried positions for outpatient directors and a growing portion of these were full-time appointments. The proliferation of full-time faculty slots, instrumental in the rise of scientific subspecialties, was crucial also in the emergence of psychosocial pediatrics. Pediatric chairs had increasing numbers of compensated positions at their disposal and were replacing voluntary academic staff with salaried faculty. Subspecialists filled most of the new slots and, by the 1950s, they populated the faculties of leading departments. But subspecialization itself encouraged the creation of salaried positions for academic generalists. As clinical research units grew, subspecialists spent less time on general pediatrics. Department chairs came to view the supervision of general ambulatory care as a discrete set of tasks and a distinct role within academic pediatrics.[21]

OPD directors had several major responsibilities. They administered outpatient services, treated clinic patients, and supervised the training of students and house staff in outpatient settings. In their teaching, service, and administrative activities, clinic directors confronted the types of problems encountered in community-based pediatric practice. The substance of their work contrasted sharply with that of research-oriented subspecialists who were highly focused in their clinical and research activities and who, for the most part, treated severely ill children. The OPD director was a dedicated generalist among pediatric subspecialists.

The spread of salaried professorships for pediatric clinic directors generated a distinct career track for academic generalists. In a
sequence often repeated in the history of the specialty, new work
patterns precipitated group formation and the move toward formal
organization. A number of clinic directors began meeting informally during the early 1950s while attending the major annual
forum for academic pediatricians, the joint meetings of the American Pediatric Society (APS) and the Society for Pediatric Research
(SPR). In 1960 this group founded the Association for Ambulatory
Pediatric Services, renamed the Ambulatory Pediatric Association
(APA) in the mid-1960s. The organization claimed fifty-six charter
members. From its early years, the APA scheduled its meetings
concurrently with those of the APS and SPR.[22]

Like members of other medical segments, academic generalists
sought to advance their common occupational interests. OPD directors found that general pediatrics accrued relatively little prestige
within pediatric departments of the 1950s. Academic norms re-
warded biological research and technically sophisticated clinical
interventions. Pediatrics was endeavoring to raise its standing
within medical schools by promoting the scientifically grounded
subspecialties. Many academic pediatricians viewed general ambulatory care as necessary to departmental teaching functions but
peripheral to the norms of scientific medicine. Abraham Bergman,
a charter member of the APA, alludes with some irony to the
strains experienced by contemporary generalists.

I entered pediatrics [in the late 1950s] when the subspecialties were
bursting forth into full bloom. The diagnostic and therapeutic tools used
by the cardiologists, hematologists, endocrinologists and others have pro-
foundly improved the care of sick children. Where the unique talent of all
pediatricians used to be applied to the care of the newborn, now few of us
"generalists" dare enter the sanctum of flashing lights, clicking machines,
and hissing vapors.[23]

Leaders of the ambulatory pediatrics movement set out to raise the
standing of general pediatrics within academic medicine. They did
so by formulating an ideology that justified greater attention to
psychosocial issues in pediatric teaching and research. Spokesmen
argued that more time should be devoted to ambulatory care in
pediatric training and that more resources should be allocated for

this purpose. They promoted the study of behavioral issues and sought to establish psychosocial pediatrics as a legitimate arena of clinical investigation. Academic generalists directed this ideology both toward their new collectivity and toward the leadership of academic pediatrics.

Arguing for the importance of ambulatory care without criticizing the prestigious scientific subspecialties was a delicate ideological task. Direct challenges to the prevailing normative system within academic medicine would not have advanced the generalists' cause. Instead, movement leaders pointed to the real and widening gap between pediatric education and professional practice. J. Philip Ambuel, outpatient director at the Ohio State University Children's Hospital and a founding member of the APA, wrote of this tension in 1957.

The traditional, inpatient-oriented, laboratory-dominated training program for pediatric residents is no more designed to prepare the physician for pediatric practice than a life of ease would prepare a man for duty in the front line trenches. Recently, a new graduate of an excellent training center returned to complain to his professor that while he had been trained to race at the Hialeah race track, he was now out pulling the chuck wagon like any other old dray horse.[24]

Several APA members noted that the problem arose at least in part from a growing emphasis in pediatric training on inpatient care and subspecialty rotations. Ambuel comments:

The tendency in pediatric residencies is to concentrate more and more of the resident's time on study of the complex and rare problems of pediatrics. Thus he is spending much of his time acquiring knowledge and skills which he will, in the private practice of pediatrics, rarely be called upon to use.[25]

But more frequently, movement leaders attributed tensions between training and practice to shifts in the content of community pediatrics. Modern medicine had so effectively eradicated major childhood disease that behavioral problems now dominated office-based practice. This formulation had the advantage of applauding scientific medicine while at the same time asserting a pressing need for more attention to psychosocial issues. It was the specialty's responsibility to find solutions to the "new morbidities" just as it had to infectious disease.[26]

To meet its social responsibilities and correct the imbalance between education and practice, academic pediatrics should address
itself to the type of problems encountered in community practice.
This would require more teaching and research on social behavior
and child development and more numerous and better-trained faculty in these areas. Julius Richmond, charter member of the APA
and one of the senior spokesmen of the psychosocial movement,
formulated a program of action.

What we need now is a strategy for incorporating teaching and research in
child development into the mainstream of pediatrics. The strategy requires the development of a core of pediatric faculty members with a
disciplined background of research and teaching analogous to our academic pediatricians in metabolism, infectious disease, etc. This will neces-
sitate the establishment of fellowships for pediatricians in child development. . . . This will mean, in addition to the few such fellowships now
available in departments of pediatrics, periods of study by pediatricians in
the social sciences—sociology, cultural anthropology, psychology, economics, and urban planning, among many others.[27]

Ambulatory pediatricians set out to establish research and treatment foci in psychosocial pediatrics analogous to those in the scientific subspecialties. The APA constituted itself as a scientific association and members delivered papers on issues related to child-health
supervision. There were papers on developmental and behavioral
problems in children and on parental behavior and attitudes. But
during the early and mid-1960s, much of the research focused on the
organization of outpatient services. Authors addressed such topics as
appointment systems, record keeping, and the use of clinics and
wards in residency training. Meanwhile, spokesmen argued for the
legitimacy of such research within academic medicine. Richmond
decried prevailing attitudes within pediatric departments.

Whenever one raises the question of educating students for the management of problems in growth and development . . . one is subject to the
accusation that there will be a dilution in the quality of scientific training.[28]

And again:

The most subtle resistance to research and training in child development
has been the inference by many pediatric investigators that those who
deal with biological research have "hard data" while those interested in

the social sciences have "soft data." I would be tempted to dismiss this as rubbish were it not for the considerable credence accorded this view by otherwise critical people. . . . such positions have nothing in common with good science. . . . The question . . . is one of excellence—not of hardness or softness.[29]

At issue was not only the allocation of time and resources within departments, but the specialty's definition of its knowledge base. In pursuing "the new pediatrics" as a research arena, pediatrics was extending its intellectual foundations into the social and behavioral sciences. This was explicit in the statements of movement leaders. Richmond expounds:

Just as in previous years we faced the complex problems of preventing infectious diseases, nutritional disorders, and metabolic problems, today we are challenged to find analogous approaches to prevention and management with such complicated problems as child abuse and neglect, failure to thrive, learning problems, as well as developmental disabilities. Our research members are those of the epidemiologist, biostatistician, and the social scientist.[30]

Support from Above

How the academic leadership of the specialty responded to such arguments was critical to the new segment's continued development. In the early 1960s, there was controversy and debate about the psychosocial movement among pediatric leaders. Samuel Levine, department chairman at Cornell Medical School, articulated one position in his presidential address to the American Pediatric Society in 1960. Levine acknowledged the disparity between education and practice and invoked what was, by then, an often-repeated tale of the recently minted pediatrician, stimulated by training but bored in community practice. Levine's informant had a litany of complaints about office-based practice including

long hours of routine work; continuous harassment by parents, including night telephone calls and daylight nagging, and, most important of all, a lack of intellectual excitement, challenge and gratification. "I seldom saw a really interesting medical problem . . . and when I did, I never had the time to work it up properly. Anxious mothers and running noses are not what I was trained for."[31]

If the problem was allowed to continue, pediatrics would lose status and fail to attract talented recruits. Levine's solution was consistent with the proposals of ambulatory pediatricians: more emphasis in residency training on well-child care and normal development, and longer rotations through outpatient units. He concurred that psychosocial problems were appropriate subjects for research by pediatric faculty. Levine reasoned:

Why should a case of primary aldosteronism [a metabolic abnormality caused by an excess of adrenal secretions] be considered to be more exciting, challenging, and complex than a major reading problem or an incipient case of juvenile delinquency? Actually, I suspect the latter could be equally challenging if we were willing to admit our present ineptitude in the realm of social, cultural, and personality factors and if we tried to fill the gaps in knowledge in the behavioral sciences with the same vigor used to attack the biologic problems of organic disease.[32]

But there were other opinions as well. Charles May, editor of *Pediatrics,* warned that behavioral pediatrics brought the specialty into competition with academic disciplines and with other professions serving children. It threatened to distend the pediatrician's role and weaken the specialty's position within medicine. May objected:

There are many who can make contributions to the care of the whole child—ranging from preachers to judges, not to say economists. The unique role of most pediatricians for the foreseeable future will be as physicians rather than as psychologists or general counselors. Pediatricians become engaged in open competition with others in the social and behavioral sciences when they go beyond the legal sanction granted by the license to prescribe medical treatment. To remain a medical specialist the practicing pediatrician will be wise to make certain he continues to excel in provision of traditional medical care. . . . The cultivation of the mental health and social welfare of children will not be left entirely to pediatricians, and they should not delude themselves by supposing they can become a priestly class of counselors on all things. Let those who would choose to be primarily counselors set themselves apart or enter the ranks of other professions than medicine. Unless limits are set, the primary task of physical care will be diluted and dislocated beyond recognition and the pediatrician may no longer be considered a physician.[33]

May's solution was the turn-of-the-century conception of pediatrics as a consulting specialty. He advocated transferring child-health supervision to general practitioners, reducing the number of pediatric residencies, and transforming pediatrics into a small cadre of specialists concerned with serious physical illnesses.

The alternative is to slowly drift into a more pedestrian form of pediatric practice which will earn correspondingly lessened respect and fail to attract men of exceptional ability.[34]

But May's vision was unfeasible within modern American medicine. General practitioners were a dying breed and specialists were functioning as frontline providers. Pediatrics had established itself as a primary-care specialty in the 1930s and there was no turning back in the 1960s.

Academic pediatrics accommodated to the psychosocial movement. The status system within pediatric departments did not radically change. Biologically oriented research remained the major source of pediatrics' standing within academic medicine. But department chairs added more full-time faculty positions for general pediatricians. They acceded to demands for more emphasis on ambulatory care within residency training. With the help of external funding, many departments established post-residency fellowship programs in psychosocial pediatrics.

Support from public agencies and private foundations underwrote the growth of psychosocial pediatrics. The federal Division of Maternal and Child Health provided grants to pediatric departments for education and research in behavioral medicine beginning in the 1950s. The Division funded pediatric departments for training in child development, adolescent medicine, and mental retardation during the late 1950s and 1960s. Support for these fields continued during the 1970s and the agency added training grants in behavioral pediatrics during the mid-1980s.[35] Private foundations contributed as well. The Commonwealth Fund awarded stipends for post-residency training in pediatric psychiatry as early as the late 1930s. Recipients of these grants were pioneers in the field of behavioral pediatrics.[36] The William T. Grant Foundation funded training in adolescent medicine, psychological pediatrics, and child development during the mid-1950s. In the 1970s and early 1980s, it provided eleven medical schools with resources to improve the behavioral and developmental components of pediatric residency programs. The Robert Wood Johnson Foundation awarded grants to six pediatric departments during the 1970s for research-oriented fellowship training in general pediatrics. It supported training in adolescent medicine during the same decade. During the early 1980s, the foundation initiated a service program for high-risk youth which included a training component in adolescent medicine. The Johnson Foundation provided stipends to many academically bound pediatric generalists through their Clinical Scholars Program, begun in 1972, to support post-residency training in non-biological disciplines.[37] In addition to training grants, federal agencies and private foundations supported both research and service projects for the psychosocial care of children. Meanwhile pediatric departments received funds for behavioral medicine from state agencies and private donations.

The Pediatric Generalist as Subspecialist

Spurred by training grants and further increments in faculty positions, psychosocial pediatrics continued to evolve in the 1970s and 1980s. Interest in general outpatient care gave way to more highly differentiated arenas for patient care and clinical investigation. Beginning in the late 1960s, groups of academic generalists coalesced around discrete foci within ambulatory pediatrics and established a new generation of professional associations. These included the Society for Adolescent Medicine (SAM) founded in 1968, the Society for Developmental Pediatrics (SDP) established in 1978, and the Society for Behavioral Pediatrics (SBP) created in 1982. The three associations function like other specialty societies, promoting research and advancing the segments' professional status. Prior to the consolidation of each society, there were dedicated fellowship programs in the field and a cadre of self-identified psychosocial specialists. The great majority of the organizations' founders were pursuing careers within academic medicine.

Adolescent-health care emerged quite early as a focus for clinical research and post-residency training. In 1969, sixteen institutions offered fellowship programs in this field. The number grew to twenty-eight in 1974, forty in 1978, and fifty-one in 1984.[38] In addition to grant support, population trends and the spread of age-graded service units stimulated the growth of adolescent medicine. As the baby-boom generation reached its teens in the decade of

1960, an increasing portion of American hospitals created separate clinics and inpatient wards for adolescent patients. By the mid-1970s, almost half of all pediatric departments in the country had an inpatient ward for adolescents at an affiliated hospital and more than half had adolescent clinics.[39] The number of pediatricians with a special interest in adolescent medicine rose substantially during the 1970s. The Society for Adolescent Medicine had 260 charter members in the late 1960s. By 1985 its membership stood at 850.[40]

Behavioral pediatrics and developmental pediatrics also grew up around dedicated training programs. Directors of psychosocially oriented residency training funded by the William T. Grant Foundation established the Society for Behavioral Pediatrics. This organization had over 100 members in 1983—a year after its formation—and 300 in 1986.[41] Federal sponsorship stimulated the emergence of developmental pediatrics. Legislation enacted during the 1960s and 1970s mandated the creation of University Affiliated Facilities (UAFs) for educating health professionals in the treatment of children with developmental disabilities.[42] In 1973, nineteen pediatric departments offered training in the care of handicapped children.[43] Directors of several UAFs founded the Society for Developmental Pediatrics. While the association is relatively small—the SDP had about 120 members in 1986—leaders have been quite aggressive in their efforts to advance the field.[44]

By the late 1970s, advocates of "the new pediatrics" had mobilized a good deal of support from within the specialty at large. The movement received a substantial boost in 1978 when a specialty-wide Task Force for Pediatric Education strongly endorsed the continued strengthening of research and training in—what the Task Force report called—"biosocial" issues.[45] Meanwhile, the American Academy of Pediatrics intensified efforts to promote behaviorally oriented care in community settings. It created a Committee on the Psychosocial Aspects of Child and Family Health in 1980, published new manuals for office-based physicians, and worked to improve reimbursements for behavioral services.[46]

The evolution of psychosocial segments is far from complete and new developments will undoubtedly occur in the closing years of the century. Thus far, their emergence has followed patterns comparable to those in the rise of scientifically grounded pediatric subspecialties. Training grants and dedicated faculty positions support new career tracks within academic medicine. Fellow-ship programs (and in some cases, residencies) produce trained psychosocial specialists who carry new skills and new conceptions of core professional tasks into a widening range of treatment set-tings. Leaders have modeled the segments after established sub-specialties, promoting research and establishing journals and pro-fessional associations.

Three questions about the eventual shape of the new segments are especially intriguing. First, will changes in professional ideol-ogy and training spearheaded by the psychosocial movement result in a widespread reorientation within community practice? Will primary-care practitioners expand their role in the treatment of behavioral problems? Second, will there be relatively small num-bers of specially trained psychosocial subspecialists in community practice as there are in some subspecialties of internal medicine and pediatrics? Third, will the behaviorally oriented pediatricians create certification procedures analogous to those in the scientifi-cally based subspecialties?

On the first of these issues, recent studies suggest that pediatric residents are now receiving more systematic education on psychoso-cial care than their counterparts in the 1950s and 1960s. A survey of pediatric residency programs conducted in 1982 indicates that 49 percent have a formal behavioral component and that an additional 38 percent offered some training in the field.[47] There is a growing literature evaluating the impact of psychosocial training on pediatric residents.[48] But research examining the effect of such training on community practice has yet to be conducted. Regarding the second question, available data suggest that pediatricians with advanced training in psychosocial care are now moving into community prac-tice in modest numbers. Among a random sample of American Acad-emy of Pediatrics members drawn in 1985, 10 percent had com-pleted post-residency training in an area of ambulatory pediatrics and less than half of this group held academic appointments.[49] Stud-ies of the graduates of particular fellowship programs provide further evidence of migration into community settings. A survey of adoles-cent medicine fellows who completed their training during the early 1980s indicates that 29 percent entered private practice and that 35 percent were combining practice with academic work.[50] Whether these fellowship graduates build practices different from those of conventionally trained pediatricians or those trained in behaviorally oriented residencies is another matter.

The existence of residency and fellowship programs in psychosocial pediatrics encourages new approaches to behavioral problems in office-based practice. In recent years, specialists have published numerous articles on how to practice psychosocial pediatrics in community settings.[51] But little data exist on the extent to which pediatricians actually treat behavioral disorders in their private offices. Despite claims that "the new morbidities" have become more prevalent, it is unclear how widespread is the demand for this variety of pediatric care.

Specialists face at least three constraints in their efforts to expand the psychosocial components of community practice. First, the treatment of behavioral problems is very time consuming and, at present, poorly compensated when compared to other types of pediatric services.[52] Second, epidemiological studies show that rates of behavioral disorders are highest among children from low-income families.[53] Parents of these youngsters cannot afford out-of-pocket medical expenses, and reimbursements available for psychosocial services from Medicaid and private insurers are modest. Third, the movement into psychosocial care brings pediatricians into competition with a great many other professionals claiming expertise in the behavioral and developmental disorders of children: child psychiatrists, pediatric psychologists, special educators and practitioners within social work, speech pathology, and audiology. If pediatricians are to expand their role in treating behavioral problems of children, they will have to effect changes in the division of labor between their specialty and related child-serving professions.

The issue of certification is also far from resolved. Some members of the new segments would like to initiate qualifying procedures for psychosocial specialists. Leaders of the SDP have tried to generate support for certification in developmental pediatrics. Sentiment favoring a qualifying exam in adolescent medicine is growing within SAM. Advocates view certification as a means to define their field's knowledge base formally and enhance its overall status. But within pediatrics at large, the idea of certified psychosocial subspecialists has little legitimacy. Many, including the chairs of academic departments, consider behavioral issues to be a "natural part" of all pediatrics.[54] Leadership of the older Ambulatory Pediatric Association—

whose membership grew to over 1200 in the 1980s—object to the fragmentation implied by psychosocial subspecialties and would advance instead a unified field of general pediatrics. Spokesmen for two of the psychosocial segments disagree about the foci and boundaries of the specialties. One group objects to limiting developmental pediatrics to the problems of handicapped children and argues that behavioral and developmental pediatrics should be combined.[55] Despite these obstacles, if large numbers of psychosocial specialists establish behaviorally oriented practices in community settings, pressures for certification will be difficult to resist.

From Health Supervision to Behavioral Problems

The psychosocial movement has generated applied research as well as revisions to the specialty's professional ethos. Both outcomes encourage community practitioners to extend their regulatory functions in new areas of social life. In recent ideological formulations, the specialty's long-standing focus on preventive care has given way to heightened concern over disorders of child and family behavior and pathologies of child development. Clinical research conducted by pediatricians and an array of other child-serving professionals has identified new behavioral syndromes and new treatment modalities. There are growing literatures on managing behavioral and developmental problems like tantrums, enuresis, encopresis (unreliable bowel control), and habit disorders.[56] Studies on the prevalence of "new morbidities" document high rates of school problems, learning disorders, speech difficulties, and adolescent adjustment problems among America's youngsters.[57] Major pediatric associations endorse a redefinition of the specialty's knowledge base and advocate the delivery of behaviorally oriented care in community settings.

These trends in research and professional ideology, however, do not constitute expanded terrain in the arena of medical practice. I have emphasized that the role of the community practitioner in psychosocial care remains largely unexplored. At present, treatment of developmental, behavioral, and family problems takes place largely within institutional settings: schools, welfare agencies, hospitals, and clinics. Much of this care is provided by professionals other than pediatricians. There are a great many unanswered questions about the management of behavioral problems by community pediatricians. Are some of these primary-care providers screening children and parents for psychosocial disorders more carefully than in the past? Are they diagnosing more cases of behavioral disorders? Do they undertake the treatment of these problems? Are they referring larger numbers of patients to community agencies or private professionals for behaviorally oriented care? Reliable data on these issues are unavailable. But it is clear that redefinition of the specialty's knowledge base combined with advocacy for psychosocial care encourages the diffusion of medical approaches to psychosocial problems into new treatment settings.[58] Child abuse and hyperactivity have been brought under systematic professional management since the 1960s.[59] It is likely that the treatment of other behavioral disorders of children and families will be regularized in coming decades.

Expansion of the practitioner's regulatory functions is not new to the history of pediatrics. During the 1920s and 1930s, the specialty institutionalized well-baby care and broadened its professional terrain to include supervising normal child development. But the forces promoting today's psychosocial movement differ from those operating during the initial decades of the century. In the earlier period, a highly legitimate reform movement outside medicine fostered the spread of preventive services for children. There is no comparable social movement promoting "the new pediatrics." Processes internal to the specialty and support from private foundations and state agencies have spurred the emergence of psychosocial pediatrics. The availability of public and philanthropic funds is likely to be crucial in determining patterns in the diffusion of behaviorally oriented care.

Enduring Processes in New Contexts

The preceding analysis identified factors that encouraged the rise of psychosocial pediatrics: heightened interest in social issues within the profession at large, the availability of training grants in behavioral medicine, and a growing disparity between pediatric education and practice. Several developments aggravated the tension between education and practice including the consolidation of hospital-based residency training and the evolution of scientifically grounded subspecialties. Routinization of community pediatrics may have contributed as well. But the fact that pediatric faculty, not community practitioners, spearheaded the psychosocial movement suggests that conditions within academic departments were of primary importance to its origins.

I have argued that new career tracks within academic medicine were the immediate catalyst for "the new pediatrics." Department chairs introduced full-time professorships for academic generalists and psychosocial specialists to strengthen residency training in ambulatory care. The creation of dedicated career tracks for behaviorally oriented faculty stimulated occupational processes familiar from earlier phases of the specialty's history. Physicians with common work patterns coalesce, build formal associations, and mobilize to improve their collective occupational status. Again, nascent segments imitate established specialties. Leaders of "the new pediatrics" have fostered clinical research on psychosocial issues comparable to investigatory efforts within organ-based fields. Several spokesmen have promoted the idea of certification for psychosocial specialists.

Psychosocial pediatrics has consequences for the specialty's relation to other disciplines and professions and for its role in society at large. Academic specialists have endeavored to improve their standing within pediatric departments by pursuing research on issues related to ambulatory care. In doing so, they have enlarged the specialty's knowledge base to subsume large areas of the applied social and behavioral sciences. "The new pediatrics" has also encouraged expansion in the domain of office-based specialists and the treatment of behavioral disorders in community practice. Thus far psychosocial pediatrics has been largely an academic movement and there are impediments to its diffusion into community settings. But several factors foster such movement including the introduction of residency and fellowship training in psychosocial pediatrics and advocacy by major pediatric associations. Finally, by redefining their terrain to include the psychosocial disorders of children and families, pediatricians are enterinig arenas also claimed by a host of other child-serving professions. If community pediatricians undertake the treatment of behavioral disorders on a more routine basis, the division of labor among the child-serving professions will have to change.

Chapter Eight

Concluding Remarks

Recapitulation: Occupational Processes

This book has followed American pediatrics through five historical periods and a hundred years of development. Its focus has been the occupational institutions that structure pediatrics as a professional segment; its overriding concern, the dynamics of occupational inception. Why and how does a new professional segment come into being? How and why does it evolve? What accounts for its eventual organization?

I have argued that in each historical period, practitioners formed a collectivity and constructed a new tier of professional institutions. The first generation of child specialists coalesced during the 1880s. They founded the initial specialty associations and articulated a professional ethos that defined pediatrics and justified its cultivation as a special interest within general medicine. A second generation of child specialists mobilized in the early 1900s. This group secured autonomous pediatric departments within American medical schools. With the aid of dedicated academic units and a revised professional ethos, they established pediatrics as an independent, consulting specialty. During the 1920s and 1930s, a new generation of pediatricians moved to build formal market structures. These specialists created a certifying board and standardized residency training, fully institutionalizing pediatrics as a division of primary-care medicine. The final two periods involve the formation of pediatric subspecialties as additional tiers of professional structure. Practitioners in scientifically based pediatric subfields mobilized in the

late 1950s to establish special scientific sections. By the early 1970s
they were initiating separate associations and certifying mechanisms. Finally, and most recently, academically based pediatric
generalists have moved to raise the standing of general ambulatory
care as an arena of professional activity. Thus far, they have
founded several professional societies and articulated an ideology
that promotes research and instruction on the psychosocial problems of children and families.

The present-day organization of pediatrics is the product of layers of professional structure established by successive generations
of child specialists. As new tiers are added, older institutions typically remain intact but serve somewhat different functions. Pediatricians build such occupational institutions to augment their prestige
and improve their competitive position relative to contemporary
economic actors. They regroup when the contingencies of their
labor substantially alter and when they perceive that mutual benefit will accrue from collective action. Work contingencies change as
practitioners forge careers in shifting ideational, market, and organizational conditions.

The social context in which segmentation occurs varies dramatically across historical periods. When pediatrics first emerged
in the late nineteenth century, medical organizations were premodern in character. Hospitals were charities for the poor and
medical schools were proprietary institutions offering virtually no
clinical instruction. There were fewer than a dozen medical specialty societies and the profession as a whole was struggling to
raise its occupational status. By the 1930s, hospitals and professional colleges had assumed their near modern forms. Medicine
had substantially improved its standing and contemporary medical
segments had built numerous types of professional structures.
Pediatric subspecialties emerged in the context of mature hospitals and medical schools and fully institutionalized primary medical segments. Despite such differences, there are persistent commonalities over time in social processes underlying specialization.
I delineate four recurring dynamics.

First, in each historical period, alterations in the division of
professional labor precede and stimulate the construction of professional institutions. Numerous factors contribute to changes in work
patterns: scientific advance, normative currents, innovations with-

in work organizations, and growth in demand for specialized services. New work patterns mediate between the forces propelling specialization and the mobilization of practitioners to build formal occupational structures. The narrative identifies a sequence of modal career patterns in the historical maturation of pediatrics. Nineteenth-century pediatricians were partial specialists who donated time to children's hospitals and asylums but functioned as medical generalists in their private offices. Early twentieth-century pediatricians worked as full-scale specialists by combining hospital and teaching posts with specialized private practices. In the 1920s and 1930s, pediatricians began functioning as full-time office-based specialists and there was increasing differentiation between careers in practice and those in research and teaching. By World War II, pediatric faculty were pursuing academic tracks in distinct clinical subspecialties. During each historical period, practitioners mobilize in response to a nascent but as yet unregulated division of labor. The structures and ideologies they create serve to stabilize emerging work roles and enhance opportunities for further career building.

Second, specialties emerge into occupational environments that strongly affect the pace of a segment's growth and the shape it adopts. Pediatricians repeatedly model their professional institutions after those of earlier, more fully established segments. Existing specialties provide examples of occupational design and palpable evidence that segmentation provides competitive advantages. The presence of occupational institutions can also operate as a generative factor in the evolution of new segments. In several instances, pediatricians initiate professional structures in response to the founding of comparable institutions by other contemporary specialties. Practitioners react not only to changes in work patterns and the forces propelling such change but also to surrounding occupational institutions, the benefits these structures confer, and the imperatives they create.

Third, innovations within hospitals and medical schools are crucial to changes in work patterns and the specialty's continued development. The analysis does not challenge the causal role of scientific, normative, or market factors in the evolution of pediatrics. It does indicate that organizational innovation is a more important generative factor than the existing sociological literature leads one to anticipate. Generative forces are highly interrelated in how they affect the segment's emergence. Interplay between organizational and scientific factors is recurrent in the history of pediatrics. At several junctures, the perception of new scientific possibilities helps justify the creation of specialized organizational divisions. These units, in turn, support more highly specialized work patterns and hasten the growth of substantive specialized knowledge.

Fourth, while pediatrics was born in hospitals and medical colleges, the specialty itself affected the shape of professional organizations. This dynamic is evident in the consolidation of markets for pediatric services. In two distinct historical periods, child specialists used appointments in medical schools, hospitals, and clinics to launch office-based pediatric practices. During both periods, practitioners molded arrangements within organizations so as to perpetuate favorable market conditions. Pediatricians struggled for and won autonomous departments within American medical colleges in the decade of 1910. During the 1930s, they participated in a collective movement by medical specialties to assert control over graduate professional training. Through the certifying boards, medical segments structured residency training so that specialty markets were permanently sustained. Born within hospitals and medical schools, specialties had a lasting influence on the form these parent organizations assumed.

Recapitulation: Pediatrics and the American Family

In addition to identifying occupational processes, the analysis has shed light on the forces supporting pediatricians' advice-giving role with parents. Two periods in the specialty's history have particular relevance for the professional regulation of family life. The first is the 1920s and 1930s when pediatricians consolidated the market of office-based services and made overseeing healthy youngsters a central professional activity. The second begins in the 1960s when a segment of specialists pushed for greater emphasis on the psychosocial disorders of children and families. The factors encouraging specialists to adopt new regulatory functions in these two periods are different. But in neither case is professional dominance alone a sufficient explanation for pediatric supervision of American families.

During the 1920s and 1930s a large-scale social movement championed pediatric care for well children. The boundaries of this social movement extended well beyond the profession of medicine. Its members were largely female and predominantly middle class. Its goals were to disseminate new norms regarding age-appropriate behavior and construct new institutions for childhood socialization. Pediatricians participated in the health and welfare movement. They capitalized on the demand for professional services that activism generated. But the roots of medical services for healthy youngsters lay in structural and cultural change that originated outside the child-serving professions. Nineteenth and early twentieth-century child-welfare activists had been particularly concerned with uplifting children of the poor. One of the ironies of preventive pediatrics was that, by 1940, its principal consumers were middle-class women, not the working-class mothers for whom it was originally designed. The result was less social control of the poor than professional validation for the affluent.

Events during the 1960s and 1970s are more consistent with the depiction of professional dominance. This period had no lay child-welfare movement comparable to that in the 1920s. Forces internal to pediatrics were largely responsible for specialists' attempts to expand their regulatory functions. In the late 1950s, a newly consolidated segment of academic generalists sought to raise its standing by espousing greater emphasis on psychosocial issues. With financial support from private foundations and federal agencies, these pediatric faculty set up research and training programs in psychosocial care. By the early 1980s, major specialty associations were encouraging private pediatricians to identify and treat behavioral disorders.

But the outcome of psychosocial pediatrics is unresolved. Research and advocacy alone do not constitute changes in professional practice. Little reliable information is available on how community practitioners actually handle behavioral disorders. Furthermore, there are impediments to pediatricians' undertaking more extensive treatment of these problems. Modest reimbursement rates for psychosocial services discourage physicians from offering such care. Low-income families—identified as having the highest incidence of behavioral problems—cannot afford out-of-pocket medical expenses. Federal programs funding behavioral medicine operate with substantial budgetary constraints. Public policies supporting child and family services are vulnerable to crosscutting political currents. Thus, an established child-serving profession can move to broaden its regulatory activities but its success in implementing such change will depend upon forces over which it has only limited control.

Continuities among Medical Segments

Pediatrics is unusual among medical specialties in its ties to social movements and its impact on families. Chapter 1 identified other anomalies as well: the status of pediatrics is comparatively low and, in recent decades, the field has attracted relatively high proportions of women physicians. Yet despite the segment's distinctive features, several processes discovered here are typical of numerous medical specialties. Secondary historical sources reveal that organizational innovation and new work patterns are vital in the birth of many scientifically based fields. Scholarship on nineteenth-century medicine provides the strongest evidence of these patterns. George Rosen reports that specialized clinics and hospitals spurred the inception of ophthalmology, otolaryngology, orthopedics, and urology during the second half of the nineteenth century. Research by both Rosen and Charles Rosenberg attests to the prevalence of partially specialized work patterns among elite physicians prior to the founding of specialty associations. Furthermore, Rosen's work indicates that there was a great deal of interplay between organizational innovation and scientific advance in the development of organ-based specialties.[1]

I make no claim that there are inevitable or universal stages in the evolution of medical segments or that the particular sequence of work patterns found in the development of pediatrics would be duplicated in histories of other specialties. A great many factors affect practitioners' work activities. Even if specialties evolved in identical organizational settings, differences in the character of services, the timing of scientific developments, or the pace of market expansion would probably generate variation in labor patterns. Yet because medical specialties in America emerged in very similar institutional contexts, some commonalities in work patterns across segments are likely. I predict two long-term trends in the labor patterns of practitioners in evolving medical segments: first a movement toward increasing specialization, and then increasing bifurcation of careers in practice and those in teaching and research.

The empirical record also reveals that occupational environments influence the full range of medical segments. Several observations discussed earlier in the book support this contention. One is that emerging specialties adopt very similar institutional forms. Another is the existence of discernible waves in the creation of professional structures. An example of this phenomenon is the proliferation of certifying boards in the decade of 1930. Factors other than the surrounding professional segments undoubtedly contribute to waves of institution building. But secondary sources point to the importance of surrounding occupational structures. Rosemary Stevens' account of the multiplication of certifying boards in the 1930s makes it clear that the actions of individual specialties were part of a collective movement by medical segments.[2] A third observation corroborating the importance of occupational environments is that the timing of a segment's development, relative to that of specialization as a whole, affects its eventual organization. Once the certification system was constituted, established specialties made it difficult for emerging segments to create autonomous certifying boards. After 1940, most fields were accommodated as subspecialties under the aegis of existing boards. Emerging segments emulate established ones in an effort to raise their prestige and improve their market position. Social problem specialties may be especially vulnerable to isomorphic pressures because of their relatively low occupational status. But the patterns described here indicate that the aggregate body of specialty structures affects individual segments, whatever their origins.

Regarding the dynamics of market consolidation, my discussion of continuities among specialties becomes more complicated. Certain of the market processes discussed earlier are widespread. For example, certification serves comparable functions across segments. Qualifying boards designate discrete professional commodities. Along with standardized residency programs, the boards sustain specialties as divisions of the medical market. Another pervasive dynamic concerns demand for specialized care from private consultants. Many segments use hospital and teaching posts to launch extra-organizational markets for professional services. Rosen's work substantiates this pattern.

But two points suggest that market processes vary across specialties. First, specialties differ in the extent to which perceived need for their services rests upon social or scientific rationale. Pediatrics benefited more from social movements outside medicine than is the case with most segments. Second, specialties differ in the principal way that members obtain patients. On the latter basis, I distinguish three categories of medical segments: primary-care specialties, in which practitioners rely heavily upon recommendations from clients to attract additional patients; referral specialties, in which practitioners depend largely on colleague referrals; and hospital-based specialties, in which practitioners negotiate contracts with hospitals that grant monopolies over the provision of specialized services.[3] The first category includes pediatrics, internal medicine, and family practice; the second, endocrinology, hematology, medical oncology, and most of the surgical specialties; and the third, pathology, anesthesiology, and radiology. Because pediatrics is a primary-care specialty, generating demand among lay clientele has been critical. Constituting markets for referral and hospital-based specialties involves different organizational tasks and, very probably, different underlying processes. At present, social scientists know little about how different varieties of medical segments generate demand or consolidate markets for their service. This area is ripe for further empirical study.

The hospital-based specialties raise especially intriguing questions. These segments grew up within hospitals and during the early part of the century many of their members were salaried employees. In the 1930s, pathologists and radiologists began pressuring hospitals to allow physician groups to bill separately for professional services and obtain reimbursements on a fee-for-service basis.[4] In subsequent decades, they negotiated contracts with hospitals that granted practitioners substantial control over the social and economic organization of their labor. By the late 1970s, the bulk of pathologists and radiologists had contractual agreements with hospitals that allocated use of equipment and space to specific physician groups and excluded competing physicians from access to these resources. At that time, 87 percent of radiologists and 65 percent of pathologists were compensated by fee-for-service or percentage of department income rather than by salary. The latter method results in the lowest incomes for hospital-based practitioners.[5] Given their continued reliance upon organizational resources for patients, how radiologists and pathologists succeeded in obtaining highly advantageous economic arrangements from hospitals is a matter of great interest. Taken as a whole, my discussion of market consolidation suggests that there is no single set of market dynamics but rather systematic variation among types of medical segments.

Specialties and Medicine at Large

The book has depicted medical specialization as a status and market-driven phenomenon. I have argued that successive generations of practitioners used segmentation to improve (or maintain) their professional standing and win competitive advantages. During the late nineteenth century, medical elites of northeastern cities pursued specialization to reassert their status. They mobilized at a time when the profession as a whole was reorganizing to consolidate power and adjust to the arrival of an industrial economy. Changes within medicine threatened to undermine social class as the basis for intraprofessional prestige. Specialty societies allowed the old medical elite to claim legitimacy through association with scientific medicine and to redraw the lines between upper and middle-strata practitioners. Specialization was only briefly the exclusive purview of the east coast medical elites. By the turn of the century, physicians without pedigrees were using specialization as a vehicle for intraprofessional mobility and were pushing their way into the leadership of medical segments. If nineteenth-century pediatricians successfully excluded nonelite practitioners, early twentieth-century pediatricians opened the specialty to a broader range of physicians. The board system, created in the 1930s, democratized entrance into medical segments by establishing admission criteria independent of social class background. (American physicians resist efforts to place limits on specialization because such measures would block intraprofessional mobility.) Certification regularized competitive advantages and placed their acquisition on a legitimate basis.

This interpretation is new to the literature on medical specialties and has two implications that merit comment. The first concerns the role that specialization played in medicine's rise to power during the late nineteenth and early twentieth centuries. Paul Starr argues that segmentation contributed to medicine's authority by enhancing intraprofessional cohesion. He maintains that specialization, along with growing reliance upon hospitals, made physicians more interdependent and medicine more united. Internal cohesion facilitated profession-wide cohesive action. Starr claims specialization was having such an integrative effect before the end of the nineteenth century.[6]

My account raises serious doubts about whether specialization could have engendered cohesion that early in the profession's history. The initial impact of segmentation was by no means integrative. Specialization stimulated a tremendous amount of conflict within medicine during the nineteenth century. Middle-strata physicians were rankled by the competitive advantages that specialization conferred and by the exclusionary policies of elite specialty societies.[7] The certification system, created in the 1930s, mitigated the divisive consequences of segmentation by regularizing internal market divisions and competition among physicians. I have no difficulty with the notion that increased cohesion was an eventual consequence of specialization.[8] But it is difficult to see how specialization's impact could have been primarily integrative before the construction of boards in the decade of 1930. And by then, medicine was already very far along in consolidating its standing.

Yet specialization may have contributed to medicine's authority during the late nineteenth and early twentieth centuries in ways other than through greater cohesion. Physicians succeeded in molding arrangements within hospitals and medical schools in the decades before and after the turn of the century. This fact is a key to medicine's unusually high degree of professional authority. It was as specialists and through the agency of specialty associations that practitioners exerted much of their influence over the unfolding organization of hospitals and medical schools.

That specialization regularized competitive advantages has a second implication; this one relates to policy issues. Since the 1960s, health planners have expressed concern about the consequences of progressive specialization for medical delivery. Critics point to overspecialization (which encourages unnecessary medical procedures), maldistribution of physicians, and fragmentation of patient care. Governmental policy aimed at promoting primary medical care has had limited effectiveness. Federal sponsorship helped establish family practice as a formal specialty during the late 1960s and the number of family physicians has grown substantially. But the basic organization of the medical specialty system and its underlying incentives remain. The proliferation of new segments proceeds unabated. Physician groups established more than two dozen new certifying committees during the 1970s and 1980s. Continued criticism of specialization notwithstanding, it is very unlikely that reformers would succeed in substantially restructuring the specialty system or in disassembling established segments. Specialty structures are the product of vested interests and are crucial to maintaining the balance of power among diverse constituencies within the profession. Specialties and the institutions they have built are integral to the overall organization of American medicine.

Implications Beyond Medicine?

Inferences about professions at large made from findings on pediatrics would rest on shaky ground. Pediatrics is unusual among medical segments, and specialization within medicine involves structural complexities not found in other professions. Yet several aspects of the book's analysis could have value for scholarship on a broad range of professions and professional specialties.

First, it is my conviction that research in this field would greatly benefit from more attention to practitioners' work patterns and the contingencies surrounding their labor. Professions do not appear as full-blown occupations and then acquire a set of attributes or institutions. They come into being through the efforts of practitioners who build new types of careers amid changing social and economic circumstances. Even the transformations accompanying industrialization within the older professions, like medicine and law, are mediated by significant alterations in work contingencies and career opportunities. Further study of labor patterns within professions undergoing transformation could be a source of new contributions to the sociological literature.

Second, professions in general are powerfully influenced by surrounding occupational structures and by ongoing developments within contemporary professional segments. Even casual scrutiny attests to widespread tendencies for emerging professions to emulate more prestigious ones and for professions to adopt very similar organizational forms. As yet, very few researchers have conceived of emulation as a historical process accessible to empirical study. Pursuing this line of inquiry requires that scholars disengage the imitative propensities of these occupations from the definition *profession* and understand emulation to be a self-conscious strategy adopted by occupational leaders. Elaborating the notion of occupational environments could provide analytic tools useful in explaining many phenomena among professions.

Finally, what I would like to emphasize most is not a particular analytic point but an approach to the study of professions. It is historical actors who create professional institutions. The practitioners who build them both respond to and are agents of social change. Their actions are understood best in light of the specific settings where they negotiate careers, the particular forces that impinge upon their labor, and contemporary perceptions of their interests and options. Professionalization, a variety of social change, is best explained through genuinely historical inquiry.

Notes

1. Introduction

1. Statistics on physician visits by children under eleven are from the 1980–1981 National Ambulatory Medical Care Survey. These data were provided by the National Center for Health Statistics, Public Health Service, U.S. Department of Health and Human Services. On annual rates of office visits for children under two see National Center for Health Statistics, Beulah K. Cypress, "Patterns of Ambulatory Care in Pediatrics: The National Ambulatory Medical Care Survey, United States, January 1980–December 1981," *Vital and Health Statistics*, ser. 13, no. 75, DHHS pub. no. (PHS) 84-1736 (Washington, D.C.: U.S. Government Printing Office, 1983), p. 2, table B.

2. American Medical Association, Department of Data Release Services, Division of Survey and Data Resources, *Physician Characteristics and Distribution in the U.S.*, 1986 ed. (Chicago: American Medical Association, 1986), p. 19, table A-2. This figure includes pediatric residents. Numbers of specialists in *Physician Characteristics* are based upon self-report by physicians.

3. U.S. President's Commission on the Health Needs of the Nation, *Building America's Health*, 5 vols. (Washington, D.C.: U.S. Government Printing Office, 1952–53), 3: 160, table 208. These statistics are based upon listings of specialists in contemporary issues of the *American Medical Directory* published by the American Medical Association.

4. Computed from numbers of specialists by field in AMA, *Physician Characteristics and Distribution*, 1986 ed., p. 19, table A-2. It should be noted that among the remaining 88 percent of physicians, many practice their reported specialty on less than a full-time basis.

5. The scientific histories of pediatrics include John Ruhrah, ed.,

Pediatrics of the Past (New York: Hoeber, 1925), and George F. Still, *The History of Pediatrics* (London: Oxford University Press, 1931). Typical of the biographical approach are Borden S. Veeder, ed., *Pediatric Profiles* (St. Louis: C. V. Mosby, 1957), and Abraham Levinson, *Pioneers of Pediatrics* (New York: Froben, 1943). Principal works on pediatric associations in the United States are Harold K. Faber and Rustin McIntosh, *History of the American Pediatric Society, 1887–1965* (New York: McGraw-Hill, 1966), and Marshall C. Pease, *American Academy of Pediatrics, June 1930–June 1951* (n.p.: American Academy of Pediatrics, 1952). Early presidential addresses to the American Academy of Pediatrics have been collected by Paul W. Beaven, ed., *For the Welfare of Children* (Springfield, Ill.: American Academy of Pediatrics, 1955). Among the histories that combine various approaches is one by a well-known medical historian: Fielding H. Garrison, "History of Pediatrics," in *Pediatrics by Various Authors*, ed. Isaac A. Abt (Philadelphia: W. B. Saunders, 1923), pp. 1–170. During the 1960s this volume was expanded and republished as Arthur F. Abt, ed., *Abt-Garrison History of Pediatrics* (Philadelphia: W. B. Saunders, 1965). The most recent general history is Thomas E. Cone, Jr., *History of American Pediatrics* (Boston: Little, Brown, 1979). In addition to these volumes there are innumerable articles on the history of the specialty published in pediatric journals.

6. By *freestanding profession*, I refer to an autonomously constituted profession as distinct from an organized segment within a larger occupation.

7. George Ritzer, *Working: Conflict and Change* (Englewood Cliffs, N.J.: Prentice-Hall, 1977), p. 14, table 1.1.

8. For a discussion of specialization in law see John P. Heinz and Edward O. Laumann, *Chicago Lawyers: The Social Structure of the Bar* (New York and Chicago: Russell Sage Foundation and the American Bar Foundation, 1982), pp. 18, 36–56.

9. On the organization of medical specialties in Britain and Germany consult Rosemary Stevens, *Medical Practice in Modern England: The Impact of Specialism and State Medicine* (New Haven: Yale University Press, 1966) and Deborah A. Stone, *The Limits of Professional Power: National Health Care in the Federal Republic of Germany* (Chicago: University of Chicago Press, 1980).

10. Pediatric associations (with dates of founding) include: AMA Section of Diseases of Children (1881), American Pediatric Society (1888), Association of American Teachers of the Diseases of Children (created in 1907 and disbanded in 1930), Society for Pediatric Research (1929), American Academy of Pediatrics (1930), Ambulatory Pediatric Association

(1960), Association of Medical School Pediatric Department Chairmen (1960).

11. Jeffrey L. Berlant, *Profession and Monopoly: A Study of Medicine in the United States and Great Britain* (Berkeley, Los Angeles, London: University of California Press, 1975), pp. 43–63; Magali S. Larson, *The Rise of Professionalism: A Sociological Analysis* (Berkeley, Los Angeles, London: University of California Press, 1977). This work draws upon Weber's writing on economic action, particularly his discussion of monopolization. Max Weber, *Economy and Society,* ed. Guenther Roth and Claus Wittich, 3 vols. (Berkeley, Los Angeles, London: University of California Press, 1978), vol. 1.

12. Rosemary Stevens provides a definitive account of the history and operation of specialty certifying boards in *American Medicine and the Public Interest* (New Haven: Yale University Press, 1971).

13. There are two separate listings of medical specialists. One is in the *American Medical Association Directory* which indicates all self-reported specialists, certified or not. The other is the *Directory of Medical Specialists,* compiled by the American Board of Medical Specialties (an umbrella organization for medical certifying boards); this lists only board-certified physicians.

14. On professions' use of credentialing to create market shelters see Eliot Freidson, *Professional Powers: A Study of the Institutionalization of Formal Knowledge* (Chicago: University of Chicago Press, 1986), pp. 63–91.

15. William J. Goode, "The Theoretical Limits of Professionalization," in *The Semi-Professions and Their Organization,* ed. Amitai Etzioni (New York: Free Press, 1969), pp. 266–313; William J. Goode, "Encroachment, Charlatanism, and the Emerging Professions: Psychology, Sociology and Medicine," *American Sociological Review,* 25, 6 (1960): 902–914.

16. Rue Bucher and Anselm Strauss, "Professions in Process," *American Journal of Sociology,* 66, 4 (1961): 330–331.

17. Everett C. Hughes (1960), "The Professions in Society," in *The Sociological Eye: Selected Papers* (New Brunswick, N.J.: Transaction Books, 1984), p. 367.

18. Robert H. Wiebe, *The Search For Order, 1877–1920* (New York: Hill and Wang, 1967); Burton J. Bledstein, *The Culture of Professionalism: The Middle Class and the Development of Higher Education in America* (New York: W. W. Norton, 1976); Randall Collins, *The Credential Society: An Historical Sociology of Education and Stratification* (New York: Academic Press, 1979).

19. On specialization as a route to high income and status see Charles

Rosenberg, "The Practice of Medicine in New York a Century Ago," *Bulletin of the History of Medicine*, 41, 3 (1967): 248–249; William G. Rothstein, *American Physicians in the Nineteenth Century* (Baltimore: Johns Hopkins University Press, 1972), pp. 198–216; Stevens, *American Medicine*, pp. 44, 49. Comments on the higher fees of specialists are found in George Rosen, *The Specialization of Medicine with Particular Reference to Ophthalmology* (New York: Froben, 1944), pp. 62–64, 69. On hostility toward specialization among nineteenth-century physicians see Daniel H. Calhoun, *Professional Lives in America: Structure and Aspirations, 1750–1850* (Cambridge: Harvard University Press, 1965), pp. 20–58; Donald E. Konold, *A History of American Medical Ethics, 1847–1912* (Madison: State Historical Society of Wisconsin, 1962), pp. 36–38; Rosen, *The Specialization of Medicine*, pp. 49, 62–64; Rothstein, *American Physicians in the Nineteenth Century*, pp. 209–212.

20. Charles E. Rosenberg, "Social Class and Medical Care in Nineteenth-Century America: The Rise and Fall of the Dispensary," *Journal of the History of Medicine and Allied Health Sciences*, 29, 1 (1974): 40. On stratification within nineteenth-century medicine also see Rothstein, *American Physicians in the Nineteenth Century*, pp. 201–207.

21. On membership policies of nineteenth-century medical societies see Rothstein, *American Physicians in the Nineteenth Century*, pp. 201–204. Protective measures by professional elites were widespread during the late nineteenth century. Gilb points out that the founding of national professional societies reached a peak in America during the 1870s and 1880s. Associations of this period were typically elitist, serving the upper strata of practitioners and seeking to raise standards through good example. Corinne L. Gilb, *Hidden Hierarchies: The Professions and Government* (New York: Harper and Row, 1966), pp. 27–40.

22. Rosen, *The Specialization of Medicine*. In Kuhn's terms, the notion of localized pathology introduced a new paradigm of disease. Thomas S. Kuhn, *The Structure of Scientific Revolutions* (Chicago: University of Chicago Press, 1962).

23. On the role of the maternal and child-health movement in the development of obstetrics consult Stevens, *American Medicine*, p. 200. George Rosen documents the importance of health and sanitary reform movements to the evolution of public health in *A History of Public Health* (New York: MD Publications, 1958). On the mental hygiene movement in the development of American psychiatry see comments by Stevens, *American Medicine*, p. 223. Talcott Parsons and Joseph Ben-David argue that psychoanalytic technique is largely a systematization of interpersonal dynamics whose origins lie in the social roles of doctor and patient. Talcott Parsons, "Illness and the Role of the Physician: A Sociological Perspec-

tive," *American Journal of Orthopsychiatry*, 21 (1951): 452–60; Joseph Ben-David, "Roles and Innovation in Medicine, *American Journal of Sociology*, 65, 5 (1960): 564.

24. Low earnings among social-problem fields are long-standing. For evidence of persistent income differentials see Maurice Leven, *The Income of Physicians: An Economic and Statistical Analysis*, Committee on the Cost of Medical Care, pub. no. 24 (Chicago: University of Chicago Press, 1932), p. 115, table 11A; "How Your Earnings Compare," *Medical Economics*, 37, 22 (1960): 38–47; American Medical Association, Center for Health Services Research and Development, *Profiles of Medical Practice, 1980* (Chicago: American Medical Association, 1980), p. 217, table 45.

25. On the paucity of women among early medical specialists see note 35 in chapter 3. During the 1800s and early 1900s, women physicians were discouraged from specializing by their exclusion from both specialty societies and hospital posts providing exposure to specialized skills. Even at the time of World War II, a smaller proportion of female than male physicians was entering medical specialties. In the early 1940s, 8 percent of male MDs were certified specialists while only 5 percent of women physicians held specialty certificates. U.S. Department of Labor, Women's Bureau, "The Outlook for Women in Occupations in the Medical Services: Women Physicians," Department of Labor, bull. 203, no. 7 (Washington, D.C.: U.S. Government Printing Office, 1946), p. 3. Yet from the outset, those women physicians who specialized did gravitate toward social-problem based fields. Women's Bureau, "Women Physicians," pp. 2–3. On the entrance of women MDs into social-problem specialties in recent years see Josephine E. Renshaw and Maryland Y. Pennell, "Distribution of Women Physicians, 1969," *Woman Physician*, 26, 4 (1971): 187–191; Harrison Gough, "Specialty Preferences of Physicians and Medical Students," *Journal of Medical Education*, 50, 6, (1975): 587; Jill Quadagno, "Occupational Sex-Typing and Internal Labor Market Distributions: An Assessment of Medical Specialties," *Social Problems*, 23 (1976): 442–453.

26. Psychiatry has been described as a marginal field, public health as a secondary career choice for medical graduates. Harvey L. Smith, "Psychiatry in Medicine: Intra- or Inter-Professional Relationships?" *American Journal of Sociology*, 63 (1957): 288; Kurt W. Back et al., "Public Health as a Career of Medicine: Secondary Choice within a Profession," *American Sociological Review*, 23, 5 (1958): 534–536. Among the physicians interviewed for this study, a good portion spontaneously offered the opinion that general pediatrics has relatively low standing among medical specialties. General pediatrics should be distinguished from pediatric subspecialties, many of which are highly prestigious. Occupational pres-

tige studies vary in where they place social-problem specialties in the medical status-hierarchy. One research group reports that among twenty-two specialties, pediatrics, psychiatry, and preventive medicine rank 11.5, 13, and 20 respectively. Allan M. Schwartzbaum, John H. McGrath, and Robert A. Rothman, "The Perception of Prestige Differences among Medical Subspecialties," *Social Science and Medicine*, 7, (1973): 367.

27. Abbott suggests that intraprofessional status rests on a segment's relative ability to exclude nonprofessional issues from professional practice. Shortell points to the degree of physician dominance in typical doctor-patient interactions. Bosk observes that physicians are drawn to the high-status surgical specialties by their "gladiator dimensions"; surgery is "where the action is." Andrew Abbott, "Status and Status Strain in the Professions," *American Journal of Sociology*, 86, 4 (1981): 819–835; Stephen M. Shortell, "Occupational Prestige Differences within the Medical and Allied Health Professions, *Social Science and Medicine*, 8 (1974): 1–9; Charles Bosk, *Forgive and Remember: Managing Medical Failure* (Chicago: University of Chicago Press, 1979), p. 90.

28. George Rosen, "Whither Specialization," in *Medicine and Society: Contemporary Medical Problems in Historical Perspective*, ed. American Philosophical Society Library (Philadelphia: American Philosophical Society Library, 1971), p. 208; Rosen, *The Specialization of Medicine*, p. 42.

29. A. M. Carr-Saunders and P. A. Wilson, *The Professions* (Oxford: Oxford University at the Clarendon Press, 1933), pp. 285–286, 297.

30. Wilbert E. Moore, *The Professions: Roles and Rules* (New York: Russell Sage Foundation, 1970), pp. 143–145.

31. "The information which [mothers] seek has to do with that which cannot be obtained from books, but rather is that sort of knowledge which has passed from mouth to mouth down through the centuries. Instead of asking mother or grandmother what should be done, the doctor is consulted. . . . The doctor is taking the place more and more of the 'advice offering neighbor.' " B. R. Hoobler, "The Desirability of Teaching Students Details Concerning the Care of the Normal Infant," *Transactions of the Association of American Teachers of the Diseases of Children*, 11 (1917): 43. Following Hoobler's address, discussion continues among session participants. Dr. W. P. Northrup: "I would suggest as a heading for a chapter 'The elimination of the grandmother.' The grandmother is the great trial of my life. She probably has had eight children and I have not had any." *Transactions of the Association of American Teachers of the Diseases of Children*, 11 (1917): 45.

32. Work on medicalization includes Peter Conrad and Joseph W. Schneider, *Deviance and Medicalization* (St. Louis: C. V. Mosby, 1980).

For a feminist perspective see Barbara Ehrenreich and Deirdre English, *For Her Own Good: 150 Years of Experts' Advice to Women* (Garden City, N.Y.: Anchor Books, 1978). On present-day child-serving professions consult Carole E. Joffe, *Friendly Intruders: Childcare Professionals and Family Life* (Berkeley, Los Angeles, London: University of California Press, 1977), and Carole Joffe, *The Regulation of Sexuality* (Philadelphia: Temple University Press, 1986). Still others address policy issues pertaining to state intervention in family affairs, for example, Edward F. Zigler, Sharon L. Kagan, and Edgar Klugman, eds., *Children, Families, and Government: Perspectives on American Social Policy* (Cambridge: Cambridge University Press, 1983).

33. Remarks made by William Goode at the American Sociological Association, 1985 Annual Meeting, Washington, D.C. Noteworthy historical accounts of the origins of child and family-related services include Anthony M. Platt, *The Child Savers: The Invention of Delinquency* (Chicago: University of Chicago Press, 1969); and Murray Levine and Adeline Levine, *A History of the Helping Services* (New York: Appleton-Century Crofts, 1970).

34. Christopher Lasch, *Haven in a Heartless World: The Family Besieged* (New York: Basic Books, 1977). For another account that emphasizes professional dominance see Jacques Donzelot, *The Policing of Families*, trans. Robert Hurley (New York: Pantheon, 1979).

35. Primary historical materials were drawn from libraries at the University of California, Berkeley; the University of California, San Francisco; the University of Chicago; the New York Academy of Medicine; the College of Physicians of Philadelphia; and from the Matas Medical Library at Tulane University in New Orleans. The difficult-to-obtain *Transactions of the Association of American Teachers of the Diseases of Children*—cited extensively in chapters 4 and 5—are located in the collections in San Francisco, New York, and New Orleans. In addition to the primary sources already mentioned, I used a limited amount of archival material from the Chicago and San Francisco collections.

36. References to unpublished documents and interview data are found in notes to chapters 6 and 7.

37. Arthur L. Stinchcombe, *Theoretical Methods in Social History* (New York: Academic Press, 1978).

2. Professionalization as Historical Process

1. This borrows from Stinchcombe's formulation that professions are distinguished by continuity in a labor market external to organizations.

Arthur L. Stinchcombe, "Bureaucratic and Craft Administration of Production: A Comparative Study," *Administrative Science Quarterly*, 4, 2 (1959): 186.

2. Everett C. Hughes (1960), "The Professions in Society," in *The Sociological Eye: Selected Papers* (Chicago: Aldine-Atherton, 1971), pp. 364–373. Also in the same volume: Hughes (1965), "Professions," pp. 374–386; Hughes (1956), "The Making of a Physician," pp. 397–407.

3. Rue Bucher and Anselm Strauss, "Professions in Process," *American Journal of Sociology*, 25, 6 (1960): 902–914.

4. Anselm Strauss et al., *Psychiatric Ideologies and Institutions* (New York: Free Press, 1964); Rue Bucher and Joan Stelling, "Characteristics of Professional Organizations," *Journal of Health and Social Behavior*, 10 (1969): 3–15.

5. Over the long run, change in professional institutions does occur. An institution may perform quite different functions in different periods of a profession's development. The American Pediatric Society was the central professional association for child specialists in the 1890s. Today it is largely an honorary society. This type of change is especially likely when new layers of professional institutions are added to already existing structures. It is noteworthy that in successfully developing professions, few professional stuctures are actually dismantled. In the history of pediatrics, only one society was disbanded (The Association of American Teachers of the Diseases of Children) and it was superceded by another association.

6. Émile Durkheim (1893), *The Division of Labor in Society*, trans. George Simpson (New York: Free Press, 1964); Adam Smith (1776), *Inquiry into the Nature and Causes of the Wealth of Nations* (New York: Modern Library, 1937).

7. Neil J. Smelser, *Social Change in the Industrial Revolution* (Chicago: University of Chicago Press, 1959); Neil J. Smelser, "Sociological History: The Industrial Revolution and the British Working-Class Family," and "Toward a General Theory of Social Change," in *Essays in Sociological Explanation* (Englewood Cliffs, N.J.: Prentice-Hall, 1968), pp. 76–91, 192–280.

8. Treatments which make the inception of new occupational units problematic include C. Turner and M. N. Hodge, "Occupations and Professions," in *Professions and Professionalization*, ed. J. A. Jackson (London: Cambridge University Press, 1970), pp. 19–50; Andrew M. Pettigrew, "Occupational Specialization as an Emergent Process," *Sociological Review*, 21 (1973): 255–278. Scholars have focused more attention on the inception of academic disciplines and research fields. See, for example, Joseph Ben-David and Randall Collins, "Social Factors in the Origins of a New Science: The Case of Psychology," *American Sociological Review*,

31, 4 (1966): 451–465; Warren O. Hagstrom, *The Scientific Community* (New York: Basic Books, 1965), pp. 159–243; Nicholas C. Mullins, "The Development of a Scientific Specialty: The Phage Group and the Origins of Molecular Biology," *Minerva*, 10, 1 (1972): 51–82.

9. On the notion of a continuum of occupations see Howard M. Vollmer and Donald L. Mills, eds., *Professionalization* (Englewood Cliffs, N.J.: Prentice-Hall, 1966), p. vii. Critiques of work focusing on the traits of professions include Terence J. Johnson, *Professions and Power* (London: Macmillan, 1972), pp. 21–38; Douglas Klegon, "The Sociology of Professions," *Sociology of Work and Occupations*, 5, 3 (1978): 259–283; Julius Roth, "Professionalism: the Sociologist's Decoy," *Sociology of Work and Occupations*, 1, 1 (1974): 6–23.

10. Theodore Caplow (1954), *The Sociology of Work* (New York: McGraw-Hill, 1964), pp. 139–140; Harold L. Wilensky, "The Professionalization of Everyone?" *American Journal of Sociology*, 70 (1964): 137–158.

11. There is an extensive literature on organizational environments and institutional isomorphism. Work that I found particularly useful in thinking about professional environments includes Arthur Stinchcombe, "Social Structure and Organizations," in *Handbook of Organizations*, ed. James G. March (Chicago: Rand McNally, 1965), pp. 142–193; Paul DiMaggio and Walter W. Powell, "The Iron Cage Revisited: Institutional Isomorphism and Collective Rationality in Organizational Fields," *American Sociological Review*, 48 (1983): 147–160; Howard Aldrich, *Organizations and Environments* (Englewood Cliffs, N.J.: Prentice-Hall, 1979); John W. Meyer and W. Richard Scott, *Organizational Environments: Ritual and Rationality* (Beverly Hills, Calif.: Sage, 1983); Mary L. Fennell, "The Effects of Environmental Characteristics on the Structure of Hospital Clusters," *Administrative Science Quarterly*, 25 (1980): 485–510.

12. William J. Goode, "The Theoretical Limits of Professionalization," in *The Semi-Professions and Their Organization*, ed. Amitai Etzioni (New York: Free Press, 1969), pp. 269–270; Eliot Freidson, *The Profession of Medicine* (New York: Harper and Row, 1970), pp. 47–70; Eliot Freidson, *Professional Dominance* (Chicago: Aldine, 1970), pp. 127–164. Carol Brown provides a general discussion of the ways medicine controls allied health professions in "The Division of Laborers: Allied Health Professionals," *International Journal of Health Services*, 3, 3 (1973): 435–444. For a historical account of the impact of medical segments on the development of two ancillary professions (physical therapy and occupational therapy) see Glenn Gritzer and Arnold Arluke, *The Making of Rehabilitation: A Political Economy of Medical Specialization, 1890–1980* (Berkeley, Los Angeles, London: University of California Press, 1985).

13. Gilb suggests that professional organization is strongly determined by broader economic forces. She identifies three stages in the development of professional associations in the nineteenth century and links these to plateaus in the evolution of the industrial system. Corinne L. Gilb, *Hidden Hierarchies: The Professions and Government* (New York: Harper and Row, 1966), pp. 27–40.

14. DiMaggio and Powell, "The Iron Cage Revisited," pp. 150–152.

15. Rosen comments on this dynamic. He writes that "the very fact of the origin and continued existence of a specialty undoubtedly creates new conditions and may facilitate the occurrence of other specialties." The appearance of early specialties "established an institutional form into which . . . later developments could fit themselves. By this we mean that as new foci of interest appeared it was relatively easier for them to become organized in an institutional pattern which was already fairly well set." Rosen, *The Specialization of Medicine with Particular Reference to Ophthalmology* (New York: Froben, 1944), pp. 58, 30. It is interesting to note that the social-problem based segments coalesced as specialties somewhat after the first organ-based segments. Pediatric and obstetric associations appeared in the 1880s after societies for some eight organ-based specialties had been established. The situation with psychiatry and public health is more complicated. An Association of Medical Superintendents of American Institutions of the Insane was created in 1844. (This became the American Medico-Psychological Association in 1893 and the American Psychiatric Association in 1921.) The American Public Health Association was established in 1872. However, neither of these organizations functioned as specialty associations until well after their founding.

16. Stinchcombe identified spurts in the formation of new organizations and points to a correlation between the structure of organizations and the time of their founding. Waves in the formation of organizations of one type are followed by periods of slower growth and then by waves of new kinds of organizations in the same field. Stinchcombe, "Social Structure and Organizations," pp. 142–193. The situation with medical specialties is similar except that institutions founded in different historical periods and with different characteristics constitute the evolving structural features of a single professional segment. As new tiers of professional institutions are added, the functioning of older institutions alters.

17. American Ophthalmological Society, 1864; American Otological Society, 1867; American Neurological Association, 1875; American Gynecological Society, 1876; American Dermatological Association, 1876; the American Laryngological Society, 1879; American Surgical Association, 1880; American Orthopedic Association, 1887; American Pediatric Association, 1888; American Association of Obstetricians and Gynecologists,

1888; American Electro-Therapeutic Association (physical medicine and rehabilitation), 1891; American Proctologic Society (colon and rectal surgery), 1897; American Roentgen Ray Society, 1900; American Urological Association, 1902.

18. Primary specialties with dates of board incorporation are ophthalmology, 1917; otolaryngology, 1924; obstetrics and gynecology, 1930; dermatology, 1932; pediatrics, 1933; radiology, 1934; psychiatry and neurology, 1934; orthopedic surgery, 1934; colon and rectal surgery, 1935; urology, 1935; pathology, 1936; internal medicine, 1936; surgery, 1937; anesthesiology, 1938; plastic surgery, 1939; neurological surgery, 1940; physical medicine and rehabilitation, 1947; preventive medicine, 1948; thoracic surgery, 1950; family practice, 1969; nuclear medicine, 1971. In addition there are two conjoint boards: allergy and immunology, 1971; and emergency medicine, 1976. American Board of Medical Specialties, *Annual Report and Reference Handbook-1985* (Evanston, Ill: American Board of Medical Specialties, 1985).

19. Stinchcombe, "Social Structure and Organizations," p. 153. On other factors influencing the rate of organizational formation see Stinchcombe, "Social Structure and Organization," pp. 145–153.

20. DiMaggio and Powell make a similar distinction between coercive and mimetic isomorphism. "The Iron Cage Revisited," p. 150.

21. The incorporation of the pediatric board in 1933 was also, in part, a defensive maneuver. A contemporary pediatric leader commented that the board was necessary "as a matter of self protection." American Academy of Pediatrics, "Meeting of the Executive Board, held November 26 and 27, 1932 at Evanston, Illinois," *Journal of Pediatrics*, 2, 1 (1933): 119. See chapter 5 of this book for a discussion of events surrounding the creation of the American Board of Pediatrics.

22. Rosemary Stevens, *American Medicine and the Public Interest* (New Haven: Yale University Press, 1971), pp. 212–215, 324–327.

23. On the intellectual foundations of professions see, for example, A. M. Carr-Saunders and P. A. Wilson, *The Professions* (Oxford: Oxford University at the Clarendon Press, 1933); Talcott Parsons, "Professions," in *International Encyclopedia of the Social Sciences*, ed. David L. Sills (New York: Macmillan and the Free Press, 1968), 12: 536–547; as discussed in chapter 1, George Rosen provides an outstanding account of the intellectual roots of medical specialization in *The Specialization of Medicine*.

24. Magali S. Larson, *The Rise of Professionalism: A Sociological Analysis* (Berkeley, Los Angeles, London: University of California Press, 1977). Other treatments of the role of demand in professional consolidation include Wilbert Moore, *The Professions: Roles and Rules* (New York: Russell Sage Foundation, 1970), pp. 52–58. Gritzer and Arluke apply a

"market model" to the development of medical specialties. See Glenn Gritzer, "Occupational Specialization in Medicine: Knowledge and Market Explanations," in *Changing Structure of Health Service Occupations, Research in the Sociology of Health Care*, vol. 2, ed. Julius Roth (Greenwood, Conn.: JAI Press, 1981), pp. 251–283; Gritzer and Arluke, *The Making of Rehabilitation*.

25. Carr-Saunders and Wilson, *The Professions*, pp. 285–286, 297.

26. Larson, *The Rise of Professionalism*, p. 179.

27. Rosen, *The Specialization of Medicine*, pp. 30–49. Charles Rosenberg provides corroborating evidence by documenting the spread of specialized departments within general dispensaries beginning at mid-century and explaining the importance of these units to contemporary medical careers. Charles E. Rosenberg, "Social Class and Medical Care in Nineteenth-Century America: The Rise and Fall of the Dispensary," *Journal of the History of Medicine and Allied Health Sciences*, 29, 1 (1974): 32–54; Charles Rosenberg, "The Practice of Medicine in New York a Century Ago," *Bulletin of the History of Medicine*, 41, 3 (1967): 223–253. The first specialty divisions within general hospitals were outpatient departments; specialized inpatient units were a later development. Morris J. Vogel, *The Invention of the Modern Hospital* (Chicago: University of Chicago Press, 1980), p. 88.

28. Rosen makes essentially the same point. "The creation of specialized hospitals provided centers for the transmission and development of knowledge and skills connected with the special field of practice." *The Specialization of Medicine*, p. 39. Shryock comments on the importance of hospitals founded during the eighteenth century to subsequent medical research. Richard H. Shryock (1936), *The Development of Modern Medicine* (Madison: University of Wisconsin Press, 1979), pp. 42–45.

29. George Rosen, "Whither Specialization," in *Medicine and Society: Contemporary Medical Problems in Historical Perspective*, ed. American Philosophical Society Library (Philadelphia: American Philosophical Society Library, 1971), p. 208.

30. Joseph Ben-David links the pace of scientific advance to organizational factors and argues that progress is greatest where specialized scientific roles are institutionalized. Joseph Ben-David, "Scientific Productivity and Academic Organization in Nineteenth Century Medicine," *American Sociological Review*, 23, 6 (1960): 828–843.

31. These authors comment both on the spread of specialized hospitals and dispensaries and the emergence of partially specialized medical practices among contemporary practitioners. Rosen, *The Specialization of Medicine*, pp. 30–49, 71–72; Rosenberg, "The Practice of Medicine in New York," pp. 223–253; Rosenberg, "Social Class and Medical Care," pp. 32–54.

32. Note 18 to chapter 1 provides citations on the relative status and fees accrued by medical specialists.

33. Rosenberg, "Social Class and Medical Care," p. 40.

34. Late eighteenth-century American physicians patterned their careers in a similar manner. Among upwardly mobile practitioners, the social class of clientele rose over time. Young physicians acquired knowledge and skills working with the poor and later practiced medicine among the rich. Communication with historian Samuel Haber.

35. The use of academic appointments to build private practices diminished with the introduction of full-time salaried professorships within clinical departments of medical schools beginning in the second decade of the twentieth century. Full-time clinical professorships multiplied following World War II. Stevens, *American Medicine,* p. 359; Vernon W. Lippard, *A Half Century of American Medical Education: 1920–1950* (New York: Josiah Macy Jr. Foundation, 1974), pp. 56–59. One result was that careers in practice and those in academic medicine became increasingly differentiated.

36. Medical schools became increasingly involved in graduate professional training after World War II. During the 1960s and 1970s, universities established affiliations with a growing portion of hospitals that sponsored residency training. By the mid-1970s, 90 percent of residency programs were in hospitals with some variety of university affiliation. Irving J. Lewis and Cecil G. Sheps, *The Sick Citadel: The American Academic Medical Center and the Public Interest* (Cambridge, Mass.: Oelgeschlager, Gunn and Hain, 1983), p. 50.

37. Stevens discusses the control that medical segments have over specialty boards, the functions of certification for specialty groups, the impact of certification on graduate training, and alternative models of graduate medical education which might have been adopted during the 1930s. *American Medicine,* chaps. 8–12.

38. Richard H. Hall, "Professionalization and Bureaucratization," *American Sociological Review,* 33, 1 (1968): 103.

39. Larson argues that standardized training programs are crucial to market consolidation in *The Rise of Professionalism,* pp. 15–19, 40–52.

3. The Inception of a Medical Specialty

1. Anne L. Kuhn, *The Mother's Role in Childhood Education: New England Concepts, 1830–1860* (New Haven: Yale University Press, 1947), p. 18.

2. Commentaries on nineteenth-century American domestic tracts include Kuhn, *The Mother's Role in Childhood Education;* Robert Sun-

ley, "Early Nineteenth-Century American Literature on Child Rearing," in *Childhood in Contemporary Cultures*, ed. Margaret Mead and Martha Wolfenstein (Chicago: University of Chicago Press, 1955), pp. 150–167; Geoffrey H. Steere, *Changing Values in Child Socialization: A Study of United States Child-Rearing Literature, 1865–1929* (Ann Arbor, Mich: University Microfilms, 1964); Bernard Wishy, *The Child and the Republic: The Dawn of Modern American Child Nurture* (Philadelphia: University of Pennsylvania Press, 1968). American child-rearing advice of the twentieth century is discussed by Celia Stendler, "Sixty Years of Child Training Practices," *Journal of Pediatrics*, 36, 1 (1950): 122–134; Clark E. Vincent, "Trends in Infant Care Ideas," *Child Development*, 22, 3 (1951): 199–209; Martha Wolfenstein, "Trends in Infant Care," *American Journal of Orthopsychiatry*, 23, 1 (1953): 120–130; Elizabeth M. R. Lomax, Jerome Kagan, and Barbara G. Rosenkrantz, *Science and Patterns of Child Care* (San Francisco: W. H. Freeman, 1978), pp. 129–140; Daniel Miller and Guy Swanson, *The Changing American Parent* (New York: Wiley, 1958), pp. 6–29. Miller and Swanson discuss both the nineteenth and twentieth-century literatures. How faithfully prescriptive literature reflects attitudes within the community at large is open to question. For a discussion of problems with using child-rearing manuals as a source of information on child-rearing values, see Jay E. Mechling, "Advice to Historians on Advice to Mothers," *Journal of Social History*, 9, 1 (1975): 44–63.

3. Adolescence came to be viewed as a distinct stage of the life course during the late 1800s. On changing notions about adolescence and young adulthood consult Joseph Kett, "Adolescence and Youth in Nineteenth-Century America," *Journal of Interdisciplinary History*, 2, 2 (1971): 283–298; John Demos and Virginia Demos, "Adolescence in Historical Perspective," *Journal of Marriage and the Family*, 31, 4 (1969): 632–638; F. Musgrove, *Youth and the Social Order* (London: Routledge and Kegan Paul, 1964); Paul S. Fass, *The Damned and the Beautiful: American Youth in the 1920s* (New York: Oxford University Press, 1977). On the rising value of working-class children during the late nineteenth and early twentieth centuries see Viviana Zelizer, *Pricing the Priceless Child* (New York: Basic Books, 1985).

4. Kuhn, *The Mother's Role in Childhood Education*, p. 22.

5. The idea that experiences of early childhood powerfully influence the individual's character in adulthood predates modern psychological and psychoanalytic theories by a century.

6. The enthronement of motherhood in mid-century domestic tracts is discussed by Kuhn, *The Mother's Role in Childhood Education*; and Barbara Welter (1966), "The Cult of True Womanhood: 1820–1860," in

The American Family in Social-Historical Perspective, ed. Michael Gordon, 2d ed. (New York: St. Martin's, 1978), pp. 313–333. On the implications of the domestic ideal for women's authority in the home, see Carl N. Degler, *At Odds: Women and the Family in America from the Revolution to the Present* (New York: Oxford University Press, 1980), pp. 73–85.

7. Degler, *At Odds*, p. 189; Kuhn, *Mother's Role in Childhood Education*.

8. Richard H. Shryock (1936), *The Development of Modern Medicine* (Madison: University of Wisconsin Press, 1979), p. 327. George Rosen identifies declining birth rates as a causal factor in the inception of pediatrics. "The population factor exercises an influence on medical specialization by giving rise to social problems that become foci of interest. Such problems may be created by . . . an increase or decrease of specific population elements, for instance, a rising infant mortality, a decline in births, or an increase in the number of old people. Problems such as these become foci of interest around which specialties can develop. The outstanding instances of this type of development are the specialties of pediatrics, and . . . geriatrics, which is still in *statu nascendi*." George Rosen, *The Specialization of Medicine with Particular Reference to Ophthalmology* (New York: Froben, 1944), p. 42. See also George Rosen, "Whither Specialization," in *Medicine and Society: Contemporary Problems in Historical Perspective*, ed. American Philosophical Society Library (Philadelphia: American Philosophical Society Library, 1971), p. 207.

9. Musgrove insists that declining birth rates "came after extensive measures for child welfare, and not before." *Youth and the Social Order*, p. 60. But recent work in historical demography suggests that controlled fertility may have taken place as far back as the seventeenth and eighteenth centuries. Robert V. Wells (1975), "Family History and Demographic Transition," in *The American Family in Social-Historical Perspective*, ed. Michael Gordon, 2d ed. (New York: St. Martin's Press, 1978), p. 519. General discussions of fertility patterns and family organization include (for the early nineteenth century) Degler, *At Odds*, and (for the late nineteenth and early twentieth centuries) Paula S. Fass, *The Damned and the Beautiful* (New York: Oxford University Press, 1977), pp. 53–118.

10. Musgrove, *Youth and Social Order*, p. 60; Lawrence Stone, *The Family, Sex and Marriage in England 1500–1800* (New York: Harper and Row, 1977), p. 105; Zelizer, *Pricing the Priceless Child*, pp. 10–11. Philippe Ariès remarks that, in the eighteenth century, notions about the preciousness of children were accompanied by concerns over physical health. See *Centuries of Childhood: A Social History of Family Life*, trans. Robert Baldick (New York: Vintage, 1962), p. 133.

11. The consensus among early and mid-nineteenth century authors

was that infant mortality was rising within American cities. See, for example, Lemuel Shattuck, "On the Vital Statistics of Boston," *The American Journal of Medical Sciences, New Series*, 1 (1841): 382; D. Meredith Reese, "A Report on Infant Mortality in Large Cities; The Sources of Its Increase, and Means for Its Diminution," *Transactions of the American Medical Association*, 10 (1867): 94–95. More recent commentaries on nineteenth-century child mortality rates include Degler, *At Odds*, pp. 72–73; Maris A. Vinovskis, "Mortality Rates and Trends in Massachusetts before 1860," *Journal of Economic History*, 32, 1 (1972): 184–213; Maris A. Vinovskis, "Recent Trends in American Historical Demography: Some Methodological and Conceptual Considerations," *Annual Review of Sociology*, 4 (1978): 620–622; Gretchen A. Condran and Eileen Crimmins, "Mortality Differentials between Rural and Urban Areas of States in the Northeastern United States 1890–1900," *Journal of Historical Geography* 6,2 (1980): 179–202; Gretchen A. Condran and Eileen Crimmins-Gardner, "Public Health Measures and Mortality in U.S. Cities in the Late Nineteenth Century," *Human Ecology* 6, 1 (1978): 27–54.

12. Neil J. Smelser and Sydney Halpern, "The Historical Triangulation of Family, Economy, and Education," in *Turning Points: Historical Essays on the Family*, ed. John Demos and Sarane S. Boocock (Chicago: University of Chicago Press, 1978), pp. S288–S315. Other scholarship that links changing domestic norms to alterations in the structure of the family includes Edward Shorter, *The Making of the Modern Family* (New York: Basic Books, 1975). Early theoretical work on the emergence of the modern nuclear family includes Ernest W. Burgess and Harvey J. Locke, *The Family: From Institution to Companionship*, 2d ed. (New York: American Book, 1953); William F. Ogburn and Meyer F. Nimkoff, *Technology and the Changing Family* (Boston: Houghton Mifflin, 1955); Talcott Parsons, "The American Family: Its Relation to Personality and to the Social Structure," in *Family, Socialization, and Interaction Process* by Talcott Parsons and Robert F. Bales (Glencoe, Ill: Free Press, 1955), pp. 3–33.

13. Kuhn, *The Mother's Role in Childhood Education*, p. 68.

14. Children were only one of the foci of contemporary moral and institutional reform. During the first half of the nineteenth century, Americans built an array of institutions whose primary purpose was social control: penitentiaries, asylums, and mental hospitals. Furthermore, the temperance movement had its origins during this period. David J. Rothman, *The Discovery of the Asylum: Social Order and Disorder in the New Republic* (Boston: Little, Brown, 1971); Joseph R. Gusfield, *Symbolic Crusade: Status Politics and the American Temperance Movement* (Urbana, Ill.: University of Illinois Press, 1963).

15. For a well-documented overview of contemporary institutions for the young, see Barbara Finkelstein, "Casting Networks of Good Influence: The Reconstruction of Childhood in the United States, 1790–1870," in *American Childhood: A Research Guide and Historical Handbook*, ed. Joseph M. Hawes and N. Ray Hiner (Westport, Conn.: Greenwood, 1985), pp. 112–152. Sources on the common school movement include David B. Tyack, *Turning Points in American Educational History* (Waltham, Mass.: Blaisdell, 1967), pp. 119–177; Lawrence Cremin, *The American Common School: An Historic Conception* (New York: Teachers College, Columbia University, 1951). Michael B. Katz states that the number of these public schools in Massachusetts grew by 54 percent between 1840 and 1865. Katz, *The Irony of Early School Reform* (Boston: Beacon, 1968), pp. 11–12.

16. On the rise and decline of the infant-school movement see Dean May and Maris A. Vinovskis, "A Ray of Millennial Light: Early Education and Social Reform in the Infant School Movement in Massachusetts, 1826–1840," in *Family and Kin in American Urban Communities, 1800–1940*, ed. Tamara K. Hareven (New York: Watts, 1976), pp. 62–99; and Carl F. Kaestle and Maris A. Vinovskis, "From Apron Strings to ABCs: Parents, Children, and Schooling in Nineteenth-Century Massachusetts," in *Turning Points: Historical and Sociological Essays on the Family*, ed. John Demos and Sarane S. Boocock (Chicago: University of Chicago Press, 1978), pp. 39–80; Smelser and Halpern, "The Historical Triangulation of Family, Economy, and Education," p. 308.

17. Estimates of the number of orphanages from Robert H. Bremner et al., eds., *Children and Youth in America: A Documentary History*, 3 vols. (Cambridge: Harvard University Press, 1970–74), 1: 632, n. 2. Rothman discusses the founding of both orphan asylums and houses of refuge (reformatories) in *The Discovery of the Asylum*, pp. 206–236. Prior to the founding of orphanages, dependent children were often sent to almshouses along with destitute adults.

18. See a statement by Horace Mann from the *First Annual Report of the Massachusetts Board of Education, 1838*, excerpted in Bremner et al., eds., *Children and Youth in America*, 1: 450.

19. For examples, see Kaestle and Vinovskis, "From Apron Strings to ABCs: Parents, Children, and Schooling in Nineteenth-Century Massachusetts," p. 51; Rothman, *The Discovery of the Asylum*, pp. 210–213.

20. Fielding H. Garrison (1923), "History of Pediatrics," in *Abt-Garrison History of Pediatrics*, ed. Arthur F. Abt (Philadelphia: W. B. Saunders, 1965), pp. 121–122; Thomas E. Cone, Jr., "The History of Pediatric Ambulatory Services," in *Ambulatory Pediatrics*, ed. Morris Green and Robert J. Haggerty (Philadelphia: W. B. Saunders, 1968), pp. 11–13; Samuel X. Radbill, "A History of Children's Hospitals," *American*

Journal of Diseases of Children, 90 (1955): 416; Bremner et al., eds., *Children and Youth in America* 2: 831, n. 1. There were attempts to establish medical facilities for children during the 1840s but these institutions did not survive. Samuel X. Radbill, "Hospitals and Pediatrics, 1776– 1976," *Bulletin of the History of Medicine*, 53, 2 (1979): 289. Not all the early hospitals limited their patients to children. Garrison writes that the Nursery and Child's Hospital was at the outset also a maternity hospital. Garrison, "History of Pediatrics," p. 121. Radbill gives a somewhat different account of Nursery and Child's Hospital, suggesting it began as a nursery for the children of wet nurses and other working mothers. Children's Hospital of Philadelphia is generally credited with being the first hospital in the United States exclusively for children. Samuel X. Radbill, "The Children's Hospital of Philadelphia," *Philadelphia Medicine*, 70 (1974): 352. However, determining precedence is complicated by the fact that, during the 1850s and 1860s, there was little difference between a children's hospital and a children's asylum.

21. Francis H. Brown, "The Children's Hospital," in *Medical and Surgical Report of the Children's Hospital, 1867–1894*, ed. Thomas M. Rotch and Herbert L. Burrell (Boston: Board of Managers of the Children's Hospital, 1894), p. 4.

22. Children's Hospital, *3rd Annual Report, 1871*, pp. 7–8. Quoted in Morris J. Vogel, *The Invention of the Modern Hospital* (Chicago: University of Chicago Press, 1980), p. 24.

23. "The Children's Hospital: What 'Fireside' Thinks about It," *Boston Evening Transcript*, January 22, 1879. Quoted in Vogel, *The Invention of the Modern Hospital*, p. 25.

24. Francis Brown, "The Children's Hospital," p. 5.

25. Early dispensaries and hospitals for children in Britain and Europe included the Dispensary for the Infant Poor in London (1769), the Vienna Clinic (1787), *Hôpital des Enfant Malades* in Paris (1802), the Royal Infirmary for Sick Children in London (1816), St. Anne's Children's Hospital of Vienna (1837), The Hospital for Sick Children in Great Ormond Street, London (1852). In the decade of 1850, additional hospitals for children were established in Paris, Ludwigsburg, Leipzig as well as other European cities. Radbill, "A History of Children's Hospitals," pp. 414–415; Garrison, "History of Pediatrics," pp. 120–121. According to Joseph Stokes, the founding of the Children's Hospital of Philadelphia was stimulated by the Great Ormond Street Hospital in London. Joseph Stokes, Jr., "The Children's Hospital of Philadelphia—100 Years," *Pediatrics*, 16, 5 (1955): 693. On the early nineteenth-century pediatric literature consult Abraham Jacobi (1904), "The History of Pediatrics and Its Relation to Other Sciences and Arts," in *Collectanea Jacobi*, ed. William J. Robinson,

8 vols. (New York: Critic and Guide Co., 1909), 1: 55–93; Isaac A. Abt, "The Influence of Pathology on the Development of Pediatrics," *American Journal of Diseases of Children*, 34, 1 (1927): 17–19.

26. From *A Statement made by Four Physicians In Reference to the Establishment of a Children's Hospital in the City of Boston*. Quoted in Clement A. Smith, *The Children's Hospital of Boston* (Boston: Little, Brown, 1983), p. 17.

27. The earliest of these institutions were devoted to eye and ear disorders and were located in New York, Philadelphia, Boston, and Baltimore. Rosen, *The Specialization of Medicine*, pp. 33–34.

28. Rosen argues that work by French clinical pathologists undermined the unitary concept of disease that had dominated medical thinking and pointed to the existence of many distinct disease processes affecting discrete organs or regions of the body. Rosen, *The Specialization of Medicine*, pp. 14–30.

29. Charles E. Rosenberg, "Social Class and Medical Care in Nineteenth-Century America: The Rise and Fall of the Dispensary," *Journal of the History of Medicine and Allied Sciences*, 29, 1 (1974): 37. On the spread of specialized dispensaries also see Charles E. Rosenberg, "The Hospital in America: A Century's Perspective," in *Medicine and Society: Contemporary Medical Problems in Historical Perspective*, ed. American Philosophical Society Library (Philadelphia: American Philosophical Society Library, 1971), p. 186; Charles Rosenberg, "The Practice of Medicine in New York a Century Ago," *Bulletin of the History of Medicine*, 41, 3 (1967): 248.

30. Departmentalization of general hospitals took place first in outpatient clinics; once a specialty established itself there, it might later acquire inpatient beds. See Morris Vogel, *The Invention of the Modern Hospital*, pp. 88–92; Charles E. Rosenberg, "Inward Vision and Outward Glance: The Shaping of the American Hospital, 1880–1914," *Bulletin of the History of Medicine*, 53, 3 (1979): 370.

31. The budget of the District of Columbia hospital is from Edith A. Torkington and Hope Isherwood, "History of Children's Hospital of the District of Columbia," *Clinical Proceedings, Children's Hospital, Washington, D.C.*, 26, 6 (1970): 201. Abraham Jacobi provides information on expenditures of Nursery and Child's Hospital in "Inaugural Address, Including a Paper on Infant Asylum Foundlings," in *Collectanea Jacobi*, ed. William J. Robinson, 8 vols. (New York: Critic and Guide Co., 1909), 7: 39. Jacobi delivered this address to the Medical Society of the County of New York in 1872. On the internal organization of children's hospitals consult Torkington and Isherwood, "History of Children's Hospital," pp. 200–212 and Francis Brown, "The Children's Hospital," pp. 3–20.

32. Rosenberg, "The Hospital in America," p. 185. For additional comments on the role of hospitals in nineteenth-century medical careers see Rosenberg, "Social Class and Medical Care," pp. 39–41; Rosenberg, "The Practice of Medicine in New York," p. 227.

33. Job Lewis Smith, "Presidential Address," *Transactions of the American Pediatric Society,* 2 (1890): 7.

34. Two sisters of one of its physician founders provided initial financial support for Philadelphia's Children's Hospital. Samuel X. Radbill, "The Children's Hospital of Philadelphia," *Proceedings of the XXIII International Congress of the History of Medicine,* 2 (1972): 1061. A Chicago matron established The Maurice Porter Memorial Hospital for Children (now Children's Memorial Hospital of Chicago) in 1882. Ronald D. Greenwood, "A Children's Hospital in Chicago, 1882–1904," *Illinois Medical Journal,* 146, 5 (1974): 448. An all-female Board of Directors managed the Pacific Dispensary for Women and Children (later Children's Hospital of San Francisco) from the time of its founding in 1875. Adelaide Brown, "The History of the Children's Hospital in Relation to Medical Women," Undated typescript. The Californiana Collection, Special Collections, The Library, University of California, San Francisco. Also see comments by Kathleen W. Jones, "Sentiment and Science: The Late Nineteenth Century Pediatrician as Mother's Advisor," *Journal of Social History,* 17 (1983): 81 and n. 11.

35. On the exclusion of female doctors from hospital posts see Mary Roth Walsh, *"Doctors Wanted: No Women Need Apply"* (New Haven: Yale University Press, 1977), p. 221, and Barbara J. Harris, *Beyond Her Sphere: Women and Professions in American History* (Westport, Conn.: Greenwood, 1978), p. 108. In response to this situation, women physicians initiated their own hospitals to provide opportunities for developing skills and for practicing hospital-based medicine. The Female Medical College in New York City established an Infirmary for Women and Children in 1953. Samuel X. Radbill, "Hospitals and Pediatrics, 1776–1976," *Bulletin of the History of Medicine,* 52, 2 (1979): 289. Physician Marie Zakrzewsha founded the New England Hospital for Women and Children in 1862. Walsh, *"Doctors Wanted: No Women Need Apply,"* p. 84. Doctor Mary Thompson initiated the founding of Chicago Hospital for Women and Children (later The Mary Thompson Hospital) in 1865. Greenwood, "A Children's Hospital in Chicago, 1882–1904," p. 448. Two female physicians established the Pacific Dispensary for Women and Children in 1875. This institution became the Children's Hospital and Training School for Nurses in 1885 and later the Children's Hospital of San Francisco. Adelaide Brown, "The History of the Children's Hospital in Relation to Medical Women." Drs. Sarah and Julia McNutt established Babies Hospital of the City of New York in 1887. Jones, "Senti-

ment and Science: The Late Nineteenth Century Pediatrician as Mother's Advisor," p. 81. The presence of these hospitals raises the possibility that there were women doctors specializing in diseases of children who were not a part of organized pediatrics. Whatever the ultimate verdict on this issue, rosters of the leading nineteenth and early twentieth-century pediatric societies include no women. The American Pediatric Society admitted its first female member in 1928, forty years after its formation. Harold K. Faber and Rustin McIntosh, *History of the American Pediatric Society, 1887–1965* (New York: McGraw-Hill, 1966), p. 69.

36. Smith had chaired the Pediatric Section of the Ninth International Medical Congress held in 1887 in Washington, D.C. Following the Section meeting, a number of physicians held an impromptu meeting at which they developed plans to initiate the APS. On the founding of the APS, consult Faber and McIntosh, *History of the American Pediatric Society*, pp. 7–14.

37. Samuel X. Radbill, "Job Lewis Smith (1827–1897)," *Episteme*, 8, 2–4 (1974): 340–349. Other sources on Smith's career include John Shrady, "Memoir of J. Lewis Smith, M.D.," *Transactions of the New York State Medical Association*, 14 (1897): 524–538; Harold K. Faber, "Job Lewis Smith, Forgotten Pioneer," *Journal of Pediatrics*, 63, 2, pt. 2 (1963): 794–802.

38. Abraham Jacobi, "The Jacobi Anniversary. Address by A. Jacobi," *Pediatrics*, 9, 11 (1900): 457 (cited hereafter as "Anniversary Address"). Fielding H. Garrison, "Dr. Abraham Jacobi (1830–1919)," *Science*, 50, 1283 (1919): 102. Other sources on Jacobi's life include Jerome S. Leopold, "Abraham Jacobi," in *Pediatric Profiles*, ed. Borden S. Veeder (St. Louis: C. V. Mosby, 1967), pp. 13–19; "Abraham Jacobi," in *Dictionary of American Biography*, ed. Dumas Malone (New York: Charles Scribner's, 1961), 5: 563–564. On the founding of the AMA Section, see Frederic W. Schlutz, "The First Half-Century of the Section on Pediatrics," *Journal of the American Medical Association*, 101, 6 (1933): 417.

39. "Louis Starr," *Dictionary of American Biography*, ed. Dumas Malone (New York: Charles Scribner's, 1961), 9: 533; John L. Morse and Charles H. Dunn, "Charles Pickering Putnam," *American Journal of Diseases of Children*, 8, 3 (1914): 249–250. On Busey's activities, consult Torkington and Isherwood, "History of Children's Hospital of the District of Columbia," p. 200.

40. Among the remaining APS founders, there were six from Philadelphia, three from Boston, three from Baltimore, two from Washington, and two from Chicago. The other six were from Jersey City, St. Louis, Cincinnati, Ann Arbor, and Canadian cities. Faber and McIntosh, *History*

of the American Pediatric Society, p. 351. New York City abounded with institutions and units for children. By the early 1900s there were, according to one estimate, sixty-four hospitals "devoting some space to the medical and surgical diseases of children" and thirteen asylums for infants and young children. Henry Dwight Chapin, "New York as a Pediatric Center," *American Journal of Obstetrics and Diseases of Women and Children,* 75 (1917): 180. (Originally read to the pediatric section of the New York Academy of Medicine.) The other cities, virtually without exception, had well-established hospitals or hospital units for children.

41. APS *Transactions* of the late 1880s and 1890s have abundant references to institutional appointments and work within children's hospitals and asylums.

42. A number of the early children's hospitals—for example, those in Philadelphia and Boston—excluded youngsters under two.

43. Estimates of foundlings in New York City are from a letter written by the Medical Board of Infant's Hospital to the Commissioners of Public Charities and Corrections. This letter is reproduced by Jacobi in "Inaugural Address," p. 62.

44. J. Lewis Smith, "Recent Improvements in Infant Feeding," *Transactions of the American Pediatric Society,* 1 (1889): 87; Radbill, "Job Lewis Smith," p. 349.

45. The hospital's inmates included neonates and infants as well as children between two and ten years of age. Jacobi made a number of different calculations of the mortality rates at this institution. See Abraham Jacobi, "In Re the Nursery and Child's Hospital," in *Collectanea Jacobi,* ed. William J. Robinson, 8 vols. (New York: Critic and Guide Co., 1909), 8: 33–34; and Jacobi, "Inaugural Address," pp. 42–44, 54. Two decades later, the prognosis for hospitalized infants was still very poor. Luther Emmett Holt estimated that among 1200 children under one year of age admitted to Babies Hospital in New York City during a seven-year period in the decade of 1890, mortality ran at 50 percent. L. Emmett Holt, "The Scope and Limitations of Hospitals for Infants," *Transactions of the American Pediatric Society,* 10 (1898): 154. John Duffy reports mortality rates within foundling homes of the 1890s that are as high as those during the 1870s. Duffy, *A History of Public Health in New York City, 1866–1966* (New York: Russell Sage Foundation, 1974), pp. 462–463.

46. The New York Foundling Asylum was reorganized to include a maternity ward that supplied wet nurses. Smith, "Recent Improvements in Infant Feeding," p. 87. Also see Radbill, "Job Lewis Smith," p. 349. Jacobi objected to combining infant wards and obstetric units during the early 1870s. He argued that in hospitals with such arrangements, puer-

peral diseases infecting women quickly spread to the infants. Jacobi, "Inaugural Address," p. 33.

47. In the course of his efforts, Jacobi was fired from his appointment at Nursery and Child's Hospital. His conflicts with the institution's managers are chronicled in "In Re the Nursery and Child's Hospital," pp. 11–42. The State Medical Society set up a committee to investigate conditions in contemporary foundling homes and this group concurred with Jacobi that the best solution was to place infants in private homes. Duffy, *A History of Public Health in New York City, 1866–1966,* pp. 209–210. Boarding out foundlings was common practice before the appearance of infant asylums. For the details of Jacobi's objections to placing foundlings in institutions see "Inaugural Address." On the consequences of his position for the creation of infant asylums in other cities see comments by E. E. Graham, *Transactions of the American Pediatric Society,* 20 (1908): 149. Later pediatricians designed boarding-out programs for dependent infants. Henry D. Chapin describes one such program in "A Plan of Dealing with Atrophic Infants and Children," *Transactions of the American Pediatric Society,* 20 (1908): 138–144, 150. Writing in the 1930s, Joseph Brennemann says of Chapin: "Some years ago he told me he was devoting the rest of his life to making up for the wrong he had committed in sending babies to infant wards." Brennemann, "Periods in the Life of the American Pediatric Society: Adolescence, 1900–1915," *Transactions of the American Pediatric Society,* 50 (1938): 63.

48. On the prevalence of clinical case studies among the publications of first-generation child specialists, see Brennemann, "Periods in the Life of the American Pediatric Society," p. 56.

49. Ibid., p. 63. Brennemann comments both on efforts by early pediatricians to reduce mortality among institutionalized foundlings and on the origins of research on infant feeding. "The contribution of the crowded infant wards and foundlings homes to the appalling sum total of infant mortality was stressed again and again by [Jacobi and his colleagues]. It was here that infant feeding was at its nadir, and yet it was largely here that the solution of the problem was sought."

50. Shrady, "Memoir of J. Lewis Smith," pp. 536–538; Brennemann, "Periods in the Life of the American Pediatric Society," p. 56.

51. Jacobi, "An Address on the Claims of Paediatric Medicine," *Transactions of the American Medical Association,* 31 (1880): 711. But the situation was to change quite rapidly; only twenty years later, Jacobi acknowledged that "there are even those who restrict their practice to infants and children." Abraham Jacobi, "Anniversary Address," p. 459.

52. Early specialty associations in the United States are discussed by

George Rosen, "Special Medical Societies in the United States after 1865," *Ciba Symposium,* 9, 9 (1947): 791; Rosemary Stevens, *American Medicine and the Public Interest* (New Haven: Yale University Press, 1971), p. 46; William G. Rothstein, *American Physicians in the Nineteenth Century* (Baltimore: Johns Hopkins University Press, 1972), p. 213. The existence of a pediatric section in Germany could also have spurred the founding of pediatric associations in America. Isaac Abt, writing in the late 1920s, states that a section for diseases of children was established within the German National Medical Society in 1868. But if the first generation of American pediatricians was aware of the existence of this section, there is no mention of it in their publications. Jacobi refers to a "Gesellschaft für Kinderheilkunde connected with the German Gesellschaft der Aerzte and Naturforscher." But he states that the German pediatric section was founded in 1883, several years after the formation of the AMA pediatric section. Abt, "The Influence of Pathology on the Development of Pediatrics," (1927), p. 17; Jacobi, "The History of Pediatrics and Its Relation to Other Sciences and Arts," p. 60. Also see Isaac A. Abt, "A Survey of Pediatrics during the Past 100 Years, *Illinois Medical Journal,* 77, 5 (1940): 487–488. "When asked in his later life how the organization of the [AMA] Section came about, Jacobi had this to say. 'There is no history, we just did it. It was a clear case of spontaneous generation. The Section was in the air and we were present when it condensed.' " Schlutz, "The First Half-Century of the Section on Pediatrics," p. 417.

53. Rosen, *The Specialization of Medicine,* pp. 71–72; Rosenberg, "The Practice of Medicine in New York," pp. 247–249.

54. Paul Starr comments on the nineteenth-century elite physicians, the origins of their status, and their relation to contemporary professional reform in *The Social Transformation of American Medicine* (New York: Basic Books, 1982), pp. 81–92.

55. On tensions within the AMA surrounding policies toward specialization see Stevens, *American Medicine,* pp. 44–46; Rothstein, *American Medicine in the Nineteenth Century,* pp. 211–212; Donald E. Konold, *A History of American Medical Ethics, 1847–1912* (Madison: State Historical Society of Wisconsin, 1962), pp. 34–36. The AMA established its first scientific sections in 1959 but these were not an endorsement of specialization. The sections were mandated to consider purely intellectual concerns, not matters related to professional practice. Stevens, *American Medicine,* pp. 44–45. Conflict between the scientific elite and AMA leadership came to a head during the mid-1880s over the planning of the Ninth International Medical Congress to be held in Washington, D.C. in 1887. An organizing committee appointed by the Congress wanted the meeting's officers to be

appointed on the basis of scientific distinction, while the AMA insisted upon other criteria including geographical representation and conformity with AMA ethical codes. On disputes over the International Medical Congress and the subsequent organization of the Association of American Physicians and Congress of American Physicians and Surgeons, see James H. Means, *The Association of American Physicians* (New York: McGraw-Hill, 1961), pp. 23–29; Konold, *A History of American Medical Ethics*, pp. 34, 39–40. As mentioned earlier, the American Pediatric Society was organized following the meeting of the Congress' pediatric section.

56. Rosen discusses variants of opposition to specialization and changes in the nature of opposition over time in "Changing Attitudes to Medical Specialization," in *The Specialization of Medicine*, pp. 49–72. On hostility toward specialization in the early nineteenth century consult Daniel H. Calhoun, *Professional Lives in America, Structure and Aspirations, 1750–1850* (Cambridge: Harvard University Press, 1965), pp. 20–58.

57. On the functions of specialty and scientific associations for the medical elite consult Rothstein, *American Physicians in the Nineteenth Century*, pp. 198–216. Gilb points out that exclusive occupational associations were common among American professions during the late nineteenth century. Corinne L. Gilb, *Hidden Hierarchies: The Professions and Government* (New York: Harper and Row, 1966), pp. 30–32.

58. Rosenberg, "The Practice of Medicine in New York," pp. 227–228; Rothstein, *American Physicians in the Nineteenth Century*, p. 204.

59. Rothstein, *American Physicians in the Nineteenth Century*, pp. 214–216. Stevens, *American Medicine*, p. 53–54.

60. Faber and McIntosh, *History of the American Pediatric Society*, p. 8.

61. Jacobi went on to become president of the New York State Medical Society, the New York Academy of Medicine (1885–1889), and the American Medical Association (1912–1913). "Abraham Jacobi," in *Dictionary of American Biography*, p. 564; Jerome S. Leopold, "Abraham Jacobi," p. 17; S. Adolphus Knopf, "A Tribute to Abraham Jacobi," *New York Medical Journal*, 10 (1919): 115.

62. Osler and Vaughan were both charter members of the APS. Faber and McIntosh, *History of the American Pediatric Society*, p. 351. In 1888, Osler was studying cerebral palsies of children and writing a chapter on neurological disorders for John M. Keating, ed., *Cyclopaedia of the Diseases of Children*, 4 vols. (Philadelphia: J. B. Lippincott, 1889–90). Harvey Cushing (1925), *The Life of Sir William Osler*, in one volume (London: Oxford University Press, 1940), p. 291. On Vaughan's professional biography consult "Victor C. Vaughan," in *Dictionary of American Biography*, ed. Dumas Malone (New York: Charles Scribner's, 1928–36), 19: 236–237.

63. Thomas M. Rotch, "Iconoclasm and Original Thought in the Study of Pediatrics," *Transactions of the American Pediatric Society*, 3 (1891): 7. This paper was delivered to the APS as a presidential address.

64. *Pediatrics* ceased publication in 1913. Another journal of the same title (still published today) was initiated in 1948. A listing of major pediatric journals with dates of origin is found in the *American Journal of Diseases of Children*, 130, 7 (1976): 746. On the founding of *Archives of Pediatrics* consult R. L. Duffus and L. Emmett Holt, Jr., *L. Emmett Holt* (New York: D. Appleton-Century, 1940), p. 93. Publications dedicated to children's disorders were preceded by a *American Journal of Obstetrics and Diseases of Women and Children* created in 1869. Pediatric journals appeared somewhat earlier in Europe than in the United States. Jacobi reports that in Germany a *Journal für Kinderkrankheiten* was established in 1843. Abraham Jacobi, "Introduction," *American Journal of Diseases of Children*, 1, 1 (1911): 4.

65. "Such impetus as [the APS] can give to the profession at large in the direction of special research, such power as it can exert on the instruction in pediatrics of students in the medical schools, such influence as it may have among the wealthy public with a view to establish and endow special hospitals for infants and children, while proving beneficial to all branches of medicine, will be a lasting blessing to the community." Jacobi, "The Relations of Pediatrics to General Medicine," p. 17.

66. Jacobi, "Anniversary Address," p. 458.

67. Jacobi's role in the history of pediatrics is open to misinterpretation. Edwards Park, chairman of pediatrics at Johns Hopkins from 1927 to 1946 and a man central to the institutionalization of modern pediatric research, comments on Jacobi's contribution. Park writes: "Abraham Jacobi was the pioneer. He was a man of remarkable personality, far better educated medically and culturally, when he came to this country from Austria, than his American colleagues. He had great influence in raising the level of American medicine, particularly in New York City. But in pediatrics, so far as I can tell, his merit is limited to his having been a pioneer. He was the first, I might say, officer, to wear the pediatric uniform. If he left a permanent imprint on pediatrics, I do not know what it is." Edwards A. Park, "John Howland Award Address," *Journal of Pediatrics*, 10, 1 (1952): 107. Jacobi did leave a permanent mark, but it was ideological and normative rather than scientific. Much of the pediatrics' present-day professional ethos had its roots in the papers Jacobi wrote during the 1880s and 1890s. Jacobi had tremendous facility in articulating occupational norms and values. This ability is best understood as an organizational skill.

68. Abraham Jacobi, "An Address on the Claims of Paediatric Medicine," pp. 712–713.

69. Abraham Jacobi. "The Relations of Pediatrics to General Medicine," *Transactions of the American Pediatric Society*, 1 (1889): 15–17.

70. Ibid., pp. 7–8; Abraham Jacobi, "Introductory," in *Cyclopaedia of the Diseases of Children*, ed. John M. Keating, 4 vols. (Philadelphia: J. B. Lippincott, 1889–90), 1: 2.

71. Jacobi, "The Relations of Pediatrics to General Medicine," p. 14.

72. Borden Veeder, "The Place of Pediatrics in the Organization of a Medical School," *Transactions of the Association of American Teachers of the Diseases of Children*, 10 (1916): 37.

73. Borden Veeder, "The Trend of Pediatrics," *Transactions of the American Child Health Organization*, 1 (1923): 315.

74. Jacobi, "The Relations of Pediatrics to General Medicine," p. 8.

75. Ibid., p. 16.

76. William Osler, "Remarks on Specialism," *Transactions of the American Pediatric Society*, 4 (1892): 9–10. Emphasis in the original. This was a president's address to the APS.

77. Jacobi also spoke of "superficiality and wantonness displayed in the constant new formation of specialists in practice." Jacobi, "An Address on the Claims of Paediatric Medicine," pp. 710, 709. See, also, Jacobi, "Introductory," p. 1. During the 1860s and 1870s, *specialist* could be used as a term of derision, a fact that explains an anecdote told about Job Lewis Smith. Upon being referred to by the title, Smith is reported to have replied, "Yes, perhaps a specialist, but I trust something more." John Shrady, "Memoir of J. Lewis Smith," *Transactions of the New York State Medical Association*, 14 (1897): 528.

78. Jacobi, "An Address on the Claims of Paediatric Medicine," pp. 709–710.

79. Jacobi, "Anniversary Address," p. 459.

80. On pediatrics as a branch of general medicine rather than a specialty, see remarks by Henry D. Chapin, Alexander Blackader, and Alfred Cotton, *Transactions of the American Pediatric Society*, 5 (1893): 12–13, 15; Augustus Caillé, "The Influence of American Pediatric Societies in Promoting the Welfare of American Children," *Transactions of the American Pediatric Society*, 3 (1904): 7. The latter was a presidential address to the APS.

81. Jacobi, "An Address on the Claims of Paediatric Medicine," p. 711; Jacobi, "Anniversary Address," p. 459.

82. Hagstrom distinguishes internal and external functions of disci-

plinary ideologies. Warren O. Hagstrom, *The Scientific Community* (New York: Basic Books, 1965), p. 212. Gilb discusses the importance of professional ideology for "buttressing group identity" in *Hidden Hierarchies,* p. 69.

83. Jacobi was referring to publications not just in the United States but to those in Britain and Western Europe as well. See Jacobi, "The History of Pediatrics and Its Relation to Other Sciences and Arts," p. 60.

4. Autonomy within American Medical Schools

1. Fielding H. Garrison (1923), "History of Pediatrics," in *Abt-Garrison History of Pediatrics,* ed. Arthur F. Abt (Philadelphia: W. B. Saunders, 1965), pp. 121–122; Thomas E. Cone, Jr., "The History of Pediatric Ambulatory Services," in *Ambulatory Pediatrics,* ed. Morris Green and Robert J. Haggerty (Philadelphia: W. B. Saunders, 1968), pp. 11–13; Samuel X. Radbill, "A History of Children's Hospitals," *American Journal of Diseases of Children,* 90, (1955): 416. Fielding Garrison gives the impression that something on the order of thirty children's hospitals had been established by 1900. The number continued to grow during the early twentieth century. A White House Conference report indicated that seventy children's hospitals were in existence by 1930. White House Conference on Child Health and Protection, Subcommittees on Hospitals and Dispensaries, and on Convalescent Care and Medical Social Service, *Hospitals and Child Health* (New York: Century, 1932), p. 23.

2. On children's wards in Cleveland's hospitals, see Frederick G. Waite, *Western Reserve University Centennial History of the School of Medicine* (Cleveland: Western Reserve University Press, 1946), pp. 255–257. On those in Chicago, consult Isaac A. Abt, "A Survey of Pediatrics during the Past 100 Years," *Illinois Medical Journal,* 77, 5 (1940): 492. Inpatient departments for children within general hospitals became genuinely widespread during the late nineteenth and early twentieth centuries. Some additional examples are the children's ward started at Cleveland's Lakeside Hospital when that institution opened in 1898 and the children's department at the University of Pennsylvania Hospital begun in 1900. In Boston, special inpatient units opened at Massachusetts General Hospital, Boston City Hospital, and the Boston Dispensary in 1910, 1922, and 1909, respectively. Waite, *Western Reserve University,* pp. 255–256; George W. Corner, *Two Centuries of Medicine: A History of the School of Medicine, University of Pennsylvania* (Philadelphia: J. B. Lippincott, 1965), p. 186; John L. Morse, "The History of Pediatrics in Massachusetts," *New England Journal of Medicine,* 205, 4 (1931): 177–178.

3. Edith A. Torkington and Hope Isherwood, "History of Children's Hospital of the District of Columbia," *Clinical Proceedings, Children's Hospital, Washington, D.C.*, 26, 6 (1970): 200–204. The early development of children's hospitals in Boston, Philadelphia, and Chicago followed a similar course regarding hospital beds, facilities, and staff composition. See, for example, Francis H. Brown, "The Children's Hospital," in *Medical and Surgical Report of the Children's Hospital, 1869–1894*, ed. Thomas M. Rotch and Herbert L. Burrell (Boston: Board of Managers of the Children's Hospital, 1895), pp. 3–20; Thomas M. Rotch, "Children's Hospital of Boston, 1869–1914: The Development of the Hospital with Especial Reference to the Medical Service," *Boston Medical and Surgical Journal*, 170, 14 (1914): 483–485; Joseph Stokes, Jr., "The Children's Hospital of Philadelphia—100 Years," *Pediatrics*, 16, 5 (1955): 683–687; Samuel X. Radbill, "The Children's Hospital of Philadelphia," *Philadelphia Medicine*, 70 (1974): 351–367; Ronald D. Greenwood, "A Children's Hospital in Chicago, 1882–1904," *Illinois Medical Journal*, 146, 5 (1974): 448–450.

4. "A List of the Officers and Others Connected with the Hospital from its Organization," in *Medical and Surgical Report of the Children's Hospital, 1869–1894*, ed. Thomas M. Rotch and Herbert L. Burrell (Boston: Board of Managers of the Children's Hospital, 1895), pp. 21–25.

5. Corner, *Two Centuries of Medicine*, pp. 176–178. At Western Reserve in the late 1870s, diseases of children was taught with obstetrics while gynecology had a separate chair. Waite, *Western Reserve University*, p. 141.

6. Abraham Jacobi, "History of Pediatrics in New York," *Archives of Pediatrics*, 34, 1 (1917): 8–10; Samuel X. Radbill, "Job Lewis Smith (1827–1897)," *Episteme*, 8, 2–4 (1974): 341–342. Information on the Busey appointment from Francis R. Packard, *History of Medicine in the United States*, 2 vols. (New York: Paul B. Hoeber, 1931), 2: 1183. A few references can be found to special instruction in diseases of children within American medical colleges as early as the 1850s. J. P. Crozer Griffith states that Gunning Bedford taught childhood disorders in a "mixed women's and children's clinic" at the University Medical College in New York City during that decade and Fielding Garrison writes that Jacobi delivered special lectures at Physicians and Surgeons beginning in 1857. Neither man is reported to have held a chair at the time. J. P. Crozer Griffith, "The Rise, Progress and Present Needs of Pediatrics," *Journal of the American Medical Association*, 31, 17 (1898): 949. (Originally a chairman's address to the AMA Section on Diseases of Children.) Fielding H. Garrison, "Dr. Abraham Jacobi (1830–1919)," *Science*, 50, 1283 (1919): 102. Appointments made in the 1850s and 1860s appear to

have been short-lived. Jacobi's chair at New York Medical College terminated in 1864 when the college folded. Smith was a lecturer in diseases of children at Bellevue during the 1860s but left, apparently dissatisfied with the rank of his post. He returned in the mid-1870s when offered a clinical professorship. Jacobi, "History of Pediatrics in New York," p. 10; Radbill, "Job Lewis Smith," pp. 341–342.

7. At both the University of Pennsylvania and Harvard, lectureships or instructorships in pediatrics had existed prior to the creation of positions with professorial rank. A clinical lectureship in diseases of children was established at the latter school as early as 1871. Corner, *Two Centuries of Medicine*, p. 177; "The Department of Pediatrics," in *The Harvard Medical School, 1782–1906* (n.p., n.d.), pp. 145–148.

8. Leslie B. Arey, *Northwestern University Medical School, 1859–1959* (Evanston, Ill.: Northwestern University Press, 1959), p. 473; Thomas N. Bonner, *Medicine in Chicago, 1890–1950* (Madison, Wis.: American History Research Center, 1957), p. 99.

9. Bonner, *Medicine in Chicago*, p. 99; A. McGehee Harvey, "The First Full-Time Academic Department of Pediatrics: The Story of the Harriet Lane Home," *Johns Hopkins Medical Journal*, 137, 1 (1975): 27; Waite, *Western Reserve University*, p. 374.

10. In an additional three schools, the subject was taught by a special appointee but the incumbent did not have professorial rank. Of the remaining colleges, forty-three (37 percent) taught pediatrics in conjunction with another field within medicine. (Presumably, this was indicated by titles such as Professor of Diseases of Women and Children.) Only seven schools failed to announce that pediatrics was included in their curricula. Griffith, "The Rise, Progress and Present Needs of Pediatrics," pp. 949–950.

11. Luther Emmett Holt, a full-scale specialist by the mid-1890s, was a founding member of the APS. But he was just commencing his career at the time. Jacobi and Smith were men in their fifties.

12. On Holt's limiting his practice to pediatrics, see "Luther Emmett Holt," in *The College of Physicians and Surgeons, New York*, ed. John Shrady, 2 vols. (New York: Lewis Publishing, n.d.) 2: 21; Edwards A. Park and Howard H. Mason, "Luther Emmett Holt," in *Pediatric Profiles*, ed. Borden S. Veeder (St. Louis: C. V. Mosby, 1957), p. 35. Other sources on Holt's life include R. L. Duffus and L. Emmett Holt, Jr., *L. Emmett Holt* (New York: D. Appleton-Century, 1940).

13. Charles Rosenberg, "The Practice of Medicine in New York a Century Ago," *Bulletin of the History of Medicine*, 41, 3 (1967): 237.

14. Griffith, "The Rise, Progress and Present Needs of Pediatrics," p. 950. Ten of the twenty-four pediatric professors received no salary. Un-

paid teaching appointments were not unique to pediatrics. According to Griffith, the schools that failed to reimburse pediatrics instructors had uncompensated instructors in other clinical specialties.

15. *Transactions of the American Pediatric Society,* 11 (1899): 21. The remark was made by Samuel Adams, Professor of Pediatrics at Georgetown University.

16. Joseph Brennemann, "Periods in the Life of the American Pediatric Society: Adolescence," *Transactions of the American Pediatric Society,* 50 (1938): 63. Work on infant feeding by turn-of-the-century pediatricians is discussed also by Thomas E. Cone, Jr., *History of American Pediatrics* (Boston: Little, Brown, 1979), pp. 131–148.

17. Brennemann, "Periods in the Life of the American Pediatric Society: Adolescence," p. 65. For an illustration of the percentage method at its fullest, see five pages of equations for calculating percentages in Thomas Morgan Rotch, *Pediatrics, The Hygiene and Medical Treatment of Children,* 4th ed. (Philadelphia: J. B. Lippincott, 1903), pp. 234–239.

18. Abraham Jacobi, "The Gospel of the Top Milk," *Journal of the American Medical Association,* 51, 15 (1908): 1219. Different objections to percentage feeding were raised in David L. Edsall and Charles A. Fife, "Concerning the Accuracy of Percentage Modification of Milk for Infants," *Transactions of the American Pediatric Society,* 15 (1903): 59–75.

19. Edwards A. Park and Howard H. Mason, "Luther Emmett Holt," pp. 45, 47–48. Park was chairman of pediatrics at Yale from 1921 to 1927 and at Johns Hopkins from 1927 to 1946.

20. According to Faber and McIntosh, a paper presented at the American Pediatric Society in 1913 presaged the decline of the percentage method. Harold K. Faber and Rustin McIntosh, *History of the American Pediatric Society, 1887–1965* (New York: McGraw-Hill, 1966), p. 90.

21. Joseph Brennemann, "Pediatric Psychology and the Child Guidance Movement," *Journal of Pediatrics,* 2, 1 (1933): 9. Pediatric research in the modern sense of the term did not begin until the second or third decade of this century when full-time academic departments were created. Men like Park and Brennemann built careers during a period when research standards in the clinical fields were being significantly upgraded from what they had been in the late nineteenth and early twentieth centuries.

22. Kathleen W. Jones, "Sentiment and Science: The Late Nineteenth Century Pediatrician as Mother's Advisor," *Journal of Social History,* 17 (1983): 85–89. The author quotes Holt as stating that "the man who masters [the percentage method] will never lack for patients." Jones, p. 85. Rima Apple also comments on supervision of artificial feeding by pediatri-

cians in private practice in " 'To be Used Only Under the Direction of a Physician': Commercial Infant Feeding and Medical Practice, 1870–1940," *Bulletin of the History of Medicine*, 54, 3 (1980): 402–417.

23. Reliable information does exist on the size of contemporary pediatric societies. There were between fifty and sixty names on the APS roster during the late 1890s but the organization was still restricting its membership. Faber and McIntosh, *History of the American Pediatric Society*, p. 311. Attendance at AMA Section meeting suggests that the number of practicing pediatricians was substantially larger. One hundred seventy-five physicians participated in sessions on diseases of children held in 1895. Frederick W. Schlutz, "The First Half-Century of the Section of Pediatrics," *Journal of the American Medical Association*, 101, 6 (1933): 417. Pediatric Section meetings were open to all AMA members but physicians uninvolved with the treatment of children were not likely to be attracted. It is more probable that attendance gives an underestimation of the total number of practicing pediatricians since only a portion of all child specialists would go to the annual AMA meetings in any given year. However, the majority of contemporary child specialists were still practicing general medicine or obstetrics as well as pediatrics.

24. Kelley sent letters of inquiry to teachers of pediatrics at a large number of medical colleges. One of the questions asked was, "How many practitioners in your city devote their whole attention to pediatrics?" Among forty-six respondents, forty-one answered "none," four indicated that they each knew of one physician who restricted his practice, and one respondent reported that there were eight full-scale specialists in his city. Kelley does not indicate where his respondents were located. Samuel W. Kelley, "Pediatrics; Past, Present and Prospective," *Cleveland Medical Gazette*, 11, 11 (1896): 611.

25. Faber and McIntosh, *History of the American Pediatric Society*, p. 311.

26. Borden S. Veeder, "Trends in Pediatric Education and Practice," *American Journal of Diseases of Children*, 50, 4 (1935): 7.

27. The reorganization of medical training was part of a broader set of institutional reforms that produced the American university in its modern form. See Laurence R. Veysey, *The Emergence of the American University* (Chicago: University of Chicago Press, 1965). On integration of medical and other professional schools into American higher education consult Talcott Parsons, "Professions," in *International Encyclopedia of the Social Sciences*, ed. David L. Sills (New York: Macmillan and the Free Press, 1968) 12: 536–547; Joseph Ben-David, *The Scientist's Role in Society* (Chicago: University of Chicago Press, 1971), pp. 142–146; Donald W. Light, "The Development of Professional Schools in America," in *The*

Transformation of Higher Learning, 1860–1930, ed. Conrad H. Jarausch (Chicago: University of Chicago Press, 1983); Sydney Halpern, "Professional Schools in the American University," in *The Academic Profession: National, Disciplinary, and Institutional Settings*, ed. Burton R. Clark (Berkeley, Los Angeles, London: University of California Press, 1987), pp. 304–330.

28. Corner reports that, in the 1890s, salaried senior clinical faculty at the University of Pennsylvania were earning a third or a fourth of what their predecessors had under the fee system. "However, it must be admitted that the practitioner-professors could tolerate this reduction of income from teaching largely because professors were no longer general practitioners (as their predecessors practically were) but specialists and consultants able to collect large fees." Corner, *Two Centuries of Medicine*, p. 187.

29. Martin Kaufman, "American Medical Education," in *The Educations of American Physicians, Historical Essays*, ed. Ronald L. Numbers (Berkeley, Los Angeles, London: University of California Press, 1980), p. 12.

30. On clinical posts at Bellevue, consult Kaufman, "American Medical Education," p. 12. On those at Physicians and Surgeons, see John Shrady, ed., *The College of Physicians and Surgeons*, 2 vols. (New York: Lewis Publishing, 1900), 1: 121.

31. Frederick C. Shattuck and J. Lewis Bremer, "The Medical School, 1869–1929," in *The Development of Harvard University*, ed. Samuel E. Morison (Cambridge: Harvard University Press, 1930), pp. 566–567. For an account of the creation of specialized teaching posts in Chicago's medical schools, see Bonner, *Medicine in Chicago*, p. 66.

32. Corner, *Two Centuries of Medicine*, p. 138.

33. The first clinics at Physicians and Surgeons actually opened several decades earlier. The number grew during the 1870s as new specialized departments opened. Shrady, ed., *The College of Physicians and Surgeons*, 1: 175, 212–214; Frederic Schiller Lee, "The School of Medicine," in *A History of Columbia University, 1794–1904*, ed. Brander Matthews et al. (New York: Columbia University Press, 1904), p. 333.

34. Abraham Flexner, *Medical Education, A Comparative Study* (New York: Macmillan, 1925), p. 218.

35. "The Department of Pediatrics," *The Harvard Medical School*, pp. 147–150; Park and Mason, "Luther Emmett Holt," pp. 42–43. From the late 1880s, medical students at George Washington and Georgetown universities were being trained on the wards of the Children's Hospital in Washington, D.C. At the Philadelphia Children's Hospital, lectures were routinely conducted for students at the University of Pennsylvania; in the

mid-1880s, the hospital's staff physicians were all associated with the university. Torkington and Isherwood, "History of Children's Hospital of the District of Columbia," p. 202; Radbill, "The Children's Hospital of Philadelphia," p. 355.

36. As mentioned earlier, some schools did have their own hospitals (for example, Bellevue in New York City and the University of Pennsylvania) or outpatient clinics (for instance, New York City's College of Physicians and Surgeons). But these facilities did not provide a full range of clinical material so faculty supplemented with cases encountered at other local institutions.

37. For a description of the influence of local professional politics on appointments at Harvard during the 1890s, see Morris J. Vogel, *The Invention of the Modern Hospital* (Chicago: University of Chicago Press, 1980), pp. 80–82.

38. Flexner complained that even at the University of Pennsylvania, a school that had its own hospital, appointments during the late 1800s and early 1900s were based upon prominence within the local medical community. Flexner, *Medical Education*, p. 217.

39. Ludmerer describes the efforts of academic physicians to establish distinct career tracks and the growing differentiation of careers in research and teaching from those in medical practice. Kenneth M. Ludmerer, *Learning to Heal: The Development of American Medical Education* (New York: Basic Books, 1985), chaps. 6, 11.

40. On opposition to full-time clinical professorships and to scientific criteria as a basis of clinical appointments, see Joseph Ben-David, "Roles and Innovation in Medicine," *American Journal of Sociology*, 65, 5 (1960): 560; Joseph Ben-David, "Scientific Productivity and Academic Organization in Nineteenth Century Medicine," *American Sociological Review*, 25, 6 (1960): 842. In the United States, neither the professionalization of clinical faculty nor university control over hospitals was ever complete. Ludmerer also discusses conflicts between medical academics and medical practitioners over full-time appointments and control of medical training. Ludmerer, *Learning to Heal*, chaps. 6, 11.

41. For example, Washington University established a union with the St. Louis Children's Hospital in 1910. Ludmerer, *Learning to Heal*, p. 220. Boston Children's Hospital became formally affiliated with Harvard in 1912. Joseph C. Aub and Ruth K. Hapgood, *Pioneer in Modern Medicine: David Linn Edsall of Harvard* (Cambridge: Harvard Medical Alumni Association, 1970), p. 122. Ludmerer points out that sentiments about university affiliations for hospitals were becoming favorable in the early 1900s. *Learning to Heal*, pp. 219–220.

42. Dean F. Smiley, "History of the Association of American Medi-

below) during the first decade of the century. James G. Burrow, *Organized Medicine in the Progressive Era* (Baltimore: Johns Hopkins University Press, 1977), pp. 35–37. In 1916, there were a total of sixty-seven schools classified as Class A. Hess, "Pediatric Curriculum in Class A Medical Schools," p. 21.

71. Calculated from data supplied by Richard A. Bolt, "Progress in the Teaching of Preventive Pediatrics in the United States," *Transactions of the Association of American Teachers of the Diseases of Children*, 18 (1924): 38–47.

72. Flexner, *Medical Education*, p. 50. On the initial full-time appointments at Johns Hopkins see Alan M. Chesney, *The Johns Hopkins Hospital and the Johns Hopkins School of Medicine*, 3 vols. (Baltimore: Johns Hopkins University Press, 1963), 3: 243–255. The contribution of private foundations, particularly the Rockefeller General Education Board, to the creation of full-time clinical professorships is discussed by E. Richard Brown, *Rockefeller Medicine Men* (Berkeley, Los Angeles, London: University of California Press, 1979).

73. Julius H. Hess, "A Further Review of the Instruction in Diseases of Children," *Transactions of the Association of American Teachers of the Diseases of Children*, 17 (1923): 15.

74. "Departmentalization of pediatrics stands not only for the recognition of the importance of the subject, but also permits of a better arrangement for administrative purposes." Edgar P. Copeland, "The Standardization of Pediatric Instruction in the Undergraduate Medical Curriculum," *Transactions of the Association of American Teachers of the Diseases of Children*, 12 (1918): 35.

75. Hess continued: "It should be the one endeavor of this society to see that the department of pediatrics is separate from the department of medicine or any other department so that the man at the head may have an idea of just what his budget is going to be." *Transactions of the Association of American Teachers of the Diseases of Children*, 16 (1922): 21.

5. Consolidating the Market for Child-Health Services

1. The other ten clinical specialties were internal medicine, surgery, neuropsychiatry, dermatology and syphilology, ophthalmology, otolaryngology, orthopedic surgery, public health and hygiene, obstetrics and gynecology, and urology. The Council also designated four basic science fields: anatomy, physiology, pharmacology and therapeutics, and pathology-bacteriology. Council on Medical Education and Hospitals, "Background and Development of Residency Review and Conference Committees,"

cal Colleges, 1876–1956," *Journal of Medical Education*, 32, 7 (1957): 516–517.

43. Griffith, "The Rise, Progress and Present Needs of Pediatrics," p. 950. Others were excluded from executive faculties. Alfred C. Cotton describes such a situation at Rush Medical College when he accepted a professorship in diseases of children in 1894. "When I was called to this chair, I dropped the position of professor of *materia medica* and soon realized that there was a string to my new position. I was not invited to the faculty meetings to discuss important matters. I found that I was a member of the faculty, but not of the executive faculty." *Transactions of the American Pediatric Society*, 11 (1899): 24.

44. John Lovett Morse, "The Teaching of Pediatrics," *Journal of the American Medical Association*, 45, 8 (1905): 509.

45. Ibid.

46. According to Harry M. McClanahan, Professor of Pediatrics at the University of Nebraska, the Association "was organized primarily by those of us who attended the meetings of the A.M.A. and could attend this society [the AATDC] by holding the meetings the day before the opening of the [AMA] Children's Section." *Transactions of the Association of American Teachers of the Diseases of Children*, 13 (1919): 37. Samuel Kelley gives a somewhat different, although not necessarily contradictory, account of the AATDC's origins. He states that the organization was first conceived of by John C. Cook—who had previously helped initiate the Chicago Pediatric Society—as "a society of pediatrists in which the membership was to represent all parts of the United States." The notion of making it an association of pediatric teachers was introduced by Kelley himself. Samuel W. Kelley, "Origins and Early Development of the Association of American Teachers of the Diseases of Children," *Transactions of the Association of American Teachers of the Diseases of Children*, 22 (1928): 46–47. The AMA Section had served as a forum for pediatricians who established the AATDC. But because the Section was bound by AMA by-laws, it could not function as a genuine professional association. By the late 1890s, there were local or regional pediatric societies in Chicago, St. Louis, Philadelphia, Ohio, Indiana, New England, and the Central states. But these could not wield as much influence as a national association. On regional pediatric associations consult Garrison, *History of Pediatrics*, pp. 123–124.

47. *Transactions of the American Pediatric Society*, 19 (1907): vi–vii.

48. Kelley, "Origins and Early Development of the Association of American Teachers of the Diseases of Children," pp. 46–47. There were about four APS members among the physicians who established the AATDC.

49. Harry M. McClanahan, "The Advantages of Specializing in Pediatric Practice," *Transactions of the Association of American Teachers of Diseases of Children*, 4 (1910): 11.

50. Samuel W. Kelley, "Report of the Committee on the Teaching of Pediatrics," *Transactions of the Association of American Teachers of Diseases of Children*, 3 (1909): 71.

51. Schlutz, "First Half Century of the Section on Pediatrics," p. 418.

52. *Transactions of the Association of American Teachers of the Diseases of Children*, 4 (1910): 2.

53. Ibid., 10 (1916): 3; *American Association for Study and Prevention of Infant Mortality*, 8, pt. 1 (1917): 17.

54. Posts in all clinical fields including general medicine and surgery were part-time until the decade of 1910. The first full-time salaried appointments in clinical medicine were introduced at Johns Hopkins in 1913. Full-time positions in the preclinical or laboratory specialties had begun to appear in the 1890s.

55. At the University of Pennsylvania, for example, professors in ophthalmology and otology appointed in 1874 were on the staff of the University Hospital but were excluded from the university's medical faculty. "The medical faculty would not grant university status to the teachers of ophthalmology and otolaryngology or, presumably, to teachers of the other specialties—for example, dermatology and clinical neurology—which were then breaking away from general practice. To do so, they said, would trespass on the domain of the existing professorships, which had always included these special topics." Corner, *Two Centuries of Medicine*, p. 140. Corner's explanation for this situation is illuminating. "Reading between the lines of the Minutes [of the Trustees] on this subject, we must suppose that this was a compromise forced on the trustees by the reluctance of the seven professors [of the medical faculty] to permit an increase of their numbers, which would diminish not only their prestige but also their income from students' fees. This was, in fact, the last gasp of the dying fee system as well as of the old, 7-man control (amounting, practically, to ownership) of the medical school through personal influence on the trustees. In a couple of years, a vigorous movement of reform was to result in a general reorganization of faculty and curriculum." Corner, *Two Centuries of Medicine*, p. 139.

56. Quoted by Samuel Kelley in "Pediatrics; Past, Present and Prospective," p. 614. Kelley states that he drew the passage from a letter written to him by Matas.

57. David L. Edsall, "Annual Address of the President, American

Pediatric Society," *Transactions of the American Pediatric Society*, 22 (1910): 11.

58. Ibid., p. 13.

59. In 1919 AASPIM changed its name to the American Child Hygiene Association; in 1923 it merged with the Child Health Organization of America (itself established in 1918) to become the American Child Health Association. The latter organization disbanded in 1935. Philip Van Ingen, "The Story of the American Child Health Association," *Child Health Bulletin*, 11, 5–6 (1935): 149–188.

60. Ira S. Wile, "Do Medical Schools Adequately Train Students for the Prevention of Infant Mortality?" *Transactions of the American Association for Study and Preventions of Infant Mortality*, 1 (1910): 217. Emphasis added.

61. Ibid., pp. 218–219.

62. Borden Veeder, "The Place of Pediatrics in the Organization of a Medical School," *Transactions of the Association of American Teachers of the Diseases of Children*, 10 (1916): 36.

63. Ibid., p. 38.

64. Edsall, "Annual Address of the President," p. 8.

65. According to Ludmerer, Welch was "the most influential spokesman for academic medicine ever in this country." *Learning to Heal*, p. 128.

66. Welch backed improvements in sewerage systems, passage of federal pure food and drug legislation, the establishment of public health agencies at the municipal, state, and federal levels. He was instrumental in the creation of schools of public hygiene within American universities. For more on Welch's activities in the arena of public health, see Simon Flexner and James T. Flexner, *William Henry Welch and the Heroic Age of American Medicine* (New York: Viking Press, 1941), pp. 341–364.

67. William Henry Welch, "Address," *Transactions of the American Association for the Study and Prevention of Infant Mortality*, 1 (1910): 51.

68. *Transactions of the American Association for the Study and Prevention of Infant Mortality*, 1 (1910): 223.

69. See, for example, Charles E. Rosenberg, "Science and American Social Thought," in *Science and American Society*, ed. David Van Tassel and Michael Hall (Homewood, Ill.: Dorsey Press, 1966), pp. 153–154.

70. Julius H. Hess, "The Pediatric Curriculum as Taught in the Class A Medical Schools in the United States," *Transactions of the Association of American Teachers of the Diseases of Children*, 11 (1917): 22. "Class A" was the top rank given by the AMA's Council on Medical Education. This body began inspecting the ranking schools (grades A, B, C, or

Journal of the American Medical Association, 165, 1 (1957): 60; Rosemary Stevens, *American Medicine and the Public Interest* (New Haven: Yale University Press, 1971), pp. 151–154. Stevens comments that "the committees gave official recognition to the separate existence of specialist groups." *American Medicine*, p. 153.

2. Remarks to this effect can be found throughout the publications of contemporary pediatricians and child-health activists. For one discussion of the growth of pediatric practice during this period, see Borden S. Veeder, "Trend of Pediatric Education and Practice," *American Journal of Diseases of Children*, 50, 1 (1935): 2, 6. This paper was a president's address to the American Pediatric Society.

3. Veeder, "Trend of Pediatrics Education and Practice," p. 7. Veeder's statistics were originally drawn from editions of the *American Medical Directory* published by the AMA.

4. U.S. President's Commission on Health Needs of the Nation, *Building America's Health*, 5 vols. (Washington, D.C.: U.S. Government Printing Office, 1952–53), 3: 160, table 208.

5. Data on rates of growth by specialized field is from ibid., 160, table 209. The figures were originally drawn from the Commission on Graduate Medical Education, *Graduate Medical Education* (Chicago: University of Chicago Press, 1940), p. 261, table 9, and from editions of the *American Medical Directory* published by the AMA.

6. The establishment of milk stations in the United States is discussed by Henry Koplik, "The History of the First Milk Depot or Gouttes De Lait with Consultations in America," *Journal of the American Medical Association*, 63, 18 (1914): 1574–1575; Philip Van Ingen, "Recent Progress in Infant Welfare Work," *American Journal of Diseases of Children*, 7, 6 (1914): 476–480; G. F. McCleary, *The Early History of the Infant Welfare Movement* (London: H. K. Lewis, 1933), pp. 54–61; George Rosen, *A History of Public Health* (New York: MD Publications, 1958), pp. 351–356. Rosen also discusses European antecedents.

7. On the transition from milk stations to infant-welfare clinics, consult Van Ingen, "Recent Progress in Infant Welfare Work"; Rosen, *A History of Public Health*, pp. 351–356.

8. Hamilton Cravens describes the change as a shift from reform to scientific professionalism. See Cravens, "Child-Saving in the Age of Professionalism, 1915–1930," in *American Childhood: A Research Guide and Historical Handbook*, ed. Joseph M. Hawes and N. Ray Hiner (Westport, Conn.: Greenwood, 1985), pp. 415–488.

9. The number of units was probably higher. Authors of the study report that some organizations sponsoring numerous separate centers failed to indicate the total number in operation. White House Conference

on Child Health and Protection, Subcommittee on Health Centers, *Child Health Centers: A Survey* (New York: Century, 1932), p. 4.

10. On Chicago's clinics, see comments by Julius H. Hess, *Transactions of the Association of American Teachers of the Diseases of Children,* 17 (1923): 46. Harold C. Stuart describes Boston's child-welfare system in "Pediatric Service in City Health Department Centers Provided by Medical Schools in Boston," *Transactions of the American Child Health Association,* 5 (1928): 89. Centers in Minneapolis and Cleveland are discussed by E. J. Huenekens, "Method of Using Child Welfare Stations in the Teaching of Pediatrics," *Transactions of the Association of American Teachers of the Diseases of Children,* 17 (1923): 44; and Van Ingen, "Infant Welfare Work," p. 477. Sources on New York's welfare clinics include Neva B. Deardorff, "New York City Child Health Work," *Child Health Bulletin,* 6 (1930): 17.

11. Harold C. Stuart, "Progress of Public Health as It Relates to the Child," *Journal of Pediatrics,* 2, 6 (1933): 762.

12. White House Conference, *Child Health Centers,* p. 8. The Conference survey asked separate questions about the agencies overseeing clinic activities and the clinic's principal source of funding. Regarding the latter question, 46 percent of health centers responded "public funds," 22 percent "private funds," and 17 percent "community fund chest." Fourteen percent failed to answer the question. *Child Health Centers,* pp. 9–10.

13. Ibid., p. 24.

14. Ibid., pp. 13–15.

15. Descriptions of child-health conferences can be found in Stuart, "Pediatric Service in City Health Department Centers," pp. 96–97; H. H. Yerington, "Clinical Supervision of the Well Baby During the First Year," *Transactions of the American Medical Association Section on Diseases of Children,* 69 (1918): 71; Borden S. Veeder, *Preventive Pediatrics* (New York: D. Appleton, 1926), pp. 177–179; Edgar J. Huenekens, "Preschool Health Supervision in a Large City by a Voluntary Agency," *Transactions of the American Child Health Association,* 5 (1928): 122–127; H. F. Helmholz and Walter Hoffman, "An Analysis of the Mortality for 1915 in the Infant Welfare Stations of Chicago," *Transactions of the American Medical Association Section on Diseases of Children,* 67 (1916): 333–334.

16. Relevant discussions at the meetings of pediatric societies include H. H. Yerington, "Clinical Supervision of the Well Baby During the First Year"; E. J. Huenekens, "Method of Using Child Welfare Stations in the Teaching of Pediatrics," pp. 44–46; Eli Friedman, "The Value of the Well-Baby and Pre-School Conferences as a Teaching Clinic," *Transactions of the Association of American Teachers of the Diseases of Children,* 23 (1929): 11–16.

17. Frances Sage Bradley and Florence Brown Sherbon, "How to Conduct a Children's Health Conference," U.S. Children's Bureau, pub. no. 23 (Washington, D.C.: U.S. Government Printing Office, 1917). Both authors were physicians.

18. About the activities of the Medical Committee of the American Child Health Association, consult "American Child Health Association Medical Services Division," *Child Health Bulletin*, 3 (1927): 134–138.

19. The field of child development had its roots in the same social and historical forces that engendered pediatric primary care. On the child-study movement of the 1890s and the inception of developmental psychology as a research field in the 1920s, see Dorothy E. Bradbury, "The Contribution of the Child Study Movement to Child Psychology," *Psychology Bulletin*, 34, 1 (1937): 21–38; John E. Anderson, "Child Development: An Historical Perspective," *Child Development*, 27, 2 (1956): 181–196; Cravens, "Child-Saving in the Age of Professionalism," pp. 415–488.

20. George T. Palmer, "Weight and Height as an Index of Nutrition in Infants," *Child Health Bulletin*, 1 (1925): 7; Bird T. Baldwin, "The Use and Abuse of Weight-Height-Age Tables as Indexes of Health and Nutrition," *Journal of the American Medical Association*, 82, 1 (1924): 1–4.

21. George T. Palmer, "The Measurement of Nutritional Status," *Child Health Bulletin*, 6 (1930): 47–50; Harold K. Faber, "A Weight Range Table for Children from 5 to 15 Years of Age," *American Journal of Diseases of Children*, 38, 4 (1929): 768.

22. T. Wingate Todd, "The Developmental Health Exam," *Journal of Pediatrics*, 3, 3 (1933): 416; Anne Whitney, "The Weighing and Measuring of School Children," *Child Health Bulletin*, 6 (1930): 44.

23. Arnold Gesell, "Normal Growth as a Public Health Concept," *Transactions of the American Child Health Association*, 3 (1926): 48.

24. New York: Macmillan.

25. White House Conference on Child Health and Protection, Committee on Growth and Development, *Growth and Development of the Child, Part IV: Appraisement of the Child* (New York: Century, 1932), p. 24. Emphasis in the original.

26. Regarding dissemination of Developmental Record Forms, see *Child Health Bulletin*, 2 (1926): 50. An example of a Developmental Record Form can be found in Veeder, *Preventive Pediatrics*, p. 193. For additional comments on the adoption of developmental standards, see E. J. Huenekens, "The Preschool Child with Especial Reference to its Emotional Life and Habit Problems," *Transactions of the American Medical Association Section on Diseases of Children*, 76 (1925): 27.

27. White House Conference, *Child Health Centers*, p. 28.

28. Stuart, "Pediatric Service in City Health Department Centers," pp. 94–96. In Baltimore, 38 percent of children under six within targeted neighborhoods were registered at public clinics. Allen W. Freeman, "An Infant Welfare Clinic in Baltimore," *Child Health Bulletin*, 7, 5 (1931): 160.

29. Grace L. Meigs, "The Children's Year Campaign," *Transactions of the American Medical Association Section on Diseases of Children*, 69 (1918): 52–53.

30. Philip Van Ingen, "The Story of the American Child Health Association," *Child Health Bulletin* 11, 5–6 (1935): 177.

31. Quoted in ibid., p. 178.

32. Ibid.; Arnold Gesell, "The Pre-School Child's Mental Health: A Radio Talk in Los Angeles, California, July 7, 1925," *Child Health Bulletin*, 1 (1925): 95–97.

33. Remarks by physician William H. Peters, *Transactions of the American Child Health Association*, 5 (1928): 100.

34. Stuart, "Pediatric Service in City Health Department Centers," p. 91.

35. On the educational character of the well-baby conference, see Bradley and Sherbon, "How to Conduct a Children's Health Conference," pp. 3–4.

36. Jones' account suggests that, in the late 1800s, demand for private pediatric consultations on artificial infant feeding was restricted to relatively small numbers of highly affluent women. Kathleen W. Jones, "Sentiment and Science: The Late Nineteenth Century Pediatrician as Mother's Advisor," *Journal of Social History*, 17 (1983): 85–90.

37. Commission on Medical Education, *Second Report* (New Haven, Conn.: Office of the Director of the Study, Jan. 1928), pp. 20–23, 57–58.

38. C. Anderson Aldrich, "The Composition of Private Pediatric Practice," *American Journal of Diseases of Children*, 47, 5 (1934): 1051–1065.

39. Arthur London, Jr., "The Composition of an Average Pediatric Practice," *Journal of Pediatrics*, 10, (1937): 770.

40. After reviewing the available data, one group of researchers suggests that between the mid-1930s and the mid-1950s, care of well children remained a stable 40 percent of pediatric practices. Robert W. Deisher, Alfred J. Derby, and Melvin J. Sturman, "Changing Trends in Pediatric Practice," *Pediatrics*, 25 (1960): 713–714. On well-child care in office-based pediatrics after World War II see my discussion in chap. 7. and n. 14 of chap. 7.

41. In addition to paid employees, 368 centers utilized volunteer physicians. White House Conference, *Child Health Centers*, pp. 13–15.

42. Richard Arthur Bolt, "Progress in the Teaching of Preventive Pediatrics in the United States," *Transactions of the Association of American Teachers of the Diseases of Children*, 18 (1924): 40–41. A copy of the APS course outline can be found in "Report of the Committee on Child Welfare," *Transactions of the American Pediatric Society*, 32 (1920): 11–14. For details on the Society's survey of medical schools, see "Report of Committee on Child Hygiene," *Transactions of the American Pediatric Society*, 33 (1921): 9–10. The APS's findings regarding curriculum on preventive pediatrics are at variance with those of Julius Hess. He surveyed pediatrics departments in 1923 and found only nineteen that offered training in infant hygiene. Julius H. Hess, "A Further Review of the Instruction in Diseases of Children," *Transactions of the Association of American Teachers of the Diseases of Children*, 17 (1923): 20.

43. Unfortunately, Stuart does not elaborate on the teaching functions of this arrangement. "Pediatric Service in City Health Department Centers," pp. 89–94. Coordination with public clinics was not the only option for pediatric departments wishing to initiate practical instruction on child hygiene. Some medical schools ran their own well-baby clinics as part of their pediatric outpatient departments. For more on pediatric departments and child hygiene, see "The Medical School and Child Health," *Transactions of the American Child Health Association*, 4 (1927): 277–306. According to the White House Conference report on welfare centers, instruction of medical students was conducted in 6 percent of urban clinics, instruction of physicians in 12 percent. White House Conference, *Child Health Centers*, p. 19.

44. White House Conference on Child Health and Protection, Report of the Subcommittee on Medical Education, *Pediatrics: Education and Practice* (New York: Century, 1931), pp. 52–62, 89–94.

45. Borden S. Veeder, "Pediatrics and the Child," *Journal of the American Medical Association*, 81, 7 (1923): 518.

46. John A. Foote, "What Should a Teacher of Pediatrics Know of the Psychology of Childhood," *Transactions of the Association of American Teachers of the Diseases of Children*, 17 (1923): 11–12.

47. C. Anderson Aldrich, "Looking Forward in Pediatrics," *Transactions of the American Medical Association Section on Diseases of Children*, 82 (1931): 24.

48. Charles A. Fife, "The Child's Family Advisor," *Transactions of the American Pediatric Society*, 46 (1934): 19.

49. Veeder, *Preventive Pediatrics*, p. 169.

50. Ibid., p. 4.

51. Borden S. Veeder, "Training of the Neurologist, the Neuro-Psychiatrist, and the Pediatrician," *Archives of Neurology and Psychiatry*, 30 (1933): 629; Veeder, *Preventive Pediatrics*, p. 4.

52. "Industrial" occupations predominated in the clientele of 85 percent of the clinics surveyed in 1930. White House Conference, *Child Health Centers*, p. 13.

53. Murray Levine and Adeline Levine, *A Social History of Helping Services* (New York: Appleton-Century-Crofts, 1970), pp. 255–256.

54. *Transactions of the Association of American Teachers of the Diseases of Children*, 17 (1923): 46.

55. Ibid.

56. Authors of the White House Conference report, published in 1932, estimate that urban child-welfare clinics employed more that 1,250 part-time and 240 full-time physicians. *Child Health Centers*, pp. 13–14.

57. Stuart, "Pediatric Service in City Health Department Centers," p. 91.

58. Borden S. Veeder, "Child Hygiene and the Private Physician," *Journal of the American Medical Association*, 79, 27 (1922): 2228–2229. Not all physicians agreed that sick children received no care at the clinics. Henry F. Helmholz of the Mayo Clinic declared that "in ten years' experience of this kind in Chicago, the infractions of all other rules were as nothing compared with the tendency of the physicians in the stations to take care of the sick. In spite of written rules, in spite of constant attention to the fact that they are not allowed to take care of the sick child, it was constantly reported in practically every station that they were taking care of minor ills of the well babies that were coming to the station." *Transactions of the American Child Hygiene Association*, 13 (1922): 214.

59. Huenekens, "Child Welfare Stations in Teaching Pediatrics," pp. 44–45.

60. Calculated from data provided in E. J. Huenekens, "The Well Baby Clinic in the Office of the Family Physician and Pediatrician," *Transactions of the American Child Health Association*, 6 (1929): 142.

61. Marshall C. Pease, *American Academy of Pediatrics* (n.p.: American Academy of Pediatrics, 1952), p. 167. On the Sheppard-Towner Act, see Edward A. Schlesinger, "The Sheppard-Towner Era: A Prototype Case Study in Federal-State Relationships," *American Journal of Public Health*, 57, 6 (1967): 1034–1040.

62. The Academy's debate on the issue of Jones-Bankhead is recorded in "American Academy of Pediatrics, Proceedings of the Second Annual Meetings," *Journal of Pediatrics*, 1, 1 (1932): 126–131. Academy leaders

were constrained from opposing the bill by the realization that a society whose stated purpose was to promote child health could not reject legislation supporting child-health programs without jeopardizing the organization's credibility. "Proceedings of the Second Annual Meetings," p. 128.

63. The Academy's side of the conflict is recounted in Pease, *American Academy of Pediatrics,* pp. 156–164, 175–181.

64. Complaints in the medical press about clinic abuse began in the 1860s and reach a peak during the early decades of the twentieth century. George Rosen, "The Impact of the Hospital on the Physician, the Patient and the Community," *Hospital Administration* 9, 4 (1964): 21–26. Also see Gert H. Brieger, "The Use and Abuse of Medical Charities in Late Nineteenth Century America," *American Journal of Public Health,* 67, 3 (1977): 264–267. On the death of the dispensary during the 1920s consult Charles E. Rosenberg, "Social Class and Medical Care in Nineteenth-Century America: The Rise and Fall of the Dispensary, *Journal of the History of Medicine and Allied Sciences,* 29, 1 (1974): 49–53; Paul Starr, *The Social Transformation of American Medicine* (New York: Basic Books, 1982), pp. 180–184.

65. Rosenberg, "Social Class and Medical Care," p. 50.

66. On the formation of the Academy, see Harold K. Faber and Rustin McIntosh, *History of the American Pediatric Society, 1887–1965* (New York: McGraw-Hill, 1966), pp. 299–301. Specialty leaders used the White House Conference on Child Health and Protection of 1930 to lay groundwork for the organization of the Academy. Reports of the Conference's Section on Medical Services were used as a vehicle to define the domain of pediatrics and assert the need for expansion of child-health supervision. Leaders also built upon the organizational apparatus created by the Conference; the Academy's committee on medical education was originally a Conference subcommittee. Specialty leaders claimed that the Conference provided a mandate for the regulation and continued development of pediatric practice.

67. Isaac A. Abt, "The American Academy of Pediatrics, Its Aim and Its Scope," *American Journal of Diseases of Children,* 42, 4 (1931): 875, 878.

68. Borden S. Veeder and C. A. Aldrich, "Report of the American Board of Pediatrics, Inc.," *American Journal of Diseases of Children,* 51 (1936): 390. Emphasis in the original.

69. For sources on the creation of the pediatric board and its early activities, see ibid.; Faber and McIntosh, *History of the American Pediatric Society,* pp. 306–308; "Report of the Committee on Medical Education for 1933, Proceedings of the American Academy of Pediatrics," *Journal of*

Pediatrics, 2 (1933): 507–508; Borden S. Veeder and C. Anderson Aldrich, "Graduate Education in Pediatrics," *American Journal of Diseases of Children,* 52 (1936): 665–673. For comments on functions of the pediatric board for the specialty, see Stevens, *American Medicine,* pp. 219–222.

70. Pediatricians who had been in practice for more than ten years at the time the Board was created were not required to take the qualifying exam. They were granted certificates through a grandfather clause. Veeder and Aldrich, "Report of the American Board of Pediatrics, Inc.," p. 394.

71. On the formation of residency review committees see Council on Medical Education and Hospitals, "Background and Development of Residency Review and Conference Committees," *Journal of the American Medical Association,* 165, 1 (1957): 60–64.

72. For a list of primary boards and dates of establishment see chapter 2, note 18.

73. American Academy of Pediatrics, "Meeting of the Executive Board, held November 26 and 27, 1932, at Evanston, Illinois," *Journal of Pediatrics,* 2, 1 (1933): 119.

74. Stevens, *American Medicine,* p. 325. The Advisory Board for Medical Specialties was formed in 1933. Stevens discusses its organization and functions on p. 245.

75. Ibid., p. 161.

76. Surgeons initiated a regulatory mechanism in 1913 with the establishment of the American College of Surgeons, an organization modeled after the British Royal Colleges. Admission was restricted to physicians who had a designated amount of experience in surgery and who successfully completed a qualifying examination.

77. Rosen, "The Impact of the Hospital on the Physician, the Patient and the Community," p. 27. For a more extensive analysis of the contemporary medical market see George Rosen, "Medical Science, Professional Control, and the Stabilization of the Medical Market, 1910–1940," in *The Structure of American Medical Practice, 1875–1941,* ed. Charles E. Rosenberg (Philadelphia: University of Pennsylvania Press, 1983), pp. 37–117.

78. Stevens provides an extremely cogent account of options and the course of decision making regarding graduate medical education in *American Medicine,* chaps. 8, 10–11.

79. On the original Council position, see ibid., pp. 153–154; regarding state licensure laws, see p. 165. The possibility that specialty practice might come to be controlled by local AMA chapters or state licensing boards was repeatedly mentioned by pediatricians during discussions on the regulation of specialty practice. See, for example, Abt, "The American

Academy of Pediatrics," p. 876; "Comments," *Journal of Pediatrics*, 1, 4 (1932): 536.

80. Between 1934 and 1940, the number of residency programs doubled and growth accelerated further during World War II. Stevens, *American Medicine*, p. 258. On the boards as arms of specialty societies, see pp. 321–323.

81. For many decades there was an informal system whereby the ten or twelve most prestigious medical schools prepared a very large portion of the country's medical faculty. Stephen J. Miller, *Prescription for Leadership: Training for the Medical Elite* (Chicago: Aldine, 1970), pp. 3–16, 56–89.

82. See chapter 2, note 36.

83. See chapter 1, note 31.

84. Joseph Brennemann, "The Menace of Psychiatry," *American Journal of Diseases of Children* 42, 2 (1931): 384–387.

85. Ibid., p. 388. For more comments in this vein see Joseph Brennemann, "Pediatric Psychology and the Child Guidance Movement," *Journal of Pediatrics* 11, 1 (1933): 16–21.

6. Birth of a Scientific Subspecialty: Pediatric Endocrinology

1. Four segments won boards after 1950: family practice (1969), nuclear medicine (1971), allergy and immunology (1971), and emergency medicine (1976). The latter two are organized conjoint boards sponsored by previously established primary boards. Allergy and immunology was originally constituted as two subspecialties. Internal medicine and pediatrics began certifying candidates in allergy and immunology during the early 1940s. In the early 1970s, after years of agitation, the two sub-boards secured approval for a separate conjoint board.

2. Early subspecialties set up legally incorporated sub-boards. More recent segments have been accommodated through special examining committees which are not legally incorporated. While slightly different in organization, sub-boards and special examining committees are comparable in their operation and functions. On political processes surrounding the establishment of medical sub-boards, see Rosemary Stevens, *American Medicine and the Public Interest* (New Haven: Yale University Press, 1971), pp. 318–347.

3. Examinations in child-related subfields are conducted by several primary boards apart from the ABP. The American Board of Surgery has

offered a certificate in pediatric surgery since 1974. The American Board of Psychiatry and Neurology examines candidates in child psychiatry (begun in 1959) and in neurology with special competence in child neurology.

4. On advances in the field of endocrinology during the 1920s and early 1930s, see Lawson Wilkins, "Presidential Address," *Endocrinology,* 61, 2 (1957): 206–212; Edward A. Park, "Lawson Wilkins," *Journal of Pediatrics* 57, 3 (1960): 319.

5. Joseph Ben-David points out that American professional schools in general institutionalized the pursuit of quasi-disciplinary research. *The Scientist's Role in Society* (Chicago: University of Chicago Press, 1971), pp. 142–145.

6. Joseph Brennemann provides information on subspecialty clinics at Children's Memorial Hospital in Chicago (where he was chief of staff beginning in 1921) in an address delivered to the Association of American Teachers of the Diseases of Children. Brennemann felt that large pediatric dispensaries in teaching hospitals should have special clinics in cardiology, neurology, and psychiatry, (congenital) syphilis, and dermatology. He indicated that there was also a nephritis clinic at Children's Memorial. Brennemann, "The Outpatient Department in the Teaching of Pediatrics," *Transactions of the Association of American Teachers of the Diseases of Children,* 20 (1926): 44. The affiliation between Children's Memorial Hospital and the University of Chicago is recorded in "Board of Trustees, November 11, 1919," Minutes of the University of Chicago Board of Trustees, University of Chicago Archives, Department of Special Collections, University of Chicago Library. Brennemann's appointment at the hospital is documented in the minutes of University of Chicago Board of Trustees meetings held during the 1920s and is discussed in C. Anderson Aldrich, "Joseph Brennemann, 1872–1944," *Proceedings of the Institute of Medicine of Chicago,* 15, 7 (1944): 152.

7. From comments by two of the hospital's physicians: Philip H. Sylvester and Paul W. Emerson. Sylvester states that the neurology and syphilis clinics met a half-day per week, the neurology clinic, twice a week. "The special clinics," he remarks, "are run as an additional load on the backs of the men who are willing to take it. . . . My own clinic, the syphilis clinic, I cannot say is working perfectly but I am beginning to feel that it is worth while." *Transactions of the Associations of American Teachers of the Diseases of Children,* 20 (1926): 47–48.

8. The Yale dispensary was open all day; acute and general patients were seen in the mornings with the special clinics meeting in the afternoons. According to Grover F. Powers, chairman of the Yale department after Park, his predecessor's organization of the dispensary was a substantial innovation. "Neither the all-day outpatient session nor the allocation

of special periods to sick and to general patients on the one hand and to those with previously diagnosed chronic or subacute diseases on the other . . . were procedures currently practiced in institutions of that day." Grover F. Powers, "Edwards A. Park, Yale Professor, 1921–1927," *Journal of Pediatrics*, 41, 6 (1952): 654–656. For another account of the Yale clinic, see Edwards A. Park, "The Appointment System in the New Haven Dispensary," *The Modern Hospital*, 19, 2 (1922): 165–168.

9. Francis F. Schwentker, "Dr. Park as a Teacher," *Journal of Pediatrics*, 41, 6 (1952): 639. Some of the early specialized clinics were more strongly geared toward patient care and teaching than toward clinical investigation. Contemporary pediatric chairmen identified size as one factor influencing a clinic's orientation toward research. Powers writes: "Dr. Park once told the author early in their New Haven careers that the Yale service was too small to be as valuable as are larger services in evaluating therapy but served well as a basis for developing ideas on disease and child care." Powers, "Edwards A. Park, Yale Professor," p. 653.

10. Accounts of the Hopkins pediatric department under Howland include Edwards A. Park, "John Howland Award Address," *Journal of Pediatrics*, 10, 1 (1952): 84–108; A. McGehee Harvey, *Science at the Bedside* (Baltimore: Johns Hopkins University Press, 1981), pp. 159–166; A. McGehee Harvey, "The First Full-Time Academic Department of Pediatrics: The Story of the Harriet Lane Home," *Johns Hopkins Medical Journal*, 137, 1 (1975): 29–40. Fourteen young physicians who worked under Howland went on to become pediatric department chairmen. On these men, consult L. Emmett Holt, Jr., "John Howland: Turning Point of American Pediatrics," *Journal of Pediatrics*, 69, 5, pt. 2 (1966): 874; Edwards A. Park, "John Howland—1873–1926," *Science*, 64, 1647 (1926): 83.

11. Howland had studied in Strasbourg with Czerny before assuming his post at Johns Hopkins. Park, "John Howland Award Address," p. 88.

12. Ibid., pp. 91–92.

13. On Park's chairmanship at Hopkins, consult Schwentker, "Dr. Park as a Teacher." (Schwentker followed Park as head of the Hopkins pediatric department.) See also A. McGehee Harvey, "The First Full-Time Academic Department of Pediatrics," pp. 40–42; Helen B. Taussig, "Dr. Edwards A. Park: Physician, Teacher, Investigator, Friend," *Johns Hopkins Medical Journal*, 132, 6 (1973): 371–376.

14. Taussig reports on opposition to Park's initiation of specialized clinics. "Dr. Edwards A. Park," p. 374. Joseph Brennemann suggests one reason why objections may have been raised. He states: "If there are too many special clinics those who have none are deprived of the benefit of

seeing such cases and their material is limited." See his "The Out-Patient Department in the Teaching of Pediatrics," p. 43.

15. Park fostered the careers of his subordinates. Lawson Wilkins states that Park "always fathered all the young pediatricians with whom he came in contact, inspiring them, even goading them, to keep up their interest in new advances." Lawson Wilkins, "Acceptance of the Howland Award," *Journal of Pediatrics,* 63, 4, pt. 2 (1963): 809. Schwentker writes: "Without knowing all of [Park's] students, I count seventeen who now head departments of pediatrics in teaching hospitals or hold equivalent positions." In "Dr. Park as a Teacher," p. 640.

16. Wilkins, "Acceptance of the Howland Award," p. 809.

17. "Mention has already been made of his ability to see potential opportunities in new fields. It was because of this that he was able to guide so many of his students into successful careers in different areas of medical knowledge. He [was] always . . . on the alert for new ideas. When one came to him he presented it to a colleague or junior member of his department. He played a major role in the initiation of the work which led to the development of the operative measures for the relief of the tetralogy of Fallot." Schwentker, "Dr. Park as a Teacher," pp. 639–640.

18. Park, "Lawson Wilkins," p. 319.

19. Harvey, *Science at the Bedside,* pp. 254–257, 375–380.

20. Harvey, "The First Full-Time Academic Department of Pediatrics," p. 44.

21. Two books published in the early 1950s helped delineate the field of pediatric endocrinology: Lawson Wilkins, *The Diagnosis and Treatment of Endocrine Disorders in Childhood and Adolescence* (Springfield, Ill.: Charles C. Thomas, 1950) and Nathan B. Talbot et al., *Functional Endocrinology from Birth through Adolescence* (Cambridge: Harvard University Press, 1952). On Wilkins' work in pediatric endocrinology, see Park, "Lawson Wilkins," p. 320; Harvey, "The First Full-Time Academic Department of Pediatrics," pp. 43–44; Alfred M. Bongiovanni, "Lawson Wilkins: Memorial (1894–1963)," *Journal of Clinical Endocrinology and Metabolism,* 24, 1 (1964): 2.

22. From data collected by Julius H. Hess and published in "A Further Review of the Instruction in Diseases of Children," *Transactions of the Association of American Teachers of the Diseases of Children,* 17 (1923): 24. There were at the time eighty-three medical schools, seventy categorized as class A by the American Medical Association. Of the latter, Hess surveyed fifty-seven schools which offered a full medical program (thirteen provided only a two-year course). He received fifty-three responses. Nearly all the major pediatric departments in the country were respondents. The three departments with more than half of all full-time

slots were Johns Hopkins, Harvard, and Washington University, the latter located in St. Louis.

23. American Academy of Pediatrics, *Child Health Services and Pediatric Education* (New York: Commonwealth Fund, 1949), pp. 169–171. In 1947 there were seventy approved medical colleges in the U.S. that offered a four-year course. The American Academy of Pediatrics surveyed the pediatrics departments of all of these schools in a study conducted between 1946 and 1948.

24. American Medical Association, Walter S. Wiggins et al., "Medical Education in the United States and Canada," *Journal of the American Medical Association*, 171, 11 (1959): 1528.

25. On early NIH funding for clinical research and research training consult James A. Shannon, "The Advancement of Medical Research: A Twenty-Year View of the Role of the National Institutes of Health," *Journal of Medical Education*, 42, 2 (1967): 100.

26. References on Wilkins' career include Park, "Lawson Wilkins"; Wilkins, "Acceptance of the Howland Award"; Samuel P. Asper, Jr., "Lawson Wilkins, 1894–1963," *Transactions of the Association of American Physicians*, 77 (1964): 33–36; Alexander Schaffer, "Lawson Wilkins, 1894–1963," *Pediatrics*, 33, 1 (1964): 1–2.

27. My description of the work histories of postwar pediatric subspecialists is drawn from interview data and curriculum vitae provided by informants.

28. On the founding of the SPR, see Sydney S. Gellis, "The Society for Pediatric Research," *American Journal of Diseases of Children*, 98 (1959): 545–552.

29. "We have felt increasing pressure from [subspecialty] groups, each suggesting that the plenary sessions be devoted to a whole morning on cardiology, an afternoon on endocrinology, and so forth. To date we have largely resisted this pressure but have yielded to the extent that one evening is devoted to simultaneous meetings of the subspecialty groups." In ibid., p. 552. The other three special sections that year were in the fields of bacteriology and immunology, virology, and pathology. *American Journal of Diseases of Children*, 98 (1959): 554–556.

30. The Academy created allergy and surgery sections in 1948, and sections for cardiology and diseases of the chest in 1957. From the librarian of the American Academy of Pediatrics.

31. These estimates are drawn from the records of pediatric endocrinology associations or from intraprofessional communications among members. The source for the 1960s estimate is from LWPES's list of founding members. The Society originally designated forty founding members and

retroactively raised the number to seventy-seven. To be a founding member, a pediatric endocrinologist had to have completed his specialized training by 1961.

32. Robert G. Petersdorf underscores the importance of federal funds, particularly federal research funds, for the growth of internal medicine faculties. "The Evolution of Departments of Medicine," *New England Journal of Medicine*, 303, 9 (1980): 490–493. On the relationship between federal research funds and full-time faculty appointments, also see John G. Freymann, *The American Health Care System: Its Genesis and Trajectory* (New York: Medcom, 1974), p. 87.

33. American Medical Association, "Medical Education in the United States," *Journal of the American Medical Association*, 210, 8 (1969): 1477; American Medical Association, "Medical Education in the United States," *Journal of the American Medical Association*, 243, 9 (1980): 849.

34. Petersdorf comments on the migration of medical subspecialists into community hospitals and the implications of this dispersion for university-based fellowship programs. One result is an "out-migration" of patients from university hospitals—where patients were previously referred—to community treatment settings. See Robert G. Petersdorf, "Is the Establishment Defensible?" *New England Journal of Medicine*, 309, 17 (1983): 1054–1055.

35. The movement of subspecialists from university to community centers underlies the diffusion of numerous medical technologies.

36. Unpublished correspondences and intraprofessional memos are my sources for information on pediatric endocrinologists' rationales for a special certificate, their responses to actions by the ABIM group, and the Academy's stance on certification for pediatric subspecialists.

37. Alexander S. Nadas, "Pediatric Cardiology, and the Sub-Boards," *Pediatrics*, 32, 2 (1963): 159.

38. Nadas, "Pediatric Cardiology," pp. 159–160.

39. On fellows trained by Taussig see Mary Allen Engle, "Dr. Helen B. Taussig, The Tetralogy of Fallot, and the Growth of Pediatric Cardiac Services in the United States," *Johns Hopkins Medical Journal*, 140, 4 (1977): 148. Other sources on the history of pediatric cardiology include Forrest H. Adams, "Development of Pediatric Cardiology," *American Journal of Cardiology*, 22, 4 (1968): 452–455; William J. Rashkind, "Pediatric Cardiology: A Brief Historical Perspective," *Pediatric Cardiology*, 1, 1 (1979): 63–71.

40. Information on controversy among pediatric endocrinologists regarding certification is from unpublished correspondences and intraprofessional memos.

41. One of my informants estimated that, of approximately twenty

pediatric endocrinologists in the country in 1950, one-half to three-quarters held full-time faculty appointments.

7. Resurgence of the Generalist: Psychosocial Pediatrics

1. A. Michael Sulman, "The Humanization of the American Child: Benjamin Spock as a Popularizer of Psychoanalytic Thought," *Journal of the History of the Behavioral Sciences*, 9, 3 (1973): 258–265.

2. For research and teaching on psychosocial issues prior to 1950 see comments by Milton J. E. Senn, "The Psychotherapeutic Role of the Pediatrician," *Pediatrics*, 2, 2 (1948): 147; Julius Richmond, "Child Development: A Basic Science for Pediatrics," *Pediatrics*, 39, 5 (1967): 651; Julius Richmond, "Coming of Age: Developmental Pediatrics in the Late Twentieth Century," *Journal of Developmental and Behavioral Pediatrics*, 6, 4 (1985): 181; W. Sam Yancy, "Discussant Remarks," *Journal of Developmental and Behavioral Pediatrics*, 6, 5 (1985): 196.

3. Irving K. Zola and Stephen J. Miller comment on medicine's increasing concern with social phenomena in "The Erosion of Medicine from Within," in *The Professions and Their Prospects*, ed. Eliot Freidson (Beverly Hills: Sage, 1973), pp. 167–169. On the emergence of psychosocial orientations within obstetrics see William Ray Arney, *Power and the Profession of Obstetrics* (Chicago: University of Chicago Press, 1982).

4. Dorothy Pawluch, "Transitions in Pediatrics: A Segmental Analysis," *Social Problems*, 30, 4 (1983): 456.

5. Ibid., p. 450.

6. Ibid., pp. 449, 457.

7. Boulware reports that, between 1930 and 1950, he encountered rising incidence of several morbidities in his pediatric practice: fibrocystic disease, viral encephalomyelitis, infectious mononucleosis, leukemia, rheumatic fever, and allergies. Deisher, Derby, and Sturman suggest that, during the 1930s and 1940s, pediatricians treated increasing numbers of patients with neurological disease, congenital deformities, and allergies. J. R. Boulware, "The Composition of Private Pediatric Practice in a Small Community in the South of the United States," *Pediatrics*, 22, 3 (1958): 556–557; Robert W. Deisher, Alfred J. Derby, and Melvin J. Sturman, "Changing Trends in Pediatric Practice," *Pediatrics*, 25 (1960): 715.

8. Harold Jacobziner, Herbert Rich, and Roland Merchant, "Pediatric Care in Private Practice," *Journal of the American Medical Association*, 182 (1962): 986.

9. During the late 1940s, child specialists were handling only 11 percent of all outpatient medical visits made by children under 15; general

practitioners provided 75 percent and other specialists 14 percent. American Academy of Pediatrics, Committee for the Study of Child Health Services, *Child Health Services and Pediatric Education* (New York: Commonwealth Fund, 1949), p. 44.

10. The American Academy of Pediatrics provides data for the late 1940s. Among children seen by general practitioners, 70 percent were ill while 30 percent were well. Among the children seen by pediatricians, 43 percent were ill and 54 percent were well. American Academy of Pediatrics, *Child Health Services and Pediatric Education*, p. 51. Jacobziner, Rich, and Merchant report figures for New York City in the late 1950s. Among children under age 6 treated by general practitioners, 59 percent were sick and 41 percent were well. Among youngsters in the same age range treated by pediatricians, 59 percent were well and 41 percent ill. Calculated from statistics in "Pediatric Care in Private Practice," p. 989.

11. Pawluch, "Transitions in Pediatrics," p. 455.

12. The first study, conducted in the late 1920s, surveyed seventeen pediatricians practicing in the South who were graduates of Tulane University. This group reported that 39 percent of patient visits were for supervision of infant feeding, vaccinations, or physical exams. C. Anderson Aldrich published the second study which describes the content of his pediatric practice in a suburb of Chicago during the early 1930s. Preventive treatment and routine care of infants and children constituted 39 percent of his activities. In a third study, pediatrician Arthur London reports on the composition of his practice during the mid-1930s in Durham, North Carolina. Thirty-nine percent of his patients received routine care, routine examinations, or immunizations. Commission on Medical Education, *Second Report* (New Haven, Conn.: Office of the Director of the Study, Jan. 1928), pp. 20–23, 57–58; C. Anderson Aldrich, "The Composition of Private Pediatric Practice, *American Journal of Diseases of Children*, 47, 5 (1934): 1051–1064; Arthur H. London, Jr., "The Composition of an Average Pediatric Practice," *Journal of Pediatrics*, 10 (1937): 770.

13. Deisher, Derby, and Sturman, "Changing Trends in Pediatric Practice," pp. 714–715.

14. The six studies were conducted in 1948, 1957, 1959, 1958–1960, 1964, and 1975. The proportions of child-health supervision were (respectively) 54 percent, 40 percent, 35 percent, 40 percent, 46 to 50 percent, and 30 percent. American Academy of Pediatrics, *Child Health Services and Pediatric Education*, p. 51; Deisher, Derby, and Sturman, "Changing Trends in Pediatric Practice," p. 713; Robert A. Aldrich and Richard H. Spitz, "Appendix: Survey of Pediatric Practice in the U.S. in 1959," in *Careers in Pediatrics, Report of the 36th Ross Conference on Pediatric*

Research (Columbus, Ohio: Ross Laboratories, 1960), p. 64; B. B. Bresse, F. A. Disney, and W. Talpey, "The Nature of a Small Pediatric Group Practice," *Pediatrics*, 38 (1966): 270–271; Abraham B. Bergman, Steven W. Dassell, and Ralph J. Wedgwood, "Time-Motion Study of Practicing Pediatricians," *Pediatrics*, 38, 2 (1966): 257; Thomas K. McInerny, Klaus J. Roghmann, and Sydney A. Sutherland, "Primary Pediatric Care in One Community," *Pediatrics*, 61, 3 (1978): 392, 395.

15. I. B. Pless, "The Changing Face of Primary Pediatrics," *Pediatric Clinics of North America*, 21, 1 (1974): 229–230; John T. Geyman, "Graduate Education in Family Practice: A Ten-Year View," *The Journal of Family Practice*, 9, 5 (1979): 860.

16. The AMA began compiling this data set in the 1960s and comparable figures for the 1950s and 1940s are unavailable. But there is every reason to believe that, during those decades also, the numbers of GPs were declining.

17. Authors of a report from the AAP's Council on Pediatric Practice argue that declines in the ratio of primary-care providers to children took place steadily between 1940 and 1967. American Academy of Pediatrics, Council on Pediatric Practice, *Lengthening Shadows* (Evanston, Ill.: American Academy of Pediatrics, 1971), p. 210. William H. Stewart and Maryland Y. Pennell indicate that between 1940 and 1961, the ratio of pediatricians per 100,000 children under 15 rose from 7.3 to 16.3. But the ratio of pediatricians plus general practitioners per 100,000 children fell from 352 to 151. "Pediatric Manpower in the United States and Its Implications," *Pediatrics*, 31, 2 (1963): 316–317.

18. Changes in fertility rates are reported in National Center for Health Statistics, *Vital Statistics of the United States, 1980*, vol. 1. Natality. DHHS pub. no. (PHS) 85-1100 (Washington, D.C.: U.S. Government Printing Office, 1984), pp. 1–7, table 1-1.

19. Robert J. Haggerty and Morris Green, "The Pediatric Clinician's Job," in *Ambulatory Pediatrics*, ed. Morris Green and Robert Haggerty (Philadelphia: W. B. Saunders, 1968), p. 106. It was during the early 1970s that pediatric leaders first began questioning the presumed shortage of primary-care physicians for children. See Robert J. Haggerty, "Do We Really Need More Pediatricians?" *Pediatrics*, 50, 5 (1972): 681–683.

20. For two examples see S. Z. Levine, "Pediatric Education at the Crossroads," *American Journal of Diseases of Children*, 100, 5 (1960): 651; and Clifford F. Taylor, "Medicine's Most Frustrating Specialty," *Medical Economics*, 28, 20 (1959): 111–115.

21. Information on faculty appointments of OPD directors during the 1950s is from interviews with five charter members of the Ambulatory Pediatric Association, curriculum vitae provided by these individuals, and

from (mimeographed) APA newsletters. The latter provide data on academic posts held by association members. My discussions of work roles and research foci among ambulatory pediatricians (later in the text) also draws upon these sources.

22. On the founding of the APA consult Richard W. Olmsted, "Letters to the Editor: Association of Outpatient Directors," *Pediatrics*, 23, 1 (1959): 174; Frederic M. Blodgett, "The Ambulatory Pediatric Association—Historical Notes," *Advances in Pediatrics*, 20 (1973): 5–7; Barbara M. Korsch, "Introduction," *Advances in Pediatrics*, 20 (1973): 9–10.

23. Abraham B. Bergman, "Pediatric Education—For What?" *Pediatrics*, 55, 1 (1975): 109. At the time he wrote this article, Bergman was director of outpatient services at Children's Orthopedic Hospital and Medical Center, affiliated with the University of Washington Medical School, Seattle.

24. J. Philip Ambuel, "Letter to the Editor," *Pediatrics*, 23, 5 (1959): 1009–1010.

25. Ibid., p. 1010. Bergman linked the imbalance to the proliferation of full-time appointment and the ascendancy of scientific subspecialties. "[One] change that I witnessed was the growth of full-time faculties to teach clinical medicine. . . . At the University of Washington in 1950, there were three full-time faculty members in the pediatric department; now [in 1974] there are 50. Though the numbers might not be as dramatic in other medical schools, the general picture is the same. Who are they? With few exceptions, they are pediatric subspecialists or persons engaged in full-time research. I don't want to be misunderstood! The development of the subspecialties has dramatically improved child health care and must continue. . . . Nevertheless, it seems obvious that we are out of kilter. . . . The fact is we lack just plain ordinary pediatricians in our pediatric departments." Bergman, "Pediatric Education—For What?" p. 109.

26. "It would be inappropriate to discuss this era of preventive pediatrics without commenting on some of our social responsibilities. Our considerable successes in reducing morbidity and mortality from many diseases have brought us face to face with new problems. And, precisely because of our past successes, society looks to us for new successes. But many of our current problems are in large measure social problems." Julius B. Richmond, "Child Development: A Basic Science for Pediatrics," *Pediatrics*, 39, 5 (1967): 657.

27. Ibid., p. 656.

28. Julius B. Richmond, "Some Observations on the Sociology of Pediatric Education and Practice," *Pediatrics*, 23, 6 (1959): 1177.

29. Richmond, "Child Development: A Basic Science for Pediatrics," p. 655.

30. Julius B. Richmond, "An Idea Whose Time Has Arrived," *The Pediatric Clinics of North America*, 22, 3 (1975): 522.

31. Levine, "Pediatric Education at the Crossroads," p. 651.

32. Ibid., p. 654.

33. Charles D. May, "The Future of Pediatricians as Medical Specialists in the United States," *American Journal of Diseases of Children*, 100, 5 (1960): 662–663.

34. Ibid., p. 664.

35. The Division of Maternal and Child Health (formerly the Office of Maternal and Child Health and, before that, the Maternal and Child Health Service) received authority to award training grants in 1963. Prior to that, grants to pediatric departments were drawn from special project funds. Training grants provided stipends for fellows and support for faculty salaries. Personal communication with Vince L. Hutchins, Director, Division of Maternal and Child Health, U.S. Department of Health and Human Services. Also See Vince L. Hutchins, "The Goals of Care," in the "Proceedings of the National Conference on Behavioral Pediatrics, March 3–5, 1985," *Journal of Developmental and Behavioral Pediatrics*, 6, 4 (1985): 180.

36. Early fellowships from the Commonwealth Fund and the individuals who received them are discussed in Dane G. Prugh and Lloyd O. Eckhardt, "Child Psychiatry and Pediatrics," in *Basic Handbook of Child Psychiatry*, ed. J. D. Noshpitz, vol. 4, *Prevention and Current Issues*, ed. I. N. Berlin and L. A. Stone (New York: Basic Books, 1979), p. 564.

37. Executive officers at Robert Wood Johnson and at William T. Grant provided information on programs these foundations have sponsored.

38. *Journal of Pediatrics*, 75, 3 (1969): 534; Adele D. Hofmann, "Fellowships in Adolescent Medicine," *Journal of Pediatrics*, 83, 3 (1973): 512; Joseph L. Rauh, "Survey of Physician Fellows in Adolescent Medicine," *Journal of Adolescent Health Care*, 1, 1 (1980): 52; Joseph L. Rauh and Alice Passer, "Survey of Physicians in Adolescent Medicine, 1979–1984," *Journal of Adolescent Health Care*, 7, 1 (1986): 34.

39. Information on adolescent units in university-affiliated hospitals from personal communication with Robert M. Blizzard, Chairman, Department of Pediatrics, University of Virginia. In 1977 Blizzard surveyed 128 pediatric department chairs. Forty-four percent reported that there was an adolescent ward at their affiliated hospital, 62 percent indicated the existence of an adolescent clinic. The spread of adolescent units within hospitals during the 1960s is documented by Dale C. Garell, "Adolescent Medicine: A Survey in the United States and Canada," *American Journal*

of Diseases of Children, 109, 4 (1965): 314–317; and C. Andrew Rigg and Rona C. Fisher, "Some Comments on Current Hospital Medical Services for Adolescents," *American Journal of Diseases of Children,* 120, 3 (1970): 193–196. Sources on the general history of adolescent medicine include J. Roswell Gallagher, "The Origins, Development and Goals of Adolescent Medicine," *Journal of Adolescent Health Care,* 3, 1 (1982): 57–63.

40. Membership figures from the office of the Society for Adolescent Medicine, Granada Hills, California. The association includes physicians trained in specialties other than pediatrics as well as nonmedical health professionals. However, a majority of SAM members are pediatricians.

41. Society for Behavioral Pediatrics, "A Brief History," unpublished statement, 1986. Membership figures from the office of the Society for Behavioral Pediatrics, Philadelphia, Pennsylvania.

42. On federal funding for university-based service and training programs in the area of mental retardation and developmental disabilities see Herbert J. Cohen, "The Politics of Mental Retardation: History, Legislation and Policy Making," in *Community Services for the Mentally Retarded,* ed. Arnold Birenbaum and Herbert Cohen (Totowa, N.J.: Rowman and Allenheld, 1985), pp. 61–65; U.S. Comptroller General, Report to the Subcommittee on the Handicapped, Senate Committee on Labor and Human Resources, *How Federal Developmental Disabilities Programs Are Working* (Washington, D.C.: U.S. General Accounting Office, Feb. 20, 1980).

43. "Residencies and Fellowships," *Journal of Pediatrics,* 83, 3 (1973): 87–88. This listing also identified sixteen programs in child development.

44. Information on membership in the Society for Developmental Pediatrics from Arnold Capute, Vice President for Medical Affairs, The John F. Kennedy Institute, Johns Hopkins School of Medicine.

45. The Task Force on Pediatric Education, *The Future of Pediatric Education* (Evanston, Ill.: American Academy of Pediatrics, 1978). Michael I. Cohen describes the organization and some of the implications of the Task Force in "Importance, Implementation, and Impact of the Adolescent Medicine Components of the Report of the Task Force on Pediatric Education," *Journal of Adolescent Health Care,* 1, 1 (1980): 1–8.

46. Publications for office-based practitioners include Committee on the Psychosocial Aspects of Child and Family Health, *Guidelines of Health Supervision* (n.p.: American Academy of Pediatrics, 1985). The Committee states that future supplements to this manual will include discussions of discipline, sleep disorders, temper tantrums, separation problems, difficult-to-comfort infants, children with handicaps, and related topics. *Guidelines for Health Supervision,* pp. 2–3. Morris Green comments on the Academy's efforts to obtain more generous third-party

reimbursements for behaviorally-oriented care in "The Role of the Pediatrician in the Delivery of Behavioral Services," *Journal of Developmental and Behavioral Pediatrics*, 6, 4 (1985): 193.

47. Researchers surveyed the country's 246 approved pediatric residency programs and got a response rate of 60 percent. Bradley H. Zebal and Stanford B. Friedman, "A National Survey of Behavioral Pediatric Residency Training," *Journal of Developmental and Behavioral Pediatrics*, 5, 6 (1984): 331.

48. For a review of this literature see Christine V. Davidson, "Training the Pediatric Psychologist and the Developmental-Behavioral Pediatrician," in *Handbook of Pediatric Psychology*, ed. D. K. Routh (New York: Guilford, 1987).

49. This group had complete fellowships in one of the following fields: ambulatory pediatrics, behavioral pediatrics, general pediatrics, child development, and adolescent medicine. Forty-three percent were working in academic settings. Anne S. Bergman and Gregory K. Fritz, "Pediatricians and Mental Health Professionals: Patterns of Collaboration and Utilization," *American Journal of Diseases of Children*, 139 (1985): 156.

50. Researchers obtained responses from 151 physicians who completed adolescent medicine fellowships between 1979 and 1984. Specialists in this group were more likely to enter private practice than members of an earlier cohort of trainees. Among fellows who graduated in the mid- to late 1970s, 19 percent went into private practice. Rauh and Passer, "Survey of Physician Fellows in Adolescent Medicine, 1979–1984," p. 35.

51. Jerome T. Y. Shen, "How to Begin the Private Practice of Adolescent Medicine," *Clinical Pediatrics*, 12, 1 (1973): 6–13; W. S. Yancy, "Behavioral Pediatrics and the Practicing Pediatrician," *Pediatric Clinics of North America*, 22, 3 (1975): 684–694; Greg Prazar and Evan Charney, "Behavioral Pediatrics in Office Practice," *Pediatric Annals*, 9, 6 (1980): 220–228; Edward R. Christophersen, "Incorporating Behavioral Pediatrics into Primary Care," *Pediatric Clinics of North America*, 29, 2 (1982): 261–296; Barbara Starfield, "Behavioral Pediatrics and Primary Health Care," *Pediatric Clinics of North America*, 29, 2 (1982): 377–390.

52. Robert J. Haggerty, "Behavioral Pediatrics: Can It Be Taught? Can It Be Practiced?" *Pediatric Clinics of North America*, 29, 2 (1982): 397.

53. Philip R. Nader, Laura Ray, and Susan G. Brink, "The New Morbidity: Use of School and Community Health Care Resources for Behavioral, Educational, and Social-Family Problems," *Pediatrics*, 67, 1 (1981): 55.

54. Stanford B. Friedman, Sheridan Phillips, and John M. Parrish, "Current Status of Behavioral Pediatric Training for General Residents: A Study of 11 Funded Programs," *Pediatrics*, 71, 6 (1983): 907.

55. On the issue of developmental and behavioral pediatrics as one field see Stanford B. Friedman, "Behavioral Pediatrics: Interaction with Other Disciplines," *Journal of Development and Behavioral Pediatrics*, 6, 4 (1985): 206. Regarding the focus of developmental pediatrics consult Arthur H. Parmelee, "Developmental Pediatrics: Not Just the Care of Children with Developmental Disabilities," *Pediatrics*, 76, 2 (1985): 329–330.

56. Michael R. Cataldo, "The Scientific Basis for a Behavioral Approach to Pediatrics," *Pediatrics Clinics of North America*, 29, 2 (1982): 416.

57. Robert W. Chamberlin et al., "The 'New Morbidity,' " in *Child Health and the Community*, ed. Robert J. Haggerty, Klaus J. Roghmann, and Ivan B. Pless (New York: John Wiley, 1975), pp. 94–116; Nader, Ray, and Brink, "The New Morbidity," pp. 53–60. On difficulties in constructing valid and reliable diagnostic categories for behavioral syndromes see Robert A. Rubinstein and Janet D. Perloff, "Identifying Psychosocial Disorders in Children: On Integrating Epidemiological and Anthropological Understandings," in *Anthropology and Epidemiology: Interdisciplinary Approaches to the Study of Health and Disease*, ed. Craig R. Janes, Ron Stall, and Sandra M. Gifford (Boston: D. Reidel, 1986), pp. 303–332.

58. Conrad and Schneider argue that medicalization of social behavior begins with the publication of articles in medical journals announcing a new diagnostic category, a new conception of etiology, or a new treatment modality. Then advocacy groups work to have medical treatment broadly institutionalized. "Publication of scientific and professional articles . . . does not assure a new deviance designation's recognition or acceptance. It needs champions and moral entrepreneurs to carry the banner and bring the new problem or definition to public attention." Peter Conrad and Joseph W. Schneider, *Deviance and Medicalization* (St. Louis: C. V. Mosby, 1980), p. 267. On factors that encourage physicians to identify new disorders see Eliot Freidson, *Profession of Medicine* (New York: Harper and Row, 1970), pp. 162–172, 244–261.

59. Processes surrounding the diffusion of care for these disorders are multifaceted and involve numerous groups of actors including medical and nonmedical professionals, federal agencies, and advocacy associations. Peter Conrad, "The Discovery of Hyperkinesis: Notes on the Medicalization of Deviant Behavior," *Social Problems*, 23, 1 (1975): 12–21; Stephen J. Pfohl, "The 'Discovery' of Child Abuse," *Social Problems*, 24, 3 (1977): 310–323; Peter Conrad and Joseph W. Schneider, "Children and Medicalization: Delinquency, Hyperactivity, Child Abuse," in *Deviance and Medicalization*, pp. 145–171.

8. Concluding Remarks

1. For citations to relevant work of Rosen and Rosenberg, see notes 26 and 27 to chapter 2.

2. Rosemary Stevens, *American Medicine and the Public Interest* (New Haven: Yale University Press, 1971), p. 199.

3. This typology draws upon two others in the sociological literature. Eliot Freidson differentiates between client-dependent and colleague-dependent practices. Ann Greer distinguishes four varieties of practitioners: community generalists, community specialists, referral specialists, and hospital-based specialists. Her interest is physician involvement in hospital decision making regarding the acquisition of new equipment and technologies. Eliot Freidson, *The Profession of Medicine* (New York: Harper and Row, 1970), p. 107; Ann L. Greer, "Medical Technology and Professional Dominance Theory," *Social Science and Medicine*, 18, 10 (1984): 811–815. These categorizations have their roots in studies by Oswald Hall on the informal organization of medical communities. See "The Informal Organization of the Medical Profession," *Canadian Journal of Economics and Political Science*, 12 (1946): 30–44; and "Types of Medical Careers," *American Journal of Sociology*, 55, 3 (1949): 243–253. My typology differs from others in that I am classifying specialties rather than practitioners.

4. Stevens, *American Medicine*, pp. 225–231.

5. Bruce Steinwald, "Hospital-Based Physicians: Current Issues and Descriptive Evidence," *Health Care Financing Review*, 2, 1 (1980): 64–67. Other work on hospital-based specialties includes Eliot Freidson, "Specialties without Roots: The Utilization of New Services," *Human Organization*, 18, 3 (1959): 112–116; Marian S. Kessler, "Physician Compensation: Survey Shows Marked Increase in Contractual Arrangements," *Hospital Medical Staff*, 5, 7 (1976): 19–25.

6. Paul Starr, *The Social Transformation of American Medicine* (New York: Basic Books, 1982), pp. 18, 111.

7. For citations on hostility toward specialization among American medical practitioners see chapter 1, note 19. Starr acknowledges that conflict surrounded specialization but he does not comment on its implications for intraprofessional cohesion.

8. Before Starr, Stanley Reiser argued that specialization generated more interdependence among physicians. But in Reiser's account, cooperative relationships were forged gradually during the twentieth century. Stanley J. Reiser, "Medical Specialism and the Centralization of Medical Care," in *Medicine and the Reign of Technology* (Cambridge: Cambridge University Press, 1978), pp. 144–157.

Index

AAMC. *See* Association of American Medical Colleges

Abt, Isaac, 102

Adolescent medicine, 142–143, 145

Advisory Board for Medical Specialties (ABMS), 27, 104, 110, 120

Aldrich, C. Anderson, 92, 96–97

AMA. *See* American Medical Association

Ambuel, J. Philip, 137

Ambulatory Pediatric Association (APA), 129, 130, 138, 145–146

American Academy of Pediatrics (AAP): committee on psychosocial care, 143; founded, 80, 94, 205 n. 66; initiates certifying board, 95, 102, 103; position on Jones-Bankhead, 101; scientific sections, 119, 124

American Association for the Study and Prevention of Infant Mortality (AASPIM), 74

American Board of Internal Medicine (ABIM), 16, 26, 110, 122, 124, 125

American Board of Medical Specialties. *See* Advisory Board for Medical Specialties

American Board of Pediatrics (ABP), 80–81, 95, 102–103, 122

American Child Health Association, 88, 89–90, 91, 197 n. 59

American Medical Association (AMA), 7, 65; Council on Medical Education, 27, 69, 71, 80, 103, 105; early specialists' relation to, 47–48, 184–185 n. 55; rebukes pediatric section, 101

American Medical Association, Section on Diseases of Children, 45, 51, 53, 61, 69, 70, 71, 96; founded, 35, 184 n. 52;

goals, 49; position on Sheppard-Towner, 101, represented on pediatric board, 102; transactions, 50

American Pediatric Society (APS), 139; established 25, 35, 49, 181 n. 36; founders' ethos, 50–54; founders' origins, 45, 70–71, 78, 181–182 n. 40; founders' professional memberships, 48–49; founders' programmatic goals, 50, 186 n. 65; founders' scientific concerns, 45–46, 49–50, 63; founders' work patterns, 43–45, 46–47; full-scale specialists within, 65; joint meetings with Society for Pediatric Research, 118, 136; represented on pediatric board, 102; restricted membership, 36, 49, 71; on training in child-health supervision, 95; women first admitted to, 181 n. 35

Association of American Medical Colleges (AAMC), 69, 71

Association of American Physicians, 48, 49

Association of American Teachers of the Diseases of Children (AATDC): founded, 70, 195 n. 46; members' origins, 71, 78; programmatic activities, 71–72

Behavioral pediatrics. *See* Psychosocial pediatrics; Society for Behavioral Pediatrics

Bergman, Abraham, 136

Berlant, Jeffrey, 6

Blalock, Alfred, 123

Brennemann, Joseph, 64, 107–108

Brown, Francis, 40–41

Designer: U.C. Press Staff
Compositor: Huron Valley Graphics
Text: 11/13 Caledonia
Display: Caledonia